Don't Put Socks on the Hippopotamus

And other rules of business life

Don't Put Socks on the Hippopotamus

And other rules of business life

Terry Kelley

Gower

Published by
Gower Publishing Limited
Gower House
Croft Road
Aldershot
Hampshire GU11 3HR
England

Gower
Old Post Road
Brookfield
Vermont 05036
USA

British Library Cataloguing in Publication Data
Kelley, Terry
   Don't put socks on the hippopotamus : and other rules of
   business life
   1. Management – Quotations, maxims, etc.   2. Management –
   Anecdotes
   I. Title
   658

   ISBN 0 566 07989 5

Library of Congress Cataloging-in-Publication Data
Kelley, Terry (Terry L.). 1946–
     Don't put socks on the hippopotamus : and other rules of business
   life / Terry Kelley.
       p.   cm.
     ISBN 0-566-07989-5 (hardcover)
     1. Business–Humor.   2. Wit and humor.   I. Title
   HF5011.K45   1998
   650'02'07–dc21   97-45181
                                                                              CIP

Typeset in Palatino by Raven Typesetters, Chester and printed
in Great Britain by MPG Books, Bodmin.

Contents

Preface

You always have to wonder why people write books, especially business books. Most business people look at this type of activity as something that just doesn't make sense. We can use our time more profitably doing practically anything else. Perhaps that's why most business books are written by academics, not business people.

Besides, business books are almost invariably boring. If we read them at all, it is because we feel we should. We certainly don't do it for enjoyment. When you look at it that way, even the idea of writing to stroke one's ego deflates, at least partially. Personally, I'd rather mow the lawn.

So, why did I become involved in writing this book? Over the years, I have been called upon to give speeches now and then, a time-consuming and difficult task, at least for me. I developed a format called 'Rules of Business Life'. I could always find a rule or two which fitted any talk I had to give. It made my life easier and I did not need to expend as much time or energy in preparation.

Occasionally, people in the audience would ask when the book would be published. They wanted to see all the rules. Naturally, I laughed at them. I had much better things to do with my time. Then the company I worked for was reorganised. My job was made redundant and, for the first time in my life, I didn't have a place to go to every morning. Rather than rushing out to find another job, I decided this was an ideal opportunity to see if my thoughts about business were worth publishing. Hence the book.

But it's more than having available time that makes a person indulge in this much pain and trouble. In addition to having something to say, you must have someone to say it to. I struggled with this for a long time. Who was the book being written for? Was it for young people just starting their business career? Others just beginning to climb the management ladder? Or was it written for all the bosses I've ever had, good or bad, to tell them how they could have been better?

I finally found the answer one day through a wonderful piece of serendipity. My wife and I were in a pub with some friends when we were joined by another couple. They were a fascinating pair, he a surgeon and she a leader of management training seminars. The conversation turned to the topic of this book and she challenged me. She wanted to know who the intended readers were and what benefit they would derive from reading it.

She'll never realise how frustrated that question made me, nor will she know how desperately I wanted to avoid telling her that I did not know the answer. Out of instinct, I told her I was writing it for myself.

'Oh,' she said, 'I understand. You mean you're writing it for the person you used to be before you learned all these rules.'

Suddenly I knew the answer. She was right. I was writing this for the naïve young person I used to be twenty or thirty years ago. I was also writing it for the me of today. Knowing the rules is not always enough. I need to be constantly reminded of them so they are not overlooked in the day-to-day hustle. Finally, I realised I was writing it for the person I'll be tomorrow because there are always new rules to learn.

I have tried to present these rules as 'wisdom hidden within humour'. That doesn't mean I consider myself either wise or humorous. Far from it. However, I know that's the kind of attitude I respond to best, so I have attempted to be the person I would listen to.

Wherever possible, I have used anecdotes to clarify the message. While the stories relate loosely to something that actually happened, most have been dramatised to make a specific point. All the characters and events are fictitious and any remaining resemblance to real persons, living or dead, is purely coincidental. The exceptions are those stories where I deal with my personal lapses. Some were very painful to write about but they may strike you as amusing. If the stories and rules help, we'll both find this worthwhile.

I'll leave you with a note of caution. These rules came about because I had questions. The results are answers to my questions but that's all they are. I don't really want you to agree with my conclusions. Find your own. If you think I'm wrong, let me know. I have been known to change my mind.

Terry Kelley

Acknowledgments ──────

No work is ever done in total isolation and this book is no exception. The list of people that deserve my gratitude includes every person I have worked for and everyone who has ever worked for me – far too many to mention. However, special thanks are owed to a few who have been directly instrumental. The first is Helen Mumford, who started the process and gave me the courage to begin. Then there are three wonderful people, Kathie Nash, Dick Andrews and Alistair McKinnon, who laboured over my first awkward attempts to articulate my thoughts. No writer has had better or more patient readers. Finally, but most importantly, I need to thank my marvellous wife and children. Not only did they provide encouragement (and quiet); they were my first and final proofreaders. Thank you Joan, JJ, Caroline and Lorraine.

TK

Part I
Rules about work

Your Majesty, according to our study, the shoe was lost for want of a nail, the horse was lost for want of a shoe, and the rider was lost for want of a horse, but the kingdom was lost because of over-regulation – written on a lavatory wall, London

'Hi-ho, hi-ho, it's off to work we go ...' Do you ever find yourself just a little envious of those dwarfs? They're so darn happy as they go off to work. Of course, it's only a fairy tale. It has nothing to do with real life. Right?

Well, why shouldn't we be happy in our work? There's no reason why every day shouldn't start with a song and finish with a true sense of accomplishment. That's all most of us want out of our labour. Of course a decent salary helps but, really, we just want to feel our energy has contributed to something good.

It certainly doesn't work out that way very often. It sometimes seems we are supposed to accomplish our tasks in the most awkward way possible. Much of the time, people are drained of all initiative by the end of a day, and end it with an 'I don't give a damn' attitude. It becomes harder and harder to start the next morning fresh and eager for the day's battle. Many give up entirely and surrender their business to the ankle-peckers, those anonymous bureaucrats who specialise in killing the spirit of their companies.

It doesn't have to be that way. If there was only a little better understanding about the nature of work, maybe all of us could be as happy as those maniacal dwarfs – or not, as the case may be, but at least we could

1

be a little happier than we usually are. With understanding, we can recognise situations faster and, with a little perseverance and a little more luck, maybe we can change things for the better.

Over the years, I have found that following a few basic rules can help. If you want to bring joy back into the work environment, try using them. Maybe, just maybe, one of them can make a real difference.

I once heard an irritated young woman who had just been given explicit instructions on how to go about a job say, 'Well, I can do it that way if you want. I can also file my fingernails by scraping them on a blackboard.' Being told to perform a task in an awkward way is bad enough – but having to do foolish work is worse. She would understand this first rule.

Rule of business life no. 1

Don't put socks on the hippopotamus

Roughly translated, this rule means there are jobs we should not do at all, much less try to do well. Just think about the poor hippopotamus for a moment. He doesn't want socks. He certainly doesn't need them. He's more than likely to become upset if you try to put some on him. Finally, doing it would be wet, messy and more than a little dangerous. It is not surprising that we never hear of professional zoologists or gamekeepers attempting it. It's just not done.

When we come to the business world, it's an entirely different situation. We constantly hear people complain that they are working harder and harder but receiving less and less credit. Sometimes they are honest enough to admit that they shouldn't be doing the job at all. We even hear some say 'We are just too busy doing our job to do what needs to be done.' But do they change what they are doing? Oh, no! That would be too radical.

I was once a guest at a famous and very posh hotel and golf resort. This was far above my normal standard of travel accommodation, but a major supplier was hosting a conference and picking up all expenses. After thoroughly enjoying myself, especially the golf, as the conference itself was boring, I got in line to check out of the hotel. While others ahead of me in the rather long queue threw down their room keys in disgust and left, I stayed through the entire process to see what was happening. It turned out that the hotel wanted me to pay for my morning newspaper: a grand total of 35 pence. Our conference hosts had forgotten to include this in their coverage.

First, the clerk at the hotel desk used the computer to print an invoice. Because I paid cash, he then had to make out a receipt manually. I don't know why, as I certainly did not want one. However, he told me it 'was the rule'. Finally, he had to go into the back office because he had run out of change. The entire process must have cost the hotel at least ten times the cost of the newspaper, much less their potential profit. For me, it was a waste of almost 30 minutes of my life. I was not happy!

I subsequently called their head office to discover why they had taken the risk of irritating a customer while losing money at the same time. A very indignant accountant informed me that 'It is imperative for us to balance our books.'

A clear case of socks on the hippo! But, wait – there's more! In the same newspaper that caused me so much aggravation, there was another hippo story. I quote: 'a bank has spent 38p on postage to tell a woman she must pay a 1p overdraft before she could close her account. [She] sent [them] a cheque.' Now, just think about the hidden costs of this bureaucratic exercise. For the bank, look at the computer time, the paper, labour in franking etc. Also, think of the cost to her: the cheque, postage, clearing charges. Well, I could go on and on, but you see my point.

We have to remember that not everything is worth doing. The elegance of having the books balance or crossing every 't' and dotting every 'i' is just not worth the time, effort and money involved. Do things, even difficult and dangerous work when necessary, by all means. But only when necessary!

The difficulty is deciding when something is really needed. There will always be multiple perspectives on the requirement for any given job. Each point of view will be rational and worth serious consideration. Nevertheless, attempts to satisfy everyone when establishing boundaries around a job will result in an excessively complicated process that achieves little and fails to really satisfy anyone.

There are no easy ways to fix this problem. A start can be made by recognising that the condition exists, something extraordinarily difficult for companies and individuals alike. However, it does exist. Whether in your company or in your personal work habits, desperately difficult work is undertaken that should never have been exposed to daylight. The sooner you come to accept this, the sooner you will begin to bring it under control.

The key to all successful endeavour is to reduce to a minimum the energy applied without reducing the value of the output. We need to get from point A to point B with the fewest steps possible. Unfortunately, need is not the same as want, and there will be those who resist this simplification of work. Every step taken today has some justification, and each will be defended vigorously. There will always be reasons not to change. Whenever you come across these 'reasons', sniff the air and ask yourself, 'Is that Rome burning?' Unless you decide consciously to ignore such reasons, any improvements they bring will be temporary and will become a disadvantage sooner rather than later. Addressing this requires a level of courage and conviction found only in the best managers.

There are three questions that will help you judge the value of work. The first asks *why* something should be done, not just if it can be done. This does not mean starting every new project with a negative view – far from it. However, it does mean you should insist on knowing the problem or opportunity before you agree to the work.

The second question asks what the work adds to profits. Now, many things must be undertaken that will not show up on the corporate bottom line, at least not immediately. For example, infrastructure investments are always vital but seldom show a clearly identifiable profit. Nevertheless, this is a useful question because it focuses the mind and forces a level of honesty into the decision to invest, especially when the investment has only a problematical financial return.

The third question, assuming the activity has got this far, asks when it should be done and what it replaces that had been planned. Always try to eliminate or delay other planned work. It is easy to pile on requirements but, unless the organisation has unlimited resources, it becomes increasingly difficult to accomplish major tasks when too many are on the schedule. Don't let your new initiatives add to the project list.

Always look for ways to reduce the workload and make progress easier. Challenge why someone is too busy, not whether they are or not. Try rewarding the lazy. Learn from them so that you can understand how they have trimmed the unnecessary. Don't reward the overworked. Instead, help them give up the labour they so jealously protect. Never, never reward those who continue in their efforts to 'put socks on the hippopotamus', regardless of how wonderful they are in other ways.

I suppose the thing I hate most about doing stupid, wasteful work is that it makes me feel stupid and wasteful myself. That's a good enough reason to fight it whenever and wherever it's found. However, it's not the only kind of work we have to worry about. There's another, much more insidious and hard to detect condition that affects the workplace. The following rule helps remind me that it's there. It's still a problem, but at least I know about it.

Rule of business life no. 2

Don't kill frogs

Have you heard the story about the frog? It may not be true but it was reported as a scientific fact. If it is true, it probably says something about scientists, or at least the one who conducted this experiment. At any rate, the story goes that if you put a frog into boiling water, it will jump out of it. However, if you put it into cold water and gradually turn up the heat, it will stay in place until it boils to death.

Fascinating, but what does it have to do with business? This little story is a reminder that businesses sometimes forget to regulate the heat. We just keep adding the work until our frogs – oops, I mean our people – collapse. Just like the frog, they cannot feel the heat slowly increasing until it's too late.

When there is a lot of pressure on the business, we recognise it. Perhaps we jump out of the heat. Perhaps we adjust our internal temperature to cope with it. Before we react, we ask questions. Is this a temporary phenomenon or is this going to continue for an extended time? Are we experiencing a true emergency or is it just something trumped up to increase our performance to unrealistic levels? Ultimately, we ask ourselves if it is worth the self-sacrifice we are being called on to make. We tend to be rather pragmatic in business. When things are really hot, we make the necessary decisions and act. After all, if a frog knows enough to jump out when the water's boiling, so do we.

What about when the water starts off cool? In business, this is when workloads seem reasonable and goals achievable. Our objectives are high but realistic enough for everyone to buy into them. There is an excitement in the workplace and morale is fine. We have all experienced this and remember the circumstances fondly. First question: do you feel that way today? Second question: if you do, how long has this feeling lasted? Last question: why hasn't it been a permanent condition? We do not ask how long this wonderful condition will last. We are all a bunch of optimists and hope it will last forever – this time.

However, we know it will not. Something will come along and blow it. It can be one of any number of things: a new assignment; a new boss; a financial change in the corporate fortunes; and so on and so on. What concerns us here, however, is the gradual increase in heat that catches us off our guard. This is called incremental work. It may be the biggest mass murderer of organisations conceivable.

Here's an example of incremental work. A medium-size company in the US wanted to improve their level of customer service. Knowing these initiatives have a tendency to grow unreasonably large, the parent company assigned a member of its operational board to provide some control on the scope of the concept. The project was originally limited to building a database of customers with products under warranty. This would be used to answer customer questions, dispatch engineers to correct problems and, when appropriate, charge for services beyond the product warranty period. In all, the entire development was expected to take two years and, of course, it had an approved budget. The head of the division, an extremely bright and creative young individual, saw this initiative as essential to his business strategy and his enthusiasm spread throughout the organisation.

The company contracted with a large technology service provider to develop and install a computer system that would support the plan. This was a very professional organisation which created a 'total quality plan' to support every aspect of the business. Computer systems were designed, training programmes developed, organisation structures modified to cope with the changing responsibilities, and so forth. Everyone recognised this new programme would mean fundamental change to the way business was conducted. They were determined to be prepared. The executive from the parent company relaxed. Everything was under control and the project started nicely.

After five years, the project was still incomplete and the budget had been overspent threefold with no end in sight. The company was on its fourth management information systems director, third operations director and second finance director, trying to control this monster. External consultants had been brought in but they could only recommend scrapping the project and starting again – with them in charge, naturally. The guy from the parent company had left and not been replaced. Meanwhile, customer service had not improved and the old existing process was in danger of collapse. The parent company was at a loss. What went wrong?

You probably noticed the comment about the bright, creative person who headed up this organisation and you've probably worked out the end of this story already. You're absolutely correct. He kept coming up with new ideas, continuously expanding the scope of the work. Each idea was good, mind you. Each could stand on its own merit and none could be countered with a logical argument. Anyway, no one wanted to disagree. Remember, everybody was enthusiastic – at least at the beginning. The work increased gradually as each new idea was accepted. The strategy still seemed to make sense. No one saw the water beginning to boil.

Before you say 'Oh, just another computer horror story', I would like you to reconsider. Yes, people who develop computer systems are often naïve and do not realise that the heat is building up. Yes, they do act like little puppies in their eagerness to please their business users. That's not the point. This type of thing happens in all firms and every functional area of every business has been guilty at some time or other. We have all sinned this way. The sad thing is that it is so easy to control.

Remember, we all have clever ideas from time to time. By itself, this is nothing to become excited about. True intelligence shows if we have the discretion to hold our ideas back when there is already too much activity. In other words, measure the temperature of the water before you turn up the heat. If your idea is a good one today, it will still be valid tomorrow.

Also, remember the poor frog. He isn't merely someone you work with – he may represent your entire firm.

Not all work is disagreeable. Most of us end up doing the things we enjoy doing the most. And we keep on working at it because we like it. Work can become as habit-forming as drugs and we run the risk of becoming workaholics. That doesn't mean we should be spending time and energy on all the work we're given to do, though. Much of what we do remains stupid and wasteful even if we don't find it objectionable. To understand how this happens, we have to look at why this type of work was started and why we allow the habit to form in the beginning.

Rule of business life no. 3

Activity ain't productivity

There is a special kind of work which requires our constant vigilance. Called 'make-work', it adds a subtle but pervasive danger to most organisations. We don't even make excuses for inflicting it on our companies. After all, idleness is something to be avoided so it's reasonable to make work for people, whether the work needs to be done or not. Isn't it?

It's how we deal with idleness that makes all the difference. Creating work merely to keep people busy can damage the morale of the individual and contaminate the spirit of the organisation. It's a temptation that's hard to avoid but one that can lead you astray in many ways. Let me give you an example.

When I was a young teenager I worked for my father, a self-employed electrical contractor. I'll be the first to admit that I wasn't much help. Actually, I think my mother was responsible as she found it an easy way to keep me out of the house and out from under her feet. Regardless, I did my best to help him in any way I could.

Unfortunately, there were not many things I could do for him. He was forced to invent some 'make-work' tasks for me. These usually involved cleaning his van and putting tools and electrical fittings into their various storage bins. Such work wasn't much to take pride in but even then I was fairly pragmatic. I was being paid, and money is, after all, money.

This situation went on for a while but I could see the writing on the wall. Let's face it, there are only so many times you can clean a van. My father was beginning to dislike having me under his feet as much as my mother did. My only source of spending money was starting to look tenuous, to say the least. Then I became clever. I started putting things away for *my* convenience, not my father's. Soon, he was unable to find anything on his own. Just that easily, my job was secure.

And that is the essential danger of created rather than required work. It can suddenly go from unimportant, meaningless activity to vital functionality. Yet, when you go back to basics, you quickly find it is actually senseless, after all.

There are other dangers with this kind of work, and they are perhaps even more important. Let's just think of some of the negative attributes that can develop. First, consider the way an unnecessarily heavy workload can create isolation. This is one of the worst results of 'make-work'. It's a common human condition for people to use their busy schedule to make you leave them alone. They can become too busy to take that customer telephone call, attend that critical staff meeting or tackle that important task. Instead they will concentrate on the unimportant details of a meaningless job.

There's a second aspect to 'make-work' which we all know about but don't always understand. There is even a business phrase to describe it. We call it 'rearranging deck chairs on the Titanic' and use it to encapsulate doing work that is routine when we can't afford to waste the time. Isn't that what most people do when a disaster is about to strike? Our old enemy, 'make-work', has hit us again. People get so engrossed in the habit of doing non-essential work, they have trouble recognising when serious issues must be dealt with.

How do situations develop that allow this to happen? Partly, this is a result of bad management. Bosses just love to be creative. They also hate seeing people idle when a salary is being paid and they don't always want to face the issues of redundancy or dismissal. After all, it might reflect badly on them. When you add these two conditions together, the scene is set for 'make-work'. If your boss is doing something of this nature to you, do everything in your power to resist. The best way, of course, is to keep busy on vital work. If there isn't any to be done, take a holiday. Or quit! You only have one career and you should not waste it doing unnecessary labour just to keep a boss happy.

However, it is not always the boss's fault. Far too often, we are the guilty party. Even the best and smartest people believe they are most productive when they are busy. Besides, being busy is satisfying. We just love to dive into problems and sort things out. This is called fire-fighting. We all do it to some extent. It's just so much fun. But, there is a huge potential for catastrophe in this. The temptation to create a fire that needs fighting often lures people into excesses.

The best way around this is to engineer situations in advance, not just react to them after they have happened. This sounds Machiavellian, and maybe it is, but that is not the reason people avoid doing it. It requires a great deal of thought, planning and fortitude to achieve. Too many of us choose the path of least resistance and just occupy our time with the trivial.

If you allow yourself that escape route, all you achieve is the act of trivialising yourself. When you learn to act, not react, you will have learned the secret of working smart, even if that is not necessarily working hard. You'll then know that you must look at the end result, not just the energy expended.

Around three hundred years ago, Isaac Watts articulated an old, old philosophy when he said, 'For Satan finds some mischief still for idle hands to do'. Perhaps that's true in a few special cases. However, the hands too busy doing useless work are the real mischief-makers in today's world.

So far, we have talked about the agonies and dangers of doing work that shouldn't be done at all. We now reverse the equation for a moment and discuss the problems involved in not being allowed to do work that needs to be done. There's no inconsistency here. The best reason to avoid useless work is to free yourself to do what's truly needed. What's the sense in doing the former if you fail to do the latter?

Rule of business life no. 4

You can't dig a well from the bottom

I'm sure all of us have experienced the problem of the boss telling us what he wants the end result to be when he doesn't want to be bothered with the effort required to achieve it. Often he'll nod off and go to sleep when it comes to the detail. He wants to drink the water without being concerned with digging the well.

It's strange, but this mistake is usually made by the best bosses. Amazingly, they almost always do it for a good reason and with the best intentions. Not only are they the ones we trust to make work decisions, but also their hearts are always in the right place. Why then, do bosses make such big mistakes? Let's look at a company where this happened to see if we can find out why it went wrong.

A few years ago, a nationwide company was doing rather well. They had established themselves in a nice market niche and over the years had grown to a dominant position. It was a terrific company in all the right ways – profitable, enjoying sustained growth and, as its employees liked to brag, a fun place to work.

The chief executive was a dynamic and charismatic individual who had been with the firm for nearly twenty years. Over that time, he had taken what was a small, family-run business and introduced a fairly high degree of professionalism among the management team. Brought in originally to save the company when it was struggling to survive, he had increased turnover more than tenfold.

All in all, he was quite a remarkable individual. Amazingly brash and energetic, he possessed one additional attribute which we all need. He had a vision. He knew exactly what he wanted the firm to become. He was determined to see it achieved.

But he was getting on in years. While retirement was not on the immediate horizon, he could see it coming. He decided to push for his end goals faster. Already dominant in its own market niche, the company decided to enter another. It bought a weak firm in a new market segment without examining the difficulties of attempting to run two dissimilar businesses. Its internal management skills were not easily transferred and the new, suddenly larger, business struggled to be comfortable.

So, following the entrepreneur's credo of never standing still, he bought another weak company in the same niche as his last acquisition rather than taking the time to digest what he now had. He believed the larger pool of skills and increased turnover would create dominance in the new market he was entering. However, two losers joined together without doing the work necessary to develop them are only that – two losers.

The businesses were not progressing fast enough to suit the chief executive. His vision of being recognised as a major business player was being delayed. Rather than invest the time and effort needed to put that right, he found another way to move towards his goal. He bought a bankrupt company in another country thousands of miles away.

By now, the sales for his combined businesses were reaching the targets he had established. This had the effect of hiding the underlying weaknesses so they did not show as overt problems. Unfortunately, all he had really achieved was to add another loser to the group, and his management was stretched ever thinner. The work to make the new ventures successful was still deferred. Meanwhile, he had another bright idea.

Remember the original company, the one that dominated its market niche? It was still the only division that was generating profits. So naturally, he had to mess around with its formula. He needed additional profits to support his other enterprises and the only way available was to increase the original division's contribution. So he added new product lines. It was a shame his management team and staff had no experience with the additional products. For a reason he never was able to fathom, profits started slipping away.

This is a very sad story. The chief executive made a huge mistake that entirely invalidated all his previous efforts. It was distressing to watch the combined businesses fight for their corporate survival and, ultimately, fail. The companies are still trading under their original names but they are now owned by a conglomerate specialising in corporate salvage operations. All the wonderful characters that made the company unique are gone, dispersed around the world. Today, it is just another faceless entity. All of this because one person wanted to start digging the well from the bottom. All of this because of impatience.

Let's look at some of the lessons we can learn from this story. If we don't understand how these mistakes are made, we run the risk of making the same errors based on the same motivations. First, it's important to understand that the worst mistakes are usually made by the smartest, most experienced people in the company. They are the ones who help the company form its vision, though the vision isn't restricted to the top leadership. We all have our visions and personal goals. If we focus solely on them and refuse to accept the labour and time necessary to achieve the goals, failure is inescapable.

We also have to accept that the gravest errors come from decisions that are well-intentioned. Just remember, whenever you want to do something because it will be 'good' for someone else, stop. Check your motivation. Check your facts. If you still think it's worthwhile, check everything again. Then, don't do it, anyway.

The biggest reason for disasters of this nature is not impatience nor is it doomed by the good intentions themselves. It is, quite simply, unbridled arrogance. You can tell when this is happening if the boss says things that boil down to 'I've said it is that way so that way must be right' or 'I have a gut feeling'. When you combine this arrogance with the need for speed and urgency, problems are inevitable and often catastrophic. There are all kinds of warnings about this in our common, everyday language. Think about some of the phrases you've heard since your childhood: 'You can't eat the meal 'till the cook's done his job' or 'You can't eat the cake till it's baked'.

Saying something is so doesn't make it so. Wanting to reach the end quickly doesn't permit you to skip the steps needed to get there. Making urgent demands doesn't make you right. You must dig the well from the top down. There is no other way.

There is still another type of work we have to understand. It's valid work. It's strategic and not incremental. And you can prepare for it properly. That doesn't mean everything is going to run smoothly. Things can still go wrong if you aren't careful. The next rule helps keep certain fundamentals in perspective.

Rule of business life no. 5

Don't make soup in a basket

For a change, the executive committee meeting was not acrimonious. It was, in fact, the closest thing to a love-in since the communes of the 1960s. To persuade that bunch of individualists to agree on the time of day was difficult enough. To get them to agree to a multi-million-dollar project seemed a miracle. Nevertheless, enthusiastic agreement was sweeping around the table.

Feeling rather satisfied, I glanced at the chairman. He was, after all, the one who had originated the concept and had been pushing for the project most aggressively. He was the real architect of the programme, not me. I was merely the tool he was using to achieve the end he wanted. I was surprised to see a frown on his face. As was his nature, he stood and began pacing the room before he addressed us.

'All right, gentlemen,' he started, 'let me see if I can summarise the situation. You have all agreed to back this new project. You realise, of course, it means spending more than 50 per cent of all the profits we made in the last fiscal year. Still, you think it's a good risk to take.

'Now, you've all agreed that it's necessary. You've also agreed that it will allow your areas to increase your contribution to the company. If that's true, and you each do what you say you will, we can easily afford to do it. Finally, you've agreed that it's absolutely necessary to undertake this if we are to achieve the business transformation needed to stay competitive.

'Okay, I'm pleased you've made this type of commitment. We wouldn't move a step forward if you hadn't. And, I agree with you. It's the right thing to do. It's essential that we move ahead as rapidly as possible. Survival isn't guaranteed if we delay.

'However, as I was listening to the discussions over the last hour or so, a nasty thought crossed my mind. Let me ask you a question. Are we building a fantastic company, only to sell it cheap? You must realise this project is not the only thing the company has to spend its money on. Doing this puts us right up against the wall for at least the next two years. And that's only if everything goes right. If any one of you fails – even the least little bit – the benefits could come too late to satisfy our shareholders. We could end up so weakened financially that some other company could buy us at a bargain-basement price.'

We all sat back in our seats to think about this. The man was absolutely right. None of us wanted to work that hard or that long only to see someone else gain the benefit. It was a real challenge. Could we afford to take the risk? On the other hand, could we afford not to take it? We were much smaller than our main competitors and they were well ahead of us in this particular area.

In the end, we took the actions any reasonably decent management team would take. We broke the project down into bite-sized elements, committed less funding up front and stretched the project life cycle over a longer period of time. A few years later, all the main elements were completed and we actually derived even greater benefits than we predicted. We even gained a few pleasant 'soft benefits' that we had hoped for but not believed possible.

The point of this little tale is to emphasise the importance of living within your corporate income. As an individual, you would not build a house you couldn't afford to maintain, would you? Well, the same thing holds for a business. You not only need to be able to build the business but you also need funds to support it as an ongoing practice. Many firms forget this. They invest so much in the future that there are no reserves left for the present.

And don't think that reserves only relate to money. You can't afford to be spendthrift with any of the company's scarce resources. You have to view your investment not just as money, but as the energy, time and the goodwill of your people. Their commitment is the most valuable commodity you have, and probably the one most often squandered.

I thought long and hard after that executive committee meeting, trying to ensure that I understood the implications of our actions and the points the chairman was making. It finally all made sense when I remembered another conversation from former years. There were three of us eating lunch at a Mexican cantina. The more senior man was trying to explain how he viewed the business. He used the analogy of basket-weaving, describing how the individual pieces of rattan cane are woven together to create something whole while the individual identities of each piece are retained.

The second person, an old friend from West Virginia, gave a wicked grin and looked us, one at a time, in the eye. 'I suppose', he said, 'it depends on what you're trying to do. Myself, I view the company as a pot you use to blend things together. Just remember, you can't make soup in a basket.'

It's not only the work we select (or have selected for us) that's important. We also have to be concerned with the sequence in which we do things. Just as you would not jump in the car and drive to work before getting dressed, there are some things at work which have to take precedence. How do you decide which are the most critical? The answer varies according to circumstances but the next rule may help in some instances.

Rule of business life no. 6

Pick the low-lying fruit first

A few years ago, I was the chief information officer in a fairly large firm. It just so happened that this was during a time when outsourcing, that is, letting another company do some of your work for you, was all the rage. The accountants loved it. The more that could be outsourced, the better it would be, according to them. They didn't care how strategic the work was, how central to the core business the functions were or how easily competitive advantages could be developed if it were not outsourced. Of course, information and technology were two of the first items to be considered.

Now I have nothing against outsourcing and have done it myself many times. As a relatively new executive with the company, I had no legacy to protect. I was also far from satisfied with some of the productivity factors of the department working for me. Outsourcing seemed to be a way to solve my problems. So, very quietly, we started looking at the opportunities to outsource.

Regardless of how confidential you attempt to keep this type of research, eventually someone will become aware of it. That's what happened in this case. A young manager approached me and asked if we were going to outsource her department. You can't lie and you can't dodge the issue in this situation, so I said it was an interesting concept and was worth looking at in an objective manner.

She glared at me for a moment and then slowly relaxed. 'Okay,' she said. 'I guess we'll have to trust your judgement. I'm not too happy about it but I can't see what we can do if that's what you decide. Just remember, please, to pick the low-lying fruit first.'

I was mortified. I had allowed myself to become so entranced with the concept of letting other people solve my problems for me for a fee that I had forgotten one of my own rules.

'Back to the beginning,' I shouted at my team. 'We're going to do this analysis again, and this time, damn it, we're going to do it right. I want every penny squeezed out of the expenses before we sign a contract. I want to see what we can do to raise our own productivity before we give up and let someone else do it for us. I screwed up the first time around but not again.'

Originally, the contract we were getting ready to sign would have saved us $1 000 000 per year. Within three weeks we picked some low-lying fruit and saved enough money to reduce the size of the cost delta by more than half, taking it to only $400 000 per year. By tightening our belts in a few other areas, it was down to less than a quarter of a million. We then changed some production schedules and finally ended up with the cost of keeping the services in-house at approximately $100 000.

Meanwhile, another team had continued to work on the contract. This was needed to ensure the service standards for the business stayed at least at the level we were already producing. Surprise, surprise! When these standards were put in writing, suddenly the bid jumped by – you guessed it, about $100 000.

In the end, I decided to keep the service in-house. I could easily have gone either way from a financial perspective. But I was so proud of my staff for their willingness to throw away their legacy thinking and grab the opportunity to pick the low-lying fruit first that it was impossible to deny them. At least, for me it was impossible.

Don't be confused. Outsourcing itself may or may not be the right thing to do in your circumstances. The point is to do certain fundamental things before jumping to conclusions. Let's take another example.

You go into your office on Monday morning. As usual, you are faced with 73 tasks that must be done immediately. Being a clever person, you apply some of the other 'rules of business life' to eliminate all those superfluous, irritating jobs developed by some superior's over-inflated ego. Still, you have three important functions that absolutely must be done.

So do the easiest one first. You know all three tasks must be tackled but isn't it much better to have one done and out of the way as soon as possible? It certainly relieves the pressure and allows you to show people that accomplishments are occurring. If nothing else, that will keep them off your back. All of this adds up eventually. It makes the hard stuff easier to do and the impossible things merely difficult.

There are other reasons to practise this rule. The most pragmatic reason is that if you don't do the easy things, someone else will. They'll be the ones who look like heroes to your boss, not you. The best business reason is that doing the easy task produces results today. However, it's not possible to over-estimate how important that is in business. Remember, your board of directors knows that today is not a dress rehearsal. It wants and needs results now – not a promise for the future.

You must be very, very careful. Remember the scenario we used earlier? Remember the seventy jobs we eliminated at the beginning of the day because they were not worth doing? If you select one of those to do because it's a low-lying fruit, you'll end up shooting yourself in the foot. Misapplication of this rule is worse than not using it at all.

Working is another way of exercising judgement. There are always multiple ways to accomplish any task. You have to choose the one that suits your circumstances at the time. Don't make lazy decisions. These are the ones that follow a formula and are applied without looking at the current situation. You know – always buy the cheapest (or the most expensive); always choose the quickest (I have never heard of a formula for choosing the slowest but it may exist); or – well, you understand. Formulas are all right in their place but their place is seldom in a profitable business environment. However, there is one formula that may help.

Rule of business life no. 7

Don't let the best be the enemy of good

Once upon a time, I worked for a chief financial officer. This is something I normally use all my skills to avoid if I possibly can. It's not that finance people wear black hats. As human beings go, some of them actually make it past the threshold. Not many, I'll admit, but a few do. I would even count one or two as friends. But I wouldn't want any of my daughters to become friendly with one.

Joking aside, there's some truth in the idea that my mind works differently from that of most financial people. They usually just want the figures to add up correctly and don't care about the sequence of the numbers. To people in my line of work, the sequence controls the entire process. We don't care if the number at the end is a little imprecise. Precision isn't that vital. We believe – correction, we *know* – that if the process is right, we will reach the right conclusion eventually. And then we can repeat the process time after time after time – without trouble and without error.

I think the CFO was quite a smart person, although I was never entirely sure. I am confident he was very, very clever. One day we were discussing a large job and looking at alternative ways to get it done. The meeting ended, as usual, with no final decision made (there I go, showing my prejudices again), but I remember his words as he was leaving the conference room.

'Remember, Terry, don't let the good be the enemy of the best,' he said, leaving utter confusion in his wake at this parting shot. 'What did he mean?' we wondered. During the entire meeting, he had been telling us to go for the cheapest solution. Now, it seemed he was telling us to go for the best.

I pondered on his phrase for quite some time. It certainly sounded smart. He even seemed, for a financial person, to give good advice. But something was wrong. I wasn't sure what, but my instincts were telling me that it was dangerous to use that advice.

We cut now to a scene a couple of years later. During lunch with the vice-chairman, he asked several probing questions, trying to determine what my decision-making criteria were. I hummed and hawed as much as possible but at last the conversation came round to a significant purchase I had made a few months previously.

'That's exactly right, young man,' he exclaimed. 'That's the way to do it! Never let the best be the enemy of good.'

I immediately remembered that meeting with the CFO and realised what had been troubling me. I told the vice-chairman about it without naming names or indicating the person involved.

'That must have been Tom,' he guessed, correctly. 'Those people in finance are always getting things back to front. If he's going to steal my quotes, he should at least get them straight.'

Well, I don't know about that. But a great weight seemed to lift from my mind. Finally, I was able to resolve the dilemma. Let me see if I can explain it.

In a nutshell, you must look at the total result, not just isolated pieces. Of course we all want to do the best possible job in everything we undertake. That's always better than a job that's merely good. Still, we have to put things into context. For example, if you're the head of a large conglomerate, you will probably find it better to buy a good company that meets your profile and fits within the structure rather than a great company that would stick out like a sore thumb. Even in personnel selection, a great talent that clashes with the entire team is probably the wrong decision. A good person who will work well with the rest of your staff is almost always a better choice.

Suppose you've decided to buy a software package for your personal computer. Maybe, at the time you buy it, it is the best. Once you've bought the package, you train yourself and the staff (or your children) how to use it.

As you know, there's always something 'new and improved' coming along. If you allow yourself to change constantly to the 'best', think of the end result. Constant retraining. Constant expense for this new 'best', whatever it is. Lost time. Lost energy. Lost money. If you just stay with something that is good and make improvements only when necessary, you will be much better off.

This doesn't mean that you should select second or third best. It doesn't mean that the best is out of the picture. We should always try to raise ourselves up by our bootstraps. Whenever the best doesn't hurt the good, go for it. When you're ready to make a change, make it for the better. Just keep your eyes on the end result. Don't let that new 'best' element destroy all the other good things you have.

So far, we have discussed the nature of work and how often our hard labour is wasted. Time after time, the focus has been to avoid doing anything that isn't absolutely necessary. There is always enough urgent work to keep us extraordinarily busy without doing foolish things. We'll close this part on work by turning things around.

Rule of business life no. 8

If it ain't broke, you haven't tried hard enough

This rule seems to fly in the face of all conventional wisdom. After all, you've been hearing for years that if it's not broke, don't fix it. So, is there an inconsistency here?

If you own or operate a car, you know exactly what this rule means. Your car is running perfectly. You glance at the odometer and see that it has passed the mileage for its scheduled maintenance. If you're smart, you don't put it off. You take the car to the garage and turn it over to the mechanic as soon as possible. You do this even though it's working perfectly. Why?

Home-owners act in the same way. The roof may not leak and the heating system may be perfect. However, the home-owner is constantly working on preventive maintenance. The work isn't easy and it's often expensive. To an outsider, the house seems perfect. Why are they doing this?

It's the old question of cost. We all know things wear out and, in the end, break down. Sooner or later, we'll have to invest some time or money in keeping things running. Through hard-won experience, we have found a small investment made sooner prevents a much larger investment later.

Business people especially recognise this fact of life. They willingly make investments every day in preventive maintenance, though almost always regarding mechanical things. We repair the office buildings, maintain the automotive fleets and make sure the engineers check the computer systems whether there is a known problem or not. Even these are sadly forgotten when businesses are involved in a cost-cutting exercise.

For many firms, however, the maintenance seems to stop there. Unfortunately, other items wear out as well. Business processes become old and stale. They may still work, but no longer fit the market environment.

A few years ago, my family and I went to the US for a wedding. By coincidence, we were not far from the first company I had worked for. I hadn't been there in twenty years but, by another strange coincidence, the company telephone number suddenly popped into my mind. I called in to see if my first boss was still there. He was, and seemed delighted to accept an invitation to lunch, when we could talk about the good old days.

It was an enjoyable reunion, not only with my old boss but with several other former workmates. While older and greyer, they were still the same wonderful people I remembered. One fact in particular struck me. A computer system I had designed and programmed had just passed its twenty-fifth anniversary. Not merely still in production, it remained a vital cog in the business machine.

Initially, I thought this was wonderful. In the fast-moving world of computers, it's rare indeed to find anything completing five years of productive life, much less twenty-five. 'This', I thought with a great deal of pride, 'is great. I must have been right on target when I designed it. How else could I have anticipated the market for that long?'

A little more thought brought home just how wrong I was. I now look back on that visit with a horrid fascination. It's the same company, the same people, the same building, the same volume of business. If it weren't for the modern cars in the parking lot, I could have thought I was lost in a time warp. Internally, little had changed. But externally it was an entirely different world. The company, once one of the brightest leaders in its industry, had fallen by the wayside. Overtaken by time, the business is now destined for a slow but peaceful death and does not seem to realise it.

The problem it faces is an old one. Everything seems to work well enough and no one single thing merits the investment to change. It isn't just the system I was so inordinately proud of that demonstrates this. Everything about the company is frozen in time.

Oh, the company directors do the basic preventive maintenance. They know enough to fix the leaks in the roof when the sun is shining. But what they elected to do was to treat the symptoms of the disease, not the disease itself.

This company may be an extreme example of the condition. However, they are not alone. All businesses suffer from this to some extent. It's a nasty problem and one of the most difficult to recognise. We have so much work needing to be done that it's difficult to address problems where none seem to exist.

You'll receive no praise if you bring this issue to the board. The bean counters – and that doesn't necessarily mean accountants – will scream at you. They'll claim there are enough real problems without bringing this to the table. Sometimes, they'll even be right.

Your business lives today on investments made in the past. Obviously, this means we must make investments today for the future. Some of these investments will be on issues which may have no perceived faults. The trick is to anticipate what will be inadequate later. Failure to recognise these situations will cause your organisation to fall slowly asleep as the rest of the world roars by.

In the final analysis, all the rules concerning work boil down to the need for you to think. There is nothing more important, nor any other activity in your working life that has greater impact. Don't waste your time reacting to events you haven't thought about. Never make judgements based solely on assumptions or intuitions. Think things through before you are pressured into action. Your workload will be lighter but, more importantly, your results will be far, far better.

There are, as you might expect, many additional rules about work, but it is now time to move on to other aspects of our business life where there are new rules to review.

Part II
Rules about advancement and promotion

Advancement and promotion are topics most often associated with the young. When you are older, it is assumed you have already reached your natural level and are satisfied with it. Poppycock! Ambition never dies. We all have it, both the good and bad parts of the drive to succeed, until we're planted in the ground. I'm not sure it can be discounted even then.

I will admit to some minor differences between the business generations. The young are ambitious in a very personal, next-step manner. They want to know when the next promotion is coming. They don't want to hear any drivel about the long term. Just tell them about tomorrow, thank you very much. For the most part, they are quite understandably concerned about their slice of the pie.

Older business people are not that much different but the approach they use is somewhat more subtle. They do tend to look at the longer term. Like chess players, they try to see options for the next five or six moves. The ambition is still there. It's just that the drive is usually directed towards building a bigger business rather than a higher position. They know a small slice of a much, much bigger pie will give them more.

The big difference is not between the young and the old but between the successful and the failures. Often, it's simply a way people view life. It's as much a matter of attitude as it is of wealth or position. Some people at the top of very large organisations are extremely frustrated while those in a smaller, more sedate role are very content.

There's a great deal of advice on how to become successful. We start learning about success in school and continue the learning process throughout life. Most of what we are taught is pure rubbish but worth listening to if only for its comical aspects. You hear advice from business executives who are undoubtedly successful. The trouble lies in their rose-coloured memories. You also hear some from academics. They have no vision problems, but they look backwards with their case studies and thus they seldom see success as it happens. You hear from management gurus, consultants, psychologists and even simple folks such as me.

We are taught that success is a journey, not a destination. But most people don't believe that. They equate success with accomplishment. Get things done, and the future is secure. That's all right; I have no bone to pick with either view. We are even taught, sometimes in excruciating detail, how to get things done. Every once in a while, the teacher even knows how to do it. Again, this is good stuff and should not be ignored.

But if you talk to any plumber or electrician, you'll learn that there are 'tricks of the trade' which make the job easier. These aren't taught in the trade schools, nor will they ever be printed in guides or manuals. They are the things learned through practical experience.

The following rules do not attempt to duplicate what you have learned in school or on management training programmes. Though never famous or successful myself, I have had the privilege of working with some men and women who were, by any standard, at the very top of their profession. By observing them, I've had an opportunity to see how they do it. Maybe some of these tricks will help you on your journey.

One of the most important rules that successful people follow is to be open-minded. They know that it's impossible to learn if you do not take the time to listen to others. This can be difficult, especially when you disagree with what is being said. When you are actually knowledgeable about the subject, it becomes even more difficult to pay attention. The best business executives work hard to overcome this trait. They know the value of the following rule.

Rule of business life no. 9

Never ignore what you don't understand

'Crap,' snorted a co-worker. Well, perhaps his language was a bit more colourful. I tried to explain my point but it was useless. He had simply decided to stop listening. I remember every aspect of the conversation vividly, even though it took place many years ago. The subject was not the reason I remember it. Nor was his reaction. People tell me my ideas are crap often enough. It's no longer unique. No, the reason I remember is because I learned a lesson.

At that time, I had another co-worker. He was someone I habitually responded to by saying, in effect, 'Crap.' I must tell you a little about this person. He was a nerd, an egghead, a six-pen geek, a ... well, you know the type. He lived in a mental place most of us can't imagine, much less visit. He mangled the English language, using either jargon or six-syllable words to express commonplace activities. I never read one of his written reports without a dictionary at my side. He always spoke in a monotone, never providing emphasis to help the listener determine what was really important. In other words, he was boring.

I thought about him during the conversation with the first guy and realised I was treating Jack the same way that I was now being treated. I had difficulty understanding Jack, so I ignored most of the things he tried to tell me. If the other person was making a mistake by telling me that my ideas were crap, perhaps I was making a mistake as well. Regardless of how difficult it was, I decided to start listening to Jack.

It was a few months later when my decision paid dividends. We were in serious trouble. A large-scale project was slowly failing and I was accountable for it. Unfortunately, I hadn't a clue as to how it could be put right. Jack came up with one of his cryptic comments that I almost automatically dismissed. Remembering my earlier promise to myself, I stopped in time. I asked Jack to repeat his idea, this time in English. After five or six tries, I finally understood his concept. It was, after translation, the best possible solution. More than that, it worked. Listening to Jack, someone I had never understood before, saved my bacon as well as several hundreds of thousands of dollars.

It was tough and it never really became any easier. He remained a difficult person to understand and it was impossible to get close to him. Still, over the next few years I came to realise that Jack was usually right in most things and always right about some. I learned never to ignore his opinions. His comments were always worth my time and effort to understand. Jack was, beyond any doubt, brilliant. It just took me far too long to recognise it.

I felt as guilty as sin and just as stupid. How, I wondered, could I have overlooked all Jack had to offer? Then I started noticing how others reacted to him. They were just the same. They ignored him as well, and for the same reason. They didn't understand him. More observation over time convinced me that Jack wasn't the only one to endure this. People tend to dismiss what they can't understand. Too many of us would rather suffer in ignorance than make the effort to learn.

Perhaps your experience is different, but it seems as if most of us only learn when the knowledge comes in a formal, and usually expensive, format. We don't want to learn from what's going on around us and, even more emphatically, from our peers and subordinates. Instead, we prefer to be derisive about their opinions and stand around pontificating about our own 'superior' opinions. We want to be heard rather than be right, and the more ignorant we are about a subject, the more true this seems.

This is when we must listen harder. If you catch yourself thinking about your rebuttal to an argument rather than trying to understand it, you are not really listening. We may not agree, even after fully understanding all the issues. But when you stop listening, you stop learning. If you do it often enough, you stop being told. The price of ignorance is very high but arrogant ignorance is twice as expensive.

The following rule is taught in school and is emphasised throughout every learning experience you will have in your business career. That doesn't take away from its importance, though. You cannot afford to let familiarity breed contempt. If you want to advance yourself, this rule is vital.

Rule of business life no. 10

Preparation is half the battle

Simple, isn't it? We've heard it thousands of times. It's just another old military saying that's been around since the dawn of time, but have you ever stopped to think about what it means? Have you tried to apply the principle to your business life?

Before combat begins, the successful military commander has considered his options and knows what he will do in any given set of circumstances. He may not share his options with the 'grunt' out in the mud, but the key analysis has been made. He may change one or even all of his decisions, but it will be to another pre-set selection.

Now, let's look at ourselves, the average (okay, let's say slightly better than average) business person. How good are we? Come on now. Let's be honest. How do we really compare with our military commander?

Well, we are really pretty good at making decisions when the need is urgent and the options are clear. At least, we are quick to make them. Sometimes we even make good ones. At the risk of being cynical, however, don't you think it's possible that we have the order reversed? Isn't it the case that the decision becomes urgent *after* the options are clear, not that clear options are defined *because* the need is urgent? Confused? If you're a serious student of business decision-making, I recommend you research the way Shell Oil ran scenario planning prior to the Gulf War. Then compare that to the way most of their rivals coped with the situation. Then you'll understand.

Let's return to our old friend, the military decision-maker. Assuming he's winning, he has done more than just pre-plan the main strategy. He's prepared for, or delegated to people he trusts, all the thousands and thousands of minor, detailed decisions that spell the difference between life and death for his troops. We do not always see it that way, yet it is the

29

little decisions that we business people make without preparation which can hurt us. These tend to create a backlog of errors and reversals that can grow and grow. No single issue may be important but the sum of them all is devastating.

That means there are no small decisions. They are all important, at least to someone. The reason we fail to make them, or change them when they are made, is because the options are not clear. This doesn't mean you shouldn't change your mind when necessary. The only thing worse than a late decision is the energy wasted on defending a bad one. However, you'll have to do it a lot less frequently if you've prepared yourself by understanding all the probable alternatives.

Once you have recognised the issue, there are a few 'golden rules' that will help you to see your way clear. The first is to have an opinion. I discovered this by accident many years ago during a staff meeting on a proposal about a truly arcane subject that no one in their right mind could care about. As always happens in this type of situation, the group was leaning towards a decision in favour of the proposal. After all, the person making it was the only one who knew anything about the asinine subject. I don't like decisions by abdication so I made a few controversial comments and stated an adversarial opinion to provoke an honest debate.

In the end, I decided to accept the proposal, but in a considerably modified form, with many of the team now familiar with the issue and able to contribute to the project. The person who had made it his personal 'pet' turned to me and asked, 'Terry, is there anything you don't have an opinion on?'

'No,' I answered. 'That's what they pay me for.' At the time, I was just being facetious. After thinking about it, I realised I was right. That is what all of us are paid for, whether in management or not. It may be better to have an informed opinion but even that is not necessary – just have one. Then, when required to make a decision, you will have a basis for some judgement and will not go about it blindly.

This is much harder, by the way, than you may think at first. Having an opinion means you should know something about the subject. You must keep yourself broadly knowledgeable about all potential topics – not easy in today's business world. It is also extraordinarily difficult for most people to keep their opinion to themselves once they have formed it. However, this is vital. An opinion is just a vehicle for making the decision when necessary, and should not be confused with the actual decision. Allow yourself the time to form better judgements if you can.

Another guideline is to make decisions within a framework. All your decisions should be seen as consistent and, in some fashion, linked with each other. Your framework can be called a strategic plan, a 'process map' of the way you wish to work, a policy handbook, or whatever works best for you. It is not important what you use for a framework, as long as you use one that is familiar to everyone affected by your decisions. Failure to make decisions within some type of framework means that if the decision is changed you may not understand the implications.

Remember also, being prepared to make a decision does not mean that you have to announce it. There are times when you want to let your staff come to the same conclusion themselves. This is a useful way to teach them the process of decision-making. By being prepared, you are in a position to guide their decision without being seen as a 'know-it-all' or allowing them to put the monkey on your back.

The final point is: prepare yourself to decide now. You don't have to tell people. You can change your mind. Use your instinct by all means. Justify your position in any way you want. But be prepared, damn it!

Okay, we all want to succeed. We are more than willing to work hard to achieve success, however elusive it may be. Some want it more than others and are willing to work that much harder. Some, no matter what they say, want it less; you can see that from the amount of effort they put into their work. But hard work alone is not enough, as the next rule attempts to show.

Rule of business life no. 11

Trying is nice – succeeding is better

I've talked about writing this book for some time. When I finally decided to do something about it, my wife's comment was 'Sure, sure – but show it to me when it's done.' Well, after all, she knows me pretty well by now. She was a little surprised but not too curious when I actually started. I showed her the results after the first few rules. She still wasn't very impressed.

She then made several suggestions to improve the approach and contents. I listened to her closely – I've learned through my pain that it's dangerous not to. She finished by saying, 'It's okay for a first effort but you'll have to do better if you want a decent result.' This reminded me of an incident early in my career that taught me one of the first rules I learned in business.

Back in those days, I was responsible for a new and very difficult project. It was one of those jobs that absolutely, positively, had to be done by a certain date, no matter what. As the number of days remaining before the deadline grew smaller and smaller, we all worked longer and longer hours. On the final weekend, the entire project team was on-site. We worked all through that final weekend, taking turns using the bed in the nurse's room for short naps. Around 8.30 on Sunday evening it was done. We were so tired that we didn't even bother to have a celebration. We all just packed up and went home.

The next day, I went to work tired but with that great sense of accomplishment that keeps us going through difficult times. I was called into the chief financial officer's office, expecting to be thanked. Imagine my surprise when I was chewed up and spat out insted. The test criteria were flawed and the project was incomplete. It took us another two days to finish.

I'll never forget that chief financial officer or the lecture he gave me. He was a fascinating person. Only slightly older than myself, he'd risen to his position in a multi-billion-dollar company as if he'd been equipped with rocket assist. It was even more amazing because he suffered from severe stuttering, a handicap that must have been tremendously difficult to overcome. He was a brilliant man and I held him in the highest regard. He also did not tolerate fools.

Listening to him describe my shortcomings was one of the more painful moments of my career, at least to that point. Although it seemed to take hours, he threw me out after five or ten minutes. I remember walking out of his office with his final words ringing in my ears. 'Remember T-T-T-Terry,' he said. 'T-t-trying is nice – succeeding is b-b-b-better.'

This story isn't about embarrassment, however. It has to do with credibility. My reputation within the company, or so I believed, was based on my ability to get the job done, whatever the job was and however difficult it seemed. No one cared how hard I worked or how much effort I put into it. Results were all that counted. Failing to achieve the needed results meant I lost credibility.

I have always told people who work for me that the biggest compliment I can give is to say 'Do it'. It means you don't have to explain, you don't have to rationalise, you don't have to ask for support. 'Do it' means that I know you will do more than try; I know you'll succeed. It's a rare compliment for me to give. It means I trust the person to know the difference between effort and result.

We must always remember that moral victories don't matter. Any attempt to turn a failure into a moral victory will only cost you time and money. If you have a failure, admit it and get on with making it right again. Don't expect your boss to congratulate you on working hard. Yes, hard work is important. But it counts for naught if there is a failure. As my wife and my old chief financial officer both reminded me, results and not efforts are what count.

Pressure is something we all have to deal with in business. It comes in many different guises and affects all of us in unique ways. It would be an over-simplification to say that successful executives counter pressure with aggression, losers with panic and the rest of us with as much dignity as possible. The truth is far more complex. Every situation causes us to react differently from what we might normally expect. A little pressure can be good, but it's far too easy to cross the line and put too much on people. Good executives always seem to remember the following rule in their treatment of others.

Rule of business life no. 12

It's hard to stand up and look around when there's a sword hanging over your head

Things were tough when I first started my career. My wife and I used to go with the baby to my parents every Friday evening after work and stay until Sunday dinner. It was one sure way to eat on a regular basis for at least two and a half days of the week. Imagine, seven free meals! Even then, the money never stretched as far as it needed to go. I took a second job to help make ends meet.

I'm not complaining or trying to portray myself as a martyr, however. It turned out that my second job was one of the best moves I could have made. Because of it, I got to know Mr Henry, one of the grandest old gentlemen you can imagine. Although he was almost forty years older, he and I became good friends and he took me under his wing. I came to know something of his past over the next two or three years because of that friendship. He's gone now, but I think you may appreciate his story.

Back in the early 1950s, Mr Henry was the senior vice-president of operations for a small but growing firm in the construction industry. It had started off as a local builder but had quickly outgrown its base, in large part because of Mr Henry's commitment to quality workmanship. At the time catastrophe struck, the firm was accepting work from a six-state area and had several large government projects. It employed over two hundred full-time staff and at least that number again in casual labour. Margins were high and the cash flow was surprisingly good. In other words, it was a solid company about to enter into the big time.

One Monday morning, Mr Henry entered the company's head office and was surprised to find that the president, the treasurer and the treasurer's husband, a contracts manager, were all missing. Throughout the day, no word was heard and all attempts to contact them failed. Finally, the police were notified and an investigation started. Later that evening, the body of the treasurer's husband was found, an apparent suicide. The next day, the company discovered that the bank accounts were empty and that all tangible assets had been sold the previous weekend. The president and treasurer had run off together, never to be seen again.

Mr Henry was left in an invidious position. As the only remaining board-level officer, he was responsible for all company debts. There was no money left to pay them. His options were limited. He could declare personal bankruptcy or agree to a long-term payment schedule. Being an honourable person, he chose the latter. It took him ten years but every penny was paid.

By the time I met him, he was a proud but beaten man. A once promising career had died early. He was resigned to a mediocre position in life, running a small store for his brother-in-law. It was sad to see someone of his calibre live without hope. That bloody great sword of debt had hung over him too long. He couldn't raise his head high enough to see the world around himself and what it had left to offer.

There are many swords that can hang over us. Most of the time, we have no one to blame but ourselves. It is something we do every time we make a commitment. We make them at home with spouses and children. We make them socially with our friends. Equally important, we make commitments in our work. Each time we do so, there is a possibility that we are hanging a new sword over our head. Okay, that's what commitments are all about.

But sometimes others try to do it for us. That was the case with Mr Henry. You might say he hung the sword himself, and there is some consolation in that. It was a commitment he chose to make when he could have done otherwise. He didn't have to act as honourably as he did, but that's the type of person he was. The president knew him and knew what he would do. As long as the bills were being paid, there was little likelihood of a hue and cry to find the guilty parties.

If you're an employee and your boss tries to threaten or in some way hang a sword over your head, don't let it happen. You must resist. A commitment made on your behalf that you cannot believe in is not a commitment. It's only pressure. Don't be blackmailed. Don't give in.

If you're the boss, don't try it. Even if you feel it's ethical to coerce people to do what you want, it won't work. Commitments must be made voluntarily or they will not be honoured in the end. Worse, you and your firm may miss the best your staff can give. Just think what may be possible if they are free to look around and see what they might do for the firm.

Mr Henry tried to teach me a sense of honour and conduct. To some degree, he failed. It's not his fault, but mine. I refuse to let another person hang a sword over me, financial or otherwise. I won't accept it. I hang enough for myself. At least this way, I can stand up and look around at the opportunities once in a while.

Some people complain that life isn't fair. They've been unlucky, they'll tell you. Well, few of us are born with a silver spoon in our mouth. In many ways, success is nothing but a lottery, and not everyone can win. It's passing strange, however, that those who keep plugging away, not wasting their time complaining, seem to overcome this. Lady Luck seems to favour those who try. The next rule is for the others.

Rule of business life no. 13

If you don't want to dance, don't come to the party

'I wanna be promoted,' he whined. 'I've got all the qualifications. I've been here longer than you. I deserve a promotion and more money.'

I wasn't very happy with him to begin with, and was becoming less so with every passing minute. 'What about last week?' I asked. 'Your people were here working late to complete that project. Where were you? While I'm on the subject, what about that project? You promised it would be done. Why isn't it? This isn't the first time, either. If you fail to deliver for me, why should I work to deliver a promotion for you?'

Although I wasn't pleased with him, I was forced to admit he was talented. He was very capable in many ways and, as he would quickly tell anyone, his qualifications were first-class. A very ambitious person, he did everything possible to gain recognition, including volunteering himself and his team to work on high-profile projects. I had to question myself and my motivations about him. Was it personal animus that prevented me from promoting him? Or were there more tangible reasons? What was it about him that warned me to be very careful?

'Only losers have to work late,' he explained. 'I have a life to lead and work isn't everything. Besides, my staff said they could take care of it. It's not my fault they were late with the project. The other times it happened were out of my control. Anyway, you expect too much.'

That clinched it for me. He considered his people 'losers' because they had to work late and he was too good to join them. At the same time, he was more than willing to let them take the blame for things he had accepted responsibility for. All this and he expected me to promote him too!

I put him on the company's 'drone list' with an official written warning. A drone is a non-worker bee. Having only one function that is soon completed, he is relatively useless to the hive except for that limited skill. People on a 'drone list' are viewed as non-productive and a company can easily do without them.

I must stress that this wasn't solely because of his many failures to deliver the developments he had promised. It wasn't just his lack of credibility. I'm always willing to work with people who make the effort to succeed, especially when they have the talent. Sometimes, they need a little more patience from the people they work for and I realise that. This had to do with effort and commitment.

In his case, I could see no alternative. As long as he believed that the causes of failure were out of his control, he wasn't trying. It was too easy to put the blame on someone else. Yes, he was talented and that certainly counts. But talent by itself isn't enough. A willingness to work, sometimes damned hard, is necessary as well. There's a great deal of truth and wisdom in that old saying that genius is 10 per cent inspiration and 90 per cent perspiration. Business works in the same proportions.

There was one other factor that contributed to his failure. He worked in the mistaken belief that his staff were responsible to him. I was never able to convince him that the reverse was the only way to view management. He was responsible for his staff. He was also responsible *to* them. This is a basic principle for anyone who wants to succeed in management. While he wanted to dance at the management party, he wasn't willing to listen to our music.

The next stage was to put him into the 'departure lounge', and I did that soon afterwards. I hate it when I have to dismiss someone. I feel as if I am the one who failed, not the one I'm firing. In fact, it *is* a failure on my part. This time, I felt I had no choice. When someone's ambition exceeds his competence, willingness to do the job or positions available, you have to remove him from the organisation. If not, he'll eat his guts out with frustration, play politics and potentially cause enormous damage. He would leave anyway, but on his schedule, not yours. Meanwhile, neither you nor he would be happy.

Not everyone can reach the top in any given company. The right to achieve is tentative, at best. None of us has a manifest destiny to achieve all we want, and sometimes it's just not possible to be happy. It isn't fair, but it's the only party out there and you had better accept it. Under some circumstances, you're just not going to win. At times, the best action you can take is to leave the firm. That is better by far than letting frustration and anger creep in. They can only lead to eventual burn-out.

Apply this rule to yourself. Are you willing to dance at the management ball? Do you accept the music as it's played? There's no place for wallflowers who want to sit on the sidelines and watch others do the work. There's room for you only if you're willing and able to participate fully in all the activity on the dance floor.

The next rule originated in the American West during the cattle drives of the late 1800s. In those days, the leaders and scouts were the successes. They were able to ride in the front. The losers were the ones relegated to the middle and back of the long train of cattle, swallowing the dust raised by thousands of feet. Sounds very much like any business of today, doesn't it?

Rule of business life no. 14

If you don't make dust, you'll eat dust

You hear the same complaints from the same people, time after time. 'Oh, so-and-so was just lucky,' they moan. 'I could be in his position if I only had a lucky break once in a while.' Of course, they're dead wrong but those types of people usually are. Those that have the time and energy to complain about someone else's success rarely have any left to achieve some for themselves.

There is an old Chinese curse that condemns enemies to 'live in interesting times'. Maybe they were trying to explain that only the unlucky are forced into a position where they have to make progress. The people who succeed in life are not so much fortunate as pushy. They are constantly sticking their noses into things, often when they shouldn't. Then they find themselves in a position where they have to do something about it. If they do the right things and do them the right way, they advance one or two pegs on the board. If they don't, well, they can always start playing the game from the beginning again.

Joe and I were at the same level, working for the same executive in a division of a large conglomerate. Joe really liked our boss, almost to a point that was sickening. He would have done anything the boss asked. As for me, well, I got along with him; I've never expected more than that with anybody I work for. The two of them together got on my nerves, however, and when the opportunity came to move to the conglomerate's head office, I accepted happily. It would be goodbye to the pair of them, as soon as the children finished the school year and we sold the house.

But, out of the blue, our old president was gracefully retired and a new one hired. Our boss had a few meetings with the new president and, suddenly, he too was gone. New presidents have an even lower tolerance for bullshit than old ones, and I guess our boss forgot that simple fact of life. Joe and I continued to run the department between us while the search was conducted for a new director. As we both reported to the president, we saw him frequently and he became well versed in our part of the business.

It was soon apparent to all that a major project we were embarking on needed a key decision urgently. An executive committee meeting was scheduled to review the issue. Joe and I were charged to prepare the options. We were told we should not work together but each develop our own approach. The big day finally came and, with it, a change in my life.

Joe elected a 'steady hands' option. He proposed to continue the programme adopted by our old boss, with no changes. He presented a well-balanced argument, showing that money already spent would not be lost if we continued forward on that path. His approach was 'better safe than sorry' and he knew he had presented it well. I didn't care for the smile he gave me when he finished and it was my turn.

I'm afraid I was not nearly as sensible as Joe in my approach to the problem. As I was leaving the division soon, I felt I had little to lose. Thus, I had looked at all the alternatives. There was one in particular that I favoured, but it would be costly, to say the least. My closing argument was emotional, rather than logical. 'If we don't make dust,' I claimed, 'we'll eat dust. If we choose any of the other options, the best we will be doing is copying the competition – and they have a three-year head start.'

'You're crazy, Terry,' Joe told me after the meeting. 'You'll never be transferred now. You'll be fired first. You didn't have to say he'd be stupid if he didn't do it your way. You can't say those kind of things to presidents.'

Of course, Joe was right. You can't say that to presidents. The next day he called me into his office and gave me hell about it. He also mentioned that he had contacted my future boss at the conglomerate head office to tell him I would not be transferring as planned.

Instead, the president went on to explain, he had cancelled the search for a new director. The job was mine and the company would handle the project my way. Now I just had to make sure we delivered the goods. Oh, by the way, the first job he gave me was to fire Joe. Anyone who was so stuck in the past as to recommend an approach that had ended his boss's career wasn't someone the president wanted around.

It's all very simple and straightforward. If you want to advance in life, you must engage in competition. It may be a direct one-to-one or it may be an undefined struggle where the opponents are not well known, but it's still competition. You may choose the nature of the competitions you enter but you can't change the nature of competition. There are winners and there are losers. It's up to you. No one is going to fight your battles for you. That's life.

I was not attempting to compete with Joe, although the reverse may not have been true. Remember, I was planning to accept a different job. I have always found that I have all the competition I crave from the other companies fighting mine. But the principles are the same whether the competition is between companies or individuals. You should never, ever compete unless you plan to win. Standing still is a sure way to lose. You have to eat too much dust as the others pass you by.

There has always been an abundance of advice about success. 'Do this,' we are told. 'Do that,' we are admonished. It seems that almost everyone has an opinion about success and they are all willing to share it with us. That's okay. Most of what they tell us to do is useful. Invariably, however, it is those things we should not do that are overlooked.

Rule of business life no. 15

A closed mouth gathers no feet

We all put our foot in it at some time during our life. We say things we regret for years. Sometimes it is just a little hiccup in our careers. At other times, it can be a big jolt. It's never entirely harmless and it's never pleasant when it happens. The thing to remember is that it's really easy to avoid. All you have to do is think before you open your mouth.

Of course, it goes against human nature to do that. If it were otherwise, we would all avoid making fools of ourselves. Instead, we practise talking when we should keep quiet. I've certainly done that often enough. What I hate most is that it makes me feel so silly. That's why I remember in particular one time I put my foot in my mouth. It didn't hurt me much but it should never have happened at all.

To call him an autocrat would have been inadequate. Tyrant is a word that fitted him much better. He was a senior executive of the 'old school' and ruled his department with an iron fist. I used to thank my lucky stars that I did not work for him and our paths crossed only infrequently. We still worked for the same firm, however, and some contact was as inevitable as the conflict between us.

These thoughts crossed my mind as I answered the telephone and heard him on the other end of the line. There had been a foul-up in some things my department was supposed to achieve which affected him. He wanted an explanation and he wanted it right now.

I was vaguely aware that there had been a problem but had not troubled myself to find out all I could about the issue. Still, I wasn't going to admit that to him. I dislike bullies in any circumstance and he was sounding especially belligerent that morning. I decided to bluff my way through the conversation until I could find out more about what had happened. Without further thought, I made a few comments totally void of any meaning, expecting that to be enough.

'What do you think you're on about, Kelley?' he barked. 'You don't have the foggiest idea about what's going on, do you? You're just pretending you have a handle on things. Well, you should keep your mouth shut, boy, or you'll just keep putting both feet in it.'

That hurt. Of all the people I did not want to receive a lecture from, he was the top of the list. The fact that he was right made it even worse. I tried to make excuses for myself. I remembered all the senior staff meetings when he had made inane comments. I thought about the times he had been caught bluffing by others and how he had tried unsuccessfully to brazen his way out. It didn't make any difference. I had still screwed up.

Naturally, most of the company knew before the day was out that Kelley had tried to bluff his way out of something when he didn't know the facts. That hurt too, but I was able to recover. More importantly, I remembered a lesson that I had forgotten, if only for a moment. Never talk when you have nothing to say, say nothing unless it needs to be said and, most of all, never, never talk when you don't know what you're talking about.

In some ways, advancement in business is similar to receiving a medal for hero-ism in the military. In both cases, you have to be seen by someone in authority before your efforts are rewarded. Just as there are always more brave people in the service than there are awards for valour, there are large numbers of talented, hard-working men and women in business who never make it to the top. Recognition is an important component of success. Unfortunately, some people take the need too far.

Rule of business life no. 16

Squeaky wheels get replaced, not lubricated

I rather like to use old platitudes and aphorisms – well, you've probably gathered that by now. They serve a number of useful purposes. They are easy to remember, which makes them ideal for teaching. Recalling one can often help make a complex situation simpler to grasp. They have an exceptional amount of wisdom buried in their simple words. A phrase doesn't become a cliché unless it has proven itself over time.

There is a problem, however. While the shelf-life of a proverb may be long, it's not forever. Unfortunately, it is difficult, perhaps impossible, to kill off proverbs when they no longer give the right message. The old one that says 'the squeaky wheel gets the oil' is a case in point. It hasn't been true since we stopped putting horses in front of wagons, but we still use it. No, today we treat people who squeak all the time in the same way as we treat our cars. We replace the noisy bit because we think it has become faulty.

Years and years ago, I already knew the value of having staff who were willing to fight with me as well as for me. I actively sought those who would not back down, even when I was at my most arrogant. If my staff would not stand up to me, how could I expect them to face our competition? I also knew the importance of keeping a cynic around. I wanted someone to challenge all our most deeply held assumptions. Besides, if you can convince a cynic to do something about it, he will work harder than anyone else to correct all the things he believes are wrong.

When I hired Harry, I thought I had found the perfect employee. He had plenty of self-confidence and was willing to disagree. In fact, he seemed to be fighting with me all the time. He also fought with everyone else, but I was willing to put up with that. He was steeped in cynicism and never took anything at face value. In other words, he was a massive pain in the neck but, so I thought, valuable enough to make up for it. Finally, he was a very good technician, the kind of person I have a great deal of time for. He was particularly knowledgeable in an area where I and most of the other members of the team were totally ignorant. That helped. We automatically listened whenever he talked. We thought we had to.

It didn't take too long before it dawned on me that I may have made a mistake – maybe a very big mistake. Harry was willing to disagree, that was true. He disagreed with everyone and everything. It was simply that his disagreements never took us anywhere. His cynicism didn't just challenge assumptions. It destroyed beliefs. Doubt crept into our management meetings and progress in every area became more difficult.

I took Harry aside and had a long talk with him. I explained that I didn't mind disputes but there had to be a point to them. Saying something would not work was just not good enough. He had to offer an alternative and be willing to prove that it was a better solution. I also told him that pessimism, suspicion and doubt all had their uses, but never if they were the only tools used.

In the end, I told Harry of my expectations and tried to convey my willingness to work with him to develop what I continued to feel was his high potential. He looked me straight in the eye and told me I was wasting my breath. He was perfectly happy with himself. I was wrong, he told me, and it wasn't his job to tell me what was right.

Harry was a squeaky wheel and had to go. He went. Unfortunately, it's not really that simple. You have to listen to the noise to find out what it is. Maybe it's just an irritating squeak. Maybe it's something much more important. Telling the difference is a great skill. Having the patience to practise it is an even greater one. You can take it too far, though, and this can hurt as much as not going far enough.

There's an assumption among business people that you need to call attention to yourself in order to be noticed. While this may be true, you have to exercise care about the type of attention you are drawing. Complainers, doom-sayers and general critics, even when right, tend to fall from grace very quickly. You have to change the situation rather than merely complain about it.

If you expect to succeed by following these few rules, you will have to think again. You'll find that attitude and aptitude are much more important. Those two plus plenty of hard work are the main ingredients for success. Still, the rules will help, even if that's all they can do. If you want better ones, and there are many, many more great rules for advancement, you'll have to find a truly successful person willing to share their secrets with you.

In the meantime, let's assume that these humble rules, along with your natural talents and perseverance, suffice. You are moving up the ladder of business success. What do you have to look forward to on the next rung? Among other features, even tougher rules and harder work. Whatever step you're on today, the journey never becomes easier.

Let's leave this subject and look at some of the problems you'll have to deal with when you take on the next level of management responsibility.

Part III
Rules about management _____

*One of life's golden rules is best stated in
the common courtesies used in the game of
golf: you must play immediately behind the
party in front – not just in front of the
party behind.*
Anonymous

It's not too strange that a great many business people want to be in management. Just think of all the benefits. Somehow, you know you'll be richer if you're in management. Sure you will. In fact, if you were paid just barely over the average wage per hour and earned overtime, you'd probably be better off financially. The sad truth is that in management the hours are long, often in excess of seventy hours a week, and few people reap the really big rewards. The odds are probably as long as those of a kid who loves playing ball getting into the pros. Rich people are, well – rich. Some of them became that way as business managers but few came up through normal management channels.

Nevertheless, we still want to be in management. There must be other rewards if the money doesn't really count. It must be the respect of your subordinates and peers, right? Wrong. You can sometimes earn their respect, and if you're really good, maybe it happens more than once. But, for every time you do earn that respect, think of the other times. You know – the pettiness, the jealousy, the back-stabbing. How about the times when everyone agrees with you and then, the minute you turn your back, the opposite plan is adopted. Sure, there's lots of respect in management!

How about recognition? Not really. Other than the well-known fifteen minutes of fame made familiar by Andy Warhol, most of us see little public recognition for the things we do in business. We might get some lasting distinction at the end of our careers, but few of us see much before then. It's similar to earning a real fortune. It'll happen for some, but the odds are not good.

It must be the great lifestyle, you say. Well, maybe, if you ignore the stress, the long hours and the total commitment to business at the expense of your family life. Yeah, it's a wonderful lifestyle – for those who live long enough to enjoy it.

No, the truth is that the only reason anyone goes into management is simple: the higher you go in management ranks, the fewer of those idiot managers you'll have to take orders from. We don't become managers to join the ranks, but to escape from them.

I've learned a great many rules over the years to help me remember the follies of business management. It's a subject that could fill a book by itself. I have exercised some control and limited myself to a small selection for this Part. I believe these apply at every level, from the junior management trainee to the soon-to-retire CEO. The first of these is the one we must be aware of at all times.

Rule of business life no. 17

Steering is not the same as rowing

There is a great deal of talk in business about 'ownership' and shared responsibility. We have invented various incentive programmes, from employee ownership and profit-sharing to stock options and bonus programmes, just to enhance this concept. All such programmes are designed to make people feel accountable for their actions and make them understand the impact they may have on the organisation. To some extent, these measures succeed, but they can miss the point if not actively supported by the style of management practised within the company.

Ownership is not merely a financial position. It has far deeper meaning to most people. It can and should grab everyone at an emotional level. We should feel this is *my* company and no one is going to hurt it! Senior managers have the power to create this type of environment. Misuse of this power can, and often does, destroy it. They need to learn that power must be shared to develop ownership.

To a large extent, good bosses like to (need to?) exercise power. They must remember that their colleagues and associates have the same urges and desires concerning power as they do. If the only incentive people have is financial, they will end up viewing the company as an investor, which is not the same as an owner. The power to control events is the trigger that activates ownership. It is this we must share to develop that attitude throughout the company.

There are many ways to achieve this. One of the easiest is to separate the power of decision-making from the power of the idea. Most of us are quite satisfied if our ideas have an impact. If we are listened to, we feel we have some power to control events. We do not demand the power to command as well.

There is more to this statement than is apparent on the surface. The power of command and the power of the idea must not be combined in the same individual position! This inevitably leads to disaster. A good boss has to let others come up with the ideas if he or she is to make the decisions regarding them. If you decide about your own ideas, you are on a one-way street to internal conflict, bad morale and a non-creative, 'yes-boss' culture.

The following story demonstrates my point. I attended an executive committee meeting of a billion-dollar company a few years ago as an invited guest. Although the president and I both served on the same operational board of the larger parent company, we did not know each other well as we lived and worked in different countries. Afterwards, we talked about the day's result.

'I don't understand it,' he complained. 'They just don't seem to be interested in owning the problems. Maybe it's because so many of my key people are foreigners. I certainly don't have this kind of trouble with Americans.'

I thought back over the meeting. He had struggled – no doubt about that. It was also true that several of his key executives had been 'loaned' by the parent firm to help him turn the business around. Even so, I couldn't see that as the reason for the level of conflict and the number of personal agendas I had observed. There were only a few non-Americans in the room and they were not solely responsible for the problems, by any means.

Then I remembered how the meeting began. He started it by saying, 'I've had this wonderful idea. Tell me, what do you think about...'

Well, he was expecting only praise but the committee proceeded to tell him what they really thought. Because they were not 100 per cent positive, he saw every comment, even positive criticism, as a personal attack. He defended his idea and rejected every other one. The meeting started tense and became worse. In the end, nothing was accomplished. He would not let another idea prevail, so he could only reject them. At the same time, he did not wish to be seen as an autocrat and would not force people to accept his proposal.

I tried to explain this to him. 'You have to choose between rowing and steering,' I said. 'If it's both your idea and your decision, what's left for them? You allow them nothing they can be fully accountable for if you don't give up something. Remember, there's nothing worse than having your boss do your job. To them, that's what seems to be happening.'

I'll cut this rather sad story short. My comments were rejected as I had 'obviously lived over there too long and had become one of them'. Most of the meetings that followed suffered from the same paralysis and little was accomplished. Finally, he was replaced and, with a different management style in place, the company started on the long road to recovery. He wasn't a bad person, just a bad manager. He tried to do it all himself.

We have to act out many roles in business. At times, we are leaders, even if the size of our team is small. And we sometimes have to make command decisions, even if they are only little ones. At the same time, we are also members of a larger organisation and we make contributions through our ideas. It is easy to confuse the situation, which is what happens if we try to act out all these roles simultaneously. As leaders, we must be visionaries but allow others to grab the vision and expand it. As decision-makers, we must not fall in love with our own ideas. Finally, when we are acting as the supporting cast for our bosses, we have to work our concepts into a greater whole and not try to fight the vision.

Ultimately, most of us do not need to choose between rowing and steering. Instead, all we have to do is choose which to do when. If we try to do both at the same time, our boat is going to go nowhere ... fast.

There's one aspect of management that is frequently overlooked when people describe it to you. Management can be a frightening responsibility. It can make even the most phlegmatic individual nervous. Maybe that's why so many managers seem paranoid. However, there's little need to be alarmed about this part of management. As the next rule points out, if you use it wisely, it's okay to ...

Rule of business life no. 18

Be scared ...

Fear can be a very positive force. It causes the adrenaline to flow, adds excitement to life and generally helps separate the winners (those who dare to fight) from the losers (those who flee from everything or merely sit frozen in the headlights). When we have nothing to fear, everyday events start to pale and we begin to lose the special motivation that the fight for survival brings.

Often, we create situations that provide the missing element of danger. We go out of our way to generate thrills. If danger is not available in our business, we attempt to create some in our private life. Look at the kids in the amusement park. They compete to try the most frightening rides. Look at the people you know. How many ski, sky-dive or even jump head-first off bridges with nothing but an elastic cord to keep them from caving their skulls in? Their eyes seem to glow when they talk about going 'off-piste' or free-falling from ten thousand feet. We love to frighten ourselves.

Even in business, fear can be a positive factor that should never be overlooked. But there are some special considerations when we bring our business into the picture. We cannot put our company at risk merely for the thrill it brings. We cannot expose our firm to danger just to liven things up a bit. We cannot generate fear in others, especially our subordinates, just to pump up their adrenaline – or to satisfy our ego. Creating conditions to scare ourselves is barely acceptable. Creating fear in others is strictly out of bounds.

The question, then, is how can we use fear as a positive factor in business without involving any of its potentially negative attributes? This is a question every individual must ask. Each of us has a different tolerance of fright, and we face our fears in an individual way. Just as some people fear heights, others fear spiders and some both, firms have their unique thresholds of fear and these must never be crossed. Each organisation must make its own determination of which fears to exploit and which to avoid.

To put a little perspective on the subject, we need to understand a few of the ways in which people feel fear. In business, fear usually translates into 'will I still have a job tomorrow?' although it can be more than that in some circumstances. There is also fear of the work itself. Generally, this occurs when someone is given a job beyond their level of competence. Companies in a phase of rapid growth can, and usually do, generate this type of fear, even in the most competent people.

One of the more common fears in business is fear of intellectual domination. This is seen when the boss is a particularly strong individual. Often intolerant, and 'unable to suffer fools gladly', these super authority figures scare individuals with their personality and demands for perfection. Finally, there is the most prevalent fear of all – the fear of not achieving expectations, whether self-imposed or otherwise.

Now, let's look at some of the positive uses of fear. Perhaps most importantly, fear develops the courage to try more, to do more and to achieve more. Courage comes naturally to a few but the rest of us must exercise our nerves, just as we exercise our muscles, to make them stronger. The 'thrills' discussed earlier can cause panic unless a tolerance is created. Allow yourself, and your staff if you have them, to go a little further than necessary. Take small risks so you can handle bigger ones when they inevitably occur.

You can also build on fear to create a special kind of camaraderie that only comes from adversity. The US Marines are famous for their *esprit de corps*, something every organisation should aspire to. When it comes to motivation, they are a terrific model by any standard. They adopted the Chinese phrase 'gung-ho' before the beginning of World War II and the popular definition is now 'a willingness to accept any challenge, respond to any dare'. The real definition, which explains why the Marines brought it back from China with them, is roughly 'working together in harmony'. This, perhaps, is the best possible way to handle fear – together as a team.

Fear plays an important role in business. It can increase our awareness and strengthen our will to fight. So, we're allowed to be scared, but there's a tremendous temptation to go too far and that is something we have to avoid. In business, it is not acceptable to generate fear. It turns into despair far too quickly. Our task is simply to allow people to scare themselves, but even then, not too much. Make it as innocent as the kids at the fairground – a little thrill but no real danger. Fear can become addictive.

I have a confession to make. When I was a foolish young man, I spent six years in the US Marine Corps. I came to learn a great deal about fear. While the last rule claims it's perfectly acceptable to 'be scared', that is only part of it. You can't show your fear. This is simply self-preservation. All animals, and perhaps the one known as man, more than any other, can sense fear. Predatory animals all react the same way: they attack! If you are going to use the last rule, you must also use this next one. They go together.

Rule of business life no. 19

... But don't let your hands shake

For all its positive aspects, fear remains an extraordinarily dangerous tool. When used by the best managers, it's still hazardous. When wielded by poor ones, it's an absolute disaster. Uncontrolled fear can run through an organisation as a fire will sweep through a fireworks factory – explosively.

That is because fear is contagious. It spreads from person to person faster than a rumour. If you want to survive in management, you must learn how this plague can be contained. The only way I know is to hide your personal fear from others and then help them mask their own. This reminds me of an experience from long ago. I've cleaned up the language but the essence hasn't changed.

'Sit down, stupid, and tell me what your trouble is,' the gunnery sergeant barked. All Marine Corps gunnery sergeants bark. It's part of their job description. This one was a small man, about my height but a little heavier. He was also one of the toughest SOBs I'd ever run across. When he said 'sit', I perched myself on a sandbag and laid my problem out for him.

I had just been promoted to lance corporal and was made temporary squad leader. I wasn't sure what that would mean but it worried me that I would be responsible for other people. In other words, I was so nervous I couldn't spit. When in doubt, all Marines go 'talk to the gunny' to get straight advice and that's what I had done.

'Listen,' he said. 'You can be a decent squad leader and, even as dumb as you are, you'll probably do okay. Anyway, it'll be hard to do worse than you were doing before. But, there's a couple of things you gotta do if you're gonna keep your squad.

'First, you gotta relax. You're so damned stiff, I could break planks with your head. You gotta couple of hard cases in the squad. If they think you're scared, they're gonna have you for breakfast. Remember, any damn fool can lead a squad for the day and that description suits you as well as anyone else around here. The problem is, you're smart enough to know it's the other things you have to do, such as making sure there's enough rations to go around at the end of the day. I'll help you with that crap for now, so don't you worry about it too much.

'And, son, you gotta start smiling. Stop worrying about that damn leadership crap. It all boils down to your people having confidence in you. If they see you smile, they know you're not scared so they don't have to be. If they see you look worried, they think they're the ones who'll get stuck with the problem in the end. They're usually right about that, you know. That's really all you have to know about leadership. All it is, son, is just controlling your fear so they don't have any.'

Well, I've remembered the gunny's lesson all these years and it has helped when times were rough. Obviously, it was very basic; leadership calls for much more but I was very young and he had to keep it simple. Nevertheless, he was right about one thing – you have to control your own fear if you are to be any good for those in your care.

To control it, you will have to make a judgement call. Is there too much fear or is there too little? Counter too much fear with blandness. Throw in a little charisma if you need to add a little 'thrill' to the everyday work life. We all have the capability to play either role if the situation demands it. Just make sure you are getting the mix right, then check it every day.

Whether you are the head of a large business defending your firm against an unfriendly take-over bid or a junior staff member making your first major presentation, the rule remains unchanged. Don't let the others

see the fear; don't display your nervousness; relax and smile if you can –
above all, don't let your hands shake.

*This next rule is pretty obvious. Nevertheless, we have to go over the territory.
My treatment of this issue may be no better than others but it was certainly
learned with more embarrassment than most.*

Rule of business life no. 20

The more *you* do, the less gets done

This was probably the first 'rule' I ever learned but it took decades for me
to really fully understand what it meant. The problem is that it is so basic
and makes so much sense, I just overlooked it in the belief that complex
lessons are the ones to listen to in today's frantic business society. Let me
start at the beginning.

My grandparents lived on a small farm in northern Maine. As a young-
ster, I spent a lot of time there and all my earliest memories come
from that period. One sticks out so clearly I can still visualise the entire
scene. It was fairly early in the evening (there are no late evenings on a
working farm) and the family was gathered around my grandfather as
he held court in his rocking chair. A pipe in one hand and a birch switch
to keep us kids quiet in the other, he went through the daily ritual of
reviewing accomplishments of the day and assigning work for the
next.

I'm not exactly sure how the subject came up, as he was not a braggart.
He was, however, a very proud man and I guess someone had challenged
his instructions about something that had to be done on the farm. That
was all it took. I remember hearing the crack as his switch hit the nearby
table and feeling fear as a hush fell over the rest of us.

'You'll not be telling me how to run this farm,' he growled at one of my
uncles. 'You're still wet behind the ears, my boy, and there's nothing I can
learn from you. Why, there's not one thing you or anyone else can do better than me. I can clear a field, mend a fence, sow and reap, and care for
the animals better than all of you combined. I can ... '

Well, this went on for some time and both his voice and the tension in the room seemed to rise in concert as it did. My grandfather was a man with a terrible temper and not one to cool easily. My grandmother was up to the task, however. Just as he was shouting, 'Why, there ain't nothing I can't do on this here farm,' she leaned over and kissed him on the cheek. 'In that case,' she whispered, 'why don't you lay me some eggs for break-fast tomorrow?'

It was nearly thirty years later that I remembered this and realised what a valuable lesson I had overlooked. I had just been promoted and was determined to prove my abilities. Nothing was going to be less than per-fect while I was in charge, that was for sure. After all, I knew the tasks that each and every one of the hundred or so people working for me had to do. I could do any of their jobs better than they could. Sure!

I was smart enough to know I couldn't do everything myself, but that didn't stop me from telling everyone how to do their job. I was brought up short one day, luckily, and re-learned the lesson my grandmother had taught so many years before. It was uncanny how similar the circum-stances were.

Like my grandfather, I was giving an assignment, only in this case to a young, very pregnant woman. I was explaining how I wanted something done, not just what the end results were supposed to be. I guess (no, let's be honest – I know) I was too explicit, and one turgid instruction followed another. At some point, she interrupted and expressed some vigorous resistance to my overly precise direction.

'Listen,' she concluded with a smile. 'You may be more experienced than me, I'll admit that. But if you think you're better at everything, let me know when you've finished having my baby.'

I cringe every time I remember this event and try to avoid it happening again. Of course, you've figured it out by now. This has to do with delega-tion, one of the most difficult yet necessary things we have to do in busi-ness, especially when we're managers.

Let me run quickly through a few of the basic reasons for delegation. You know them, but a brief reminder won't hurt. First, we delegate because it just isn't physically possible to do everything ourselves. If you think it is, the job you have is too small.

Second, we must delegate because it's unreasonable to think we know everything. The world is changing too fast for us to keep up with it. Even if you knew everything yesterday, your knowledge would be obsolete today.

The biggest and best reason for delegation, however, is to build up staff confidence. They need to know that they can do 'it' and believe in themselves. Even if you can do the task better, give them the assignment and then leave them alone. Help if they ask for assistance but otherwise keep your mouth sealed. They may make mistakes along the way. In fact, they'll probably make as many as you did. So what? They'll learn the same way you learned and the lessons will stick just as yours did. In the end, everyone, including yourself, will be stronger. Your company will benefit more from that strength than it would from a job done faster or better without that learning experience.

Delegation is difficult because it requires trusting others, which we all find hard to do. And the strange thing is, it never gets any easier. It's not a lesson you can learn once, then forget. Every time you advance, you have to learn how to trust people all over again. I've known people who were absolutely wonderful at one level but never succeeded at the next, simply because they could not bring themselves to trust their subordinates with a higher level of accountability.

If you have trouble with delegating responsibility to your staff, you have my sympathy but little else. It's your problem and you'd better find a solution quickly. Perhaps if you remember that even farmers have to trust their chickens to deliver the eggs, that may help.

Most managers are fairly astute when it comes to understanding people. They have to be. They don't become managers without developing this skill. Another thing most of them have in common is the desire to generate loyalty from their staff. Here, as in other ways, business management has improved. Many of the old-fashioned, dated concepts have, thankfully, died. Today, most people recognise that loyalty is a two-way street. In order to be given loyalty, you must first give loyalty. However, some business managers still struggle to achieve this goal. This next rule should help them.

Rule of business life no. 21

If you're right too often, you're wrong

Okay, you are now a boss. Congratulations! It doesn't make any difference whether you are a big boss with thousands of people under your command or still a little one with only one or two helpers. Whichever you are, perhaps you'll be an even bigger boss tomorrow. It doesn't matter. The critical thing is that you are a boss today. If you're not one yet, pretend you are.

It's important to remember how you became a boss. Obviously, you are good at your job. Well, you're at least as good as those around you, and possibly better. You are also right much of the time, or at least more often than you are wrong. These are the two most important things. For now, we will forget your charm, charisma and good looks. All that matters is that you are good at what you do and you make the right choices.

Within the core of your success, however, are the seeds of your eventual failure. Being right some of the time generates a temptation to be right all the time. By itself, that's not too bad. Unfortunately, it's always accompanied by the need to prove to others that you are right. This almost inevitably means that you have to prove that someone else is wrong.

This idea, that in order to succeed it is necessary for someone else to fail, is all too common in business. More than any other single factor, this destroys all chances for loyalty to develop. More is involved than just loyalty to you. It also kills the birth of any loyalty to the organisation. Instead of teamwork, you end up with people working in isolation, each with their own goals and private ambitions. Hidden warfare between the competing parties can start at any time when this happens. You may be one of the casualties. If so, you probably deserve it.

True loyalty comes with a sense of belonging to a community of interests. You can't cause it to develop through any other means and expect it to last. Charisma doesn't work. It may make people listen to you in the beginning; it may fool some of them for a while, but it is never a permanent condition. Ideas may work, at least initially. People can be loyal to an idea or concept they believe in but, ultimately, they need more. Ideas are only a part of the social grouping people naturally seek. Belonging to that community means people take part in all its activities. They can't do that if they are always wrong and you are always right.

I have been lucky. Most of the people I have had the privilege of managing were at least as smart as I am and some of them a great deal smarter. I never had to worry about being right all the time. Usually, I wasn't. But it doesn't always work that way. I remember one very sharp executive who struggled to get any loyalty from his staff. The turnover rate in his department was far too high, especially in his more senior people. He used to complain to me fairly often about it.

'I don't understand it, Terry,' he once said. 'You are one of the most sarcastic, unfriendly people I have ever met. I've seen weeks go by without hearing you say one pleasant word. Yet you don't seem to have any trouble. I'd quit in a moment if I had to work for you but none of your staff seem to mind. It's just the opposite for me. Everyone loves me but they won't work for me. What's going on?'

I knew what the problem was and I tried to explain it to him, but he didn't want to listen. He was everything he said he was. He was a nice, friendly person and people really did like him. He not only knew everyone in the company; he went out of his way to know something good about them. He was one of the smarter people I've known and very, very good at his job. Yes, he was a great guy. And he knew it. And he made sure everyone else knew it too. Personally, I would rather work for Attila the Hun.

Fred never did learn that if you want to be a boss and also want to instil loyalty to both yourself and the whole organisation, you must sacrifice some of your pride. More importantly, you must let everyone else contribute in a way that allows them to develop theirs. It's not good enough just to fight for your people when they are threatened by outsiders. Nor is it adequate to be 'one of the lads', a favourite act performed by many, in the false belief that friendliness is a valid substitute for loyalty.

Loyalty comes from your willingness to share being right. That means you have to accept the role of being wrong. Sometimes you even have to do it when you're not wrong, just not more right than the person who works for you. It may sound trite but I assure you it isn't. It will lead to everyone caring more about the business, seeing the big picture and, ultimately, being willing to make the same sacrifices you do.

There is an easy test you can use to see if the programme is working.

Forget measuring employee turnover, conducting staff opinion polls or any of the other metrics used by the average consultant. For the most part, these are just trash. Instead, ask your staff a few questions. These may vary according to your particular circumstances but, if you're smart enough to be their boss, you'll be able to ask the right ones.

I heard a distinguished person explain this once much better than I can. He gave the analogy of two stone-cutters who were asked what they were doing. One replied that he was carving stones into squares. The other said he was helping to build a cathedral. One was merely doing an assigned job but the other saw the whole picture. He was thinking for himself. I've used this anecdote to create questions for my staff and the answers have always surprised me. They have also helped a great deal.

Mao Tse-tung said, 'Political power grows out of the barrel of a gun.' Too many of our leaders still believe they can apply this type of concept in business today. Personally, I prefer another Chinese notable, the sixth century BC poet Lao-tzu, who wrote, 'Of a good leader, when his work is done, they will say: we did it ourselves.' I am convinced that if you adopt this approach, you will not only have a more loyal staff, but you will also achieve far more than otherwise seems reasonable.

One of the most important traits for a manager to develop is an excellent memory. Guessing is not good enough. You have to know and that means you must be able to recall facts whenever they are needed. Because this is so important, people often fail to realise that another trait is needed. As the next rule explains, there are times when we have to be able to forget.

Rule of business life no. 22

Some spotted leopards are just big pussy-cats

A senior executive had just finished introducing some of his management staff. One person in particular had created confusing impressions. He seemed bright and passionate about the company but there was something about him that didn't really strike the right note. Perhaps it was the shifting eyes or the nervous posture. Maybe it was just me. I asked the executive about him afterwards.

'He's a real loser, Terry,' he said. 'He had a nervous breakdown a while ago and has been completely useless ever since. As a matter of fact, he was transferred from your area and your predecessor warned me about him. I only keep him around 'cause I want to understand what your people are up to. Other than that, he doesn't actually serve a purpose. He screwed up the last big job I gave him and you only get one chance with me.'

I accepted that it was none of my business. However, I had to work closely with his department and, over the following months, I came to know a few more facts about the young man. First, I learned he hadn't really had a breakdown. He had taken some unscheduled holiday once because he had simply burned up his physical reserves. He needed a rest and had taken one. The amazing fact was that this had occurred six years previously. The way his department executive had talked had led me to believe it was only a few months ago.

Second, the project he was supposed to have screwed up had a similar story. It had been badly structured and fatally flawed long before he had been assigned to it. Perhaps no one could have succeeded. He took the blame because he had been there at the end, not because he had made a serious mistake.

I was having lunch with the vice-president of Personnel a few months later when the subject came up. 'Sure, I know all about him,' the VP explained. 'He's what we Texans call 'big hat, no cattle'. Plenty of ability there but never any performance. I keep telling John to get rid of the guy. You can't change a leopard's spots and you can't make a winner out of that guy. With all the talent available in the market, we shouldn't waste our time on a born loser.'

It wasn't long afterwards that an opening occurred in my department and we began looking for a candidate. In accordance with policy, the vacancy was announced internally so that existing staff could apply. The young man was one of them. He had the right experience and seemed eager to move back into his old profession. I decided to take a chance and gave him the job.

I would like to tell you that he became a superstar but that would be an exaggeration. I am a good manager but not that good. He remained inhibited for a time and fairly tentative in his decisions. Nevertheless, he was a good and valuable employee. Over time, his strengths grew and, the last I

59

saw of him, he was again moving up the management ladder at a good pace. I never regretted giving him that opportunity.

This is one thing in particular that a number of business men and women, especially senior executives, forget far too often – people change. Our job is to ensure they have the opportunity to change in a productive manner. We have to stop the rumours and innuendoes. We have to make sure the reputations earned are deserved and not an excuse for our own failures.

Everyone lives in their own universe. Some are very small but if we can't help them expand, we are simply failing to do our job as managers. This isn't always easy. People are not leopards. They can change, but some of them can be vicious about it if you try to push them too hard. Not every person is willing. Even dry cleaning will fail to get rid of some spots. Still, we have to try. When it works, the payoff can be huge.

The key is making people think the change is their own idea. This means using the Pygmalion theory as a rule for business conduct, both theirs and yours. They can win if they predict they will, but you have to make that prediction as well, and then let them succeed. You must ignore some of the old country wisdom we all love to quote and stop saying, 'You can't groom the wrong horse' or 'You can't make a silk purse out of a pig's ear'. Instead, forget the past as much as you can and start each new day as a separate adventure.

You'll find it surprising how small people, when given a big job, grow into the demands made on them and turn into real stars. It all depends on their willingness to put past failures behind them and start each venture fresh. Remember the legends of Robert the Bruce. Think about Winston Churchill. Failures can become successful but they need an opportunity. If nothing else, they deserve a little forgetfulness from their boss. Don't keep on repeating stories from the past to put someone down.

By now, you probably think you have figured out my approach. You've glanced ahead to the next rule and know what I'm going to say, right? Something about stress and how you have to control it, something else about the manager's responsibility to the staff and maybe even something related to the latest psycho-babble from management journals. Think again. This next rule may preach a different moral from the one you expect.

Rule of business life no. 23

Rubber bands snap

People can snap. Everyone who enters management knows this. It's just one more thing they are accountable for. There is one aspect of this rule, however, that many seem to forget.

We all know that you can push people too far. When you push too hard, they fall over. Okay, that's not a good thing to do. But people can get back up again after being pushed down. They can recover from setbacks. Often, the experience strengthens them and they become more flexible and more capable as a result. It's not nice but neither does it normally cause mortal injury. Of course, it doesn't always work that way. If you push hard enough, you can cause irreparable damage to the individual.

And, yes, you can push *yourself* too far. Whether because of your own ambition or because you are being pushed by someone higher in the organisation, you can fall over the edge as well. In its worst form, this is called executive burn-out. There are milder cases where, at least for a time, you just lose interest. Again, you have a responsibility as a manager, even though you are now managing yourself. You owe it to your family, your company and your health to watch for the signs and take preventive action. You have to learn how to push the limits of your capability. At the same time, you must control the potential damage.

These are serious issues. They are central to the job and duty of every manager. Your responsibilities should not be taken lightly. Since they have been addressed in many other publications there's no need for us to repeat them here. While I don't want to seem callous about these issues, they are not the point of this rule.

Strange as it may seem, I use this rule to remind myself about compensation. That's right: remuneration, money, filthy lucre. Call it what you will, it still lets loose tremendous forces onto individuals. These pressures have to be kept in balance. Let's look at two extreme cases to see if the pressures can be defined better.

The first involved a young man I knew casually many years ago. He worked in a manufacturing plant and, as far as I know, enjoyed his work. He had been with the firm for almost five years when an unfortunate incident occurred. Someone in the administrative section had left the payroll register in an open, accessible place. All the staff soon knew the salaries of the others, including the young man we're discussing.

This was upsetting to him. He found that his salary, as a loyal employee, was lower than many of the new people, including those less skilled. As he described it, he was the lowest-paid person in his position even though he was simultaneously the highest-rated. Whether this was true or not, it was a fact that he was both disturbed and embarrassed after the salaries became common knowledge.

His feelings about the company changed. He became the proverbial angry young man and decided to get even. Over the next few months, he stole several thousands of dollars' worth of equipment from the company. He was still dissatisfied and stepped up his campaign to include sabotaging some of the manufactured products. Of course, he was caught and punished, but he claimed it was all worth while. After all, he 'got those bastards'.

The moral of this story is simple. You must pay people what they're worth compared to others. You cannot cheat them. You cannot assume that their demonstrated loyalty allows you to count them as safe. Eventually, they will find out and try to get even. Most will be as naïve as the young individual we have been discussing. That's serious enough. Thinking that you're saving some money, you'll find that you are wasting more than you have saved. You'll also have lost what was a potentially good employee. However, there's always a few who will not be naïve. When they get even, it could cost you a tremendous amount of money and you may never catch some of them.

Now let's look at the other extreme. The CEO of a fairly substantial firm was pushing his executives hard. He desperately wanted to ratchet his firm up into the next tier. They were close and he thought, with a little more effort, they should be able to make it. Ranting and raving didn't help, but then it seldom does. Neither did preaching to the converted, something else he should have known better than to try. Every approach he tried seemed to fall short of the targets he set.

So he came up with a new scheme. He put every executive on a 100 per cent bonus programme. For the first two years, the targets were reasonable and they achieved them. The executives who were now earning twice their original salaries, which were fairly decent to begin with, thought this was wonderful! They also became accustomed to that level of income.

Then the targets were raised. They became more and more difficult to achieve. Corners were cut. The company became driven by short-term results. After all, they had to make their bonus. Ethics fell by the wayside. So too did proper accounting practices. Money was the only criterion. Cheating became endemic.

Well, the same thing happened to them as it did to the person in the first story. They were caught. The people involved in the cheating were punished. Unfortunately, so were many of the innocent. That's what always happens when corporations, not individuals, start becoming shy of following legal requirements.

This type of situation happens constantly. Hardly a month goes by without the press reporting some new scandal. Whether involving traders in the stock market, bankers, senior business executives or even low-level ones, examples of the excesses of greed abound. Read the business news for the next month and count the number of times it happens. You may be surprised.

Don't misunderstand me. I want to earn a lot of money – make that a huge amount of money. But the key word is *earn*. I want to be paid what I'm worth – no more, but definitely no less. That is what most people want. If we can't pay people too little and we can't pay them too much, what do we do? Pay them the right amount, naturally. That is where the management skill comes into play.

Rubber bands need to be stretched. If left in the drawer they'll just rot. The same is true for people to whom you give too little reward. Alternatively, they can be stretched too far. In this case, too far can be the temptation that always accompanies greed. Just remember what happens when you stretch that band too far. It hurts when it snaps back on you.

Part of the problem many people in management have, and I'm not just referring to junior managers, is that they really don't know what management is supposed to mean. They have this strange notion that it entails telling others what to do and that's all. Listen, if it were that easy, businesses would not pay big bucks for decent managers. Others in management, however, have the opposite problem. They try to make their role in management even greater than it should be. I use the following rule to control that part of my nature.

No situation is so bad that a manager can't make it worse

It was lunch-time on the third day of work at my new firm so I wandered down to the cafeteria. After selecting some food, I looked around. It was a spacious, cheerful place with tables set at random overlooking a delightful park-like area at the rear of the building. I could see a few of the people who worked for me at one table in the corner, but selected another with some folks I didn't recognise. It wasn't that I wanted to avoid my staff. I just find it better to get to know everyone in the company, not only those I work with day in and day out. I said hello, introduced myself and asked if I could join them.

They were friendly enough, welcoming me not just to their table but to the company. There were a few casual questions about what section I worked in and where I came from. It was obvious they did not recognise me as the new director. I could see they were preoccupied so I just kept my mouth shut. It's surprising what can be picked up about an organisation by just listening and I was eager to learn as much as I could about my new company.

'I can't stand working for her,' one of the males at the end of the table was saying. 'She's such an irritating, stupid bitch. Why they ever made her a manager, I'll never know. She couldn't find her backside if she used both hands.'

'Come on, Jack. She's no worse than any of the male managers we have,' came a rejoinder from one of the young ladies opposite me. 'None of them are any good. You just don't like working for a woman. You wouldn't say things like that if she weren't a female.'

'Listen,' he said, 'that's just not true. I don't care if she's a Martian. All I want is someone who won't take a good situation and work hard to make it worse so they can prove how wonderful they are. That's what she does; that's what they all do. Useless, that's what they all are. Give me one damn thing a manager is good for.'

'Target practice,' said a quiet third voice.

It makes you think, doesn't it? The issue about managers and the harm they can cause is not a local one, either. I've seen symptoms in the US, Great Britain, Australia, Holland, Belgium … the list goes on. When I joined one firm, I was appalled by the superior attitude of my management team. They were practising something they called 'man management' and took a great deal of pride in this but they were mostly held in low regard by their subordinates.

They wanted to make the most basic, low-level decisions for their people – decisions such as when to go for lunch, where to park and how much paper to use. I was surprised they didn't require passes to go to the toilet. Rather than man management, they were practising something better named as management interference. No one had explained to them that if you treat people like kids, they'll act like kids. The reverse is also true. If you treat them like adults, they will be adults.

What can you do about improving your management skills? First, give some trust and freedom to your staff. Treat them as responsible people and you'll be surprised at the results. It will be wonderful when everyone understands that there are many ways to use the Pygmalion theory in management. Just think what we might accomplish if everyone knows that what we are attempting to do *will* be achieved.

Second, as a manager, try to adopt the motto of the medical profession: *primum non nocere*, 'first, do no harm'. That seems to be a good primary function for all of us. As managers, our mistakes are like a nuclear chain reaction. One small issue can trigger a dozen more. One small mistake can destroy the progress of years.

Third, try using peer pressure to accomplish most of the more basic management functions. This can be extraordinarily successful. In one company I know of, they have no defined vacation policy. Everyone is told that they are adults and able to determine when they should go on holiday and when the company needs them to be in the office. No paperwork is expended, no management time is wasted tracking remaining entitlement for vacation days or any of the other bureaucratic drivel. I don't know what the average number of days taken off at that company is, but people are very happy, no one takes excessive holidays and the company is one of the most productive I know of. Peer pressure is the key. It makes all employees police themselves, rather than having some overpaid boss do it.

Finally, remember the words of Abraham Lincoln, who said, 'No man is good enough to govern another man without that other's consent.' We live in a free society and we can manage only by the consent of those under our supervision. When they no longer give that consent, they leave and find another employer.

If you define the verb 'manage' to simply mean 'control', it seems simple enough. Being a 'manager', however, involves far more than that. Although you do have to control, you must also nurture. You must balance the requirements of the organisation with the needs of the individuals. Your task is to blend the jobs, the events and the people to achieve a goal which is often poorly defined. An easy job? No, it's far from easy if you try to do it properly.

Still, there are more difficult skills to learn in business. We must never confuse the definition of manager with that of leader. The first tells people 'Do that for me.' The second says 'Help me as I attempt to do this.' Let's leave the management rules for now and look at the special ones needed for leadership.

Part IV
Rules about leadership

> *The world we have made as a result of the level of thinking we have done thus far, creates problems we cannot solve with the same level of thinking at which we created them.*
> *Albert Einstein*

Have you ever noticed that companies have unique 'personalities'? It doesn't matter how similar they are on the surface. You can have two companies in exactly the same business but they will be different. This is true even when they are the same size and both have equal turnover and margins. It's even true if they are located next to each other and both draw from the same labour pool. They're different. Not only that, but they recognise their uniqueness and cherish it. Neither would want to be like the other. They call it 'corporate culture' and pretend it's something mystical.

Of course, there's no great secret why this happens. Companies acquire a 'personality' from their leadership, which is a variable phenomenon. While most of it may come from the founder or CEO, it isn't exclusive to them. Real leadership can sometimes start quite low in an organisation. If you doubt that, look at the number of firms tied up in their paperwork and bureaucracy. Regardless of organisational level, it is this leadership that is the foundation of a company's 'personality'.

This is not a question of a personality cult; nor is it something the head of an organisation can achieve through showmanship. Quite simply, it's the principle of emulation. People tend to copy those they see as successful. The way to advance in a company is to do things the same way as others who have advanced. Over time, the path becomes a highway that everyone follows.

This means you can tell a great deal about a company's leadership by looking at its personality. Ask some questions. Does it take risks or is safety more important? Is every task well documented or do people respond to verbal requests? Does it have high turnover in executive ranks? What about at lower levels? Who succeeds in the company? Who fails?

The head of an organisation who wants to change its personality, or its culture, if you prefer, must look at the people who are seen by others as successful. If they do not exemplify the desired traits, new winners must be identified. Just as in any other aspect of business life, those who succeed in achieving the desired results are rewarded. Those that don't are punished. It may sound callous but it is only the old Darwinian principle of the survival of the fittest. As with evolution, it can take a while, but change will happen.

It's not quite that simple, though, is it? The person at the top may look down and say, 'I want things to change so I'll change the criteria for success', but that isn't enough. They are personally part of the equation, but they almost always fail to account for themselves. They are at the pinnacle of success in their organisation and, ultimately, they are the ones their people emulate.

Even when they see it, most leaders usually act in error. They feel they act appropriately and that everyone should copy them. After all, they'll tell you, it wouldn't be so bad if everyone were the same as them. Just as Louis XIV, who said 'I am the State' to describe how he felt he 'embodied' French society, they feel they are the company or the finance department or the XYZ division. They should understand that they are not monarchs. If they were, they could possibly end up like Louis XVI. Remember, he lost his head. They can as well.

Leaders cannot afford to forget that we live in an ever-changing world. The solutions, styles and actions which they used were good at the time. However, if they were truly successful, they created a new environment where the old ways no longer work or, at least, not as well. As usual, Einstein was right, and we would be foolish to ignore him.

Leaders need to follow rules just like the rest of us. Over the years, I created a few which I made sure were known by anyone who wanted to be my boss. Many people already at the top will claim that these rules are wrong and don't reflect their reality at all. Maybe so. For those of you who will reach the top someday in the future, I hope these rules will be remembered and will help.

Do you want to be a leader? Are you sure you understand what it means? Do you comprehend and accept the risks that are part of the job? Are you really, really determined to do it? Okay, that's fine. Just remember the following rule.

Rule of business life no. 25

Sweep the stairs from the top down

Things can sometimes go wrong in business. We know this, although we usually fail to recognise the symptoms in our own organisations until it's too late. Just a few short years ago, a middle-level scapegoat would be found and life at the top would continue as before. Sure, the big boys would feel a little embarrassed and maybe even be chastised, but they would soon get over it.

A decade or two ago, the president of a large US company wanted to change the procedure in the company's warehouse. 'The record-keeping is terrible,' he said, 'and I know how to fix it. When the stockmen are out on the floor, I want them to be able to change the counts right then and there. I don't want to hear any rubbish about audit trails, either. We don't have time to worry about that kind of bureaucratic nonsense.' The chief financial officer, who was responsible for the warehouse, thought this was a 'wonderful' idea. Well, he thought all the president's ideas were wonderful.

Have you guessed the results yet? Right! A few months and a few million dollars in stock loss later, the director of distribution was fired for an 'unrelated' cause. The president stayed on for several years and retired gracefully. The CFO? Oh, he was promoted to president afterwards, and stayed there until the company was acquired by another firm.

Today, matters are starting to become a little different. Although it depends on the size of the screw-up, heads do sometimes actually roll at the top. At the very least, controls are in place to restrict executive freedom so that problems do not recur. This is true even if the problem was just a failure to recognise problems. Why are we beginning to see this type of change? I believe it has to do with the changing definition of accountability. Let's look into the issue.

First and foremost, we need to recognise that leadership implies accepting accountability. Accountability means being responsible for the actions of everyone who works for you, whether you approved of the actions or not. When you reach a senior enough level, this expands to accountability for everyone, not merely those that report through you. Accountability does not mean finding a scapegoat.

True accountability also refuses to accept excuses, delays and indecision. Part of the leader's job is to teach subordinates the true meaning of accountability and they will never learn if they are let off the hook. Incidentally, this is also the best way for you to learn this. If you do not accept excuses from others, you eventually stop making them for yourself.

Accountability also means recognising the difference between consultation, participation and specific performance. Accountability has to do with leadership and command, and that starts at the top and goes downward, not the other way round. For those accustomed to 'passing the buck', this can be very frightening. If you do not enjoy having accountability for making decisions, start small. Graduate to higher levels slowly. That is, make more important decisions over time. Above all, use your ambition to push your personal envelope of accountability outwards.

You will know when you have reached true accountability. It will be when you stop seeing your job in relation to a section of the company and begin viewing the organisation as a whole. You will know that your business cannot have a state of affairs where 'not invented here' prevails. You will destroy the fences around divisions, countries or regions, and eliminate the alligators in the moats between operations, MIS, finance or any other vested interest in your firm.

We'll assume for a moment that you have accepted full accountability. Now you understand why we 'sweep the stairs from the top down'. Cleaning out the lower layers does not help if any dirt remains, or is even suspected, at the top. It does not matter who is at fault. It does not matter who knew about the problem but failed to fix it. It especially does not matter how well loved and respected the person at the top may be. When there is a severe failure, you start with the one in charge. Let me give you an example.

A well-respected firm had a fine chairman. He was well thought of by his colleagues on the board, people in the investment community and his management team. He was especially well liked by the people throughout the firm, as he had saved it from collapse around fifteen years previously. In other words, he was the heart and soul of the company. I counted myself lucky to know him. His friendship was a privilege and honour I worked hard to retain.

A major disaster hit his company. Accounting irregularities were uncovered that went back several years. Even though he had specifically ordered the people involved to avoid the practice (it was fairly common in that particular industry), he held himself responsible. An emergency board meeting was held the day following the discovery of the problem and he immediately resigned. He understood what accountability meant. He knew this rule about leadership and had the courage to follow it.

Let's burst one or two additional bubbles. The worst company cultures begin going bad when the leadership becomes arrogant. If the leaders cannot control their pride, no one below them is likely to do so either. The end result is usually disastrous. Sometimes, the pride and arrogance were earned, so perhaps there is an excuse. Sometimes, it exists only in some leader's fertile imagination.

Rule of business life no. 26

Even blind squirrels find some nuts

One day I was playing golf with a normally aggressive man who was having a terrible time. Finally, towards the end of the match, he managed to par a hole. 'Well, at last,' he said with great satisfaction. 'That's one in a row!' It made me think of all the other people I've met who think success can be achieved with no more than one lucky break.

So many business people tend to swell with pride when recounting their prior success. They talk (and talk and talk) about how they managed to win the gold when so many of their peers failed. They will describe in great detail how they anticipated the future and reacted before the rest of the crowd. Give them five minutes and they will take an hour to tell you 'how they succeeded'. In some cases, their stories are even true. It doesn't make any difference. It still bores me to hear the same old tale, time and time again.

For most of us, success is seldom well planned. Our skills lie more in our ability to take advantage of accidental circumstances or lucky breaks than in true planning. When we do plan, it is often just a numbers game that seldom has anything to do with the lightning strike of inspiration or unplanned piece of fortune that came our way. Nevertheless, we always look with 20/20 hindsight and see a 'strategic plan' that guided us.

This is such an easy trap to fall into and we all have to guard against it. Every once in a while, we may succeed at something. Perhaps it was luck and it was time for the dice to fall our way. Maybe it was just bloody hard work. That gets its reward too, you know. And maybe, just maybe, it was because we planned it that way. To be honest, it doesn't make any difference why we succeeded. It's what we do afterwards that counts.

If we tell ourselves there was a plan behind every success, and we will do this because that's what we tell everyone else, then we start looking to repeat the plan. We ignore the good luck and hard work. We don't need them, we say to ourselves. All we have to do is have another great strategic plan.

There are a few exceptions to this line of thinking. One is that described by the chairman of a large international firm which is spectacularly successful, in part due to its unique format and internal structure. It is so different, in fact, that the chairman has written a book about it. He gave a talk in Ireland during 1994 when he divulged the secrets of his success.

'I wish I could say it was designed,' he said, 'but it wasn't. We were facing a crisis and decisions had to be made right then. There was no plan, only instinctive reaction. It was more luck than anything else that everything turned out so well. Yes, we have a very unique structure for our business, but it just happened. It isn't what we dreamed about when we started.'

I met one other individual with this attitude. He is also the chairman of a large international company, and he too is one of the best at seeing new opportunities and not trying to repeat yesterday's story. He was and remains always dissatisfied with what has been accomplished to date, and spends his time seeking new ways to go about conducting his business. One remark of his will always stick in my memory. 'I always have a strategic plan until an opportunity comes along,' he'll say to anyone who will listen. People such as these two help keep things in perspective.

It is a delight to find honest people who have been extraordinarily successful but still do not take themselves too seriously. They are smart enough to allow relief from the pressures that success can bring. By admitting serendipity had some part to play in their company's success, they are not forced to be prescient. They do not have to repeat miracles. Not many senior business people are willing to describe their achievements this way. Instead, they struggle through life looking for a repeat of their 'infallible' strategic plan. They could take a lesson from either of these two examples.

All of us feel pride in our accomplishments. That's fine. Sometimes, even survival deserves a generous helping of self-esteem. However, before you take pride in your accomplishments, make sure they really are plural. True success is more than one in a row. When it comes to strategic planning, it's necessary to forget your past successes and determine how to make new ones. Your track record is a good indication that, having done it before, you can do it again. Don't get too big-headed about it, though. Remember, even blind squirrels find some nuts.

To be honest, I doubt if that rule punctured anything, much less some of the egos at the top of company structures. While they might admit to the presence of some squirrelly characters among their peers, they'll never see themselves in that way. Why should they? Every time they turn around, they are told how wonderful they are. The next rule is for them.

Rule of business life no. 27

If all you can hear is yesterday's praise, you've gone deaf

I love working with modern technology, perhaps because the environment changes almost every day. We techies can't afford to be satisfied with the way we did things in the past. If we do, we are knocked off our pedestal and someone new takes over. Regardless of how successful we've been, we have to be open to new concepts and ways of doing things.

Just as misery likes company, we push our associates in other parts of the business to be open to change as well. Ah, but when we get to the bosses, it becomes much harder. It's then I'm told, 'We've always done it this way and I don't see any reason to change now.' This happens every time a new idea comes up. Unfortunately, even once would be far too often. And what is most irritating is that the people who say this are some of the people I respect the most. They all have a history of success behind them. I just wish I felt as positive that they have a future of success in front of them.

If all you listen to is praise for yesterday's successes, it can go to your head. This rapidly leads to stagnation. The more you believe you understand the fundamental reasons for your success, the more the 'formula' becomes institutionalised. This prevents new ideas from being heard, much less given a fair chance. Strange as it may seem, it is always the most successful who are deaf to new ideas for future success.

This forms one of the basic principles of the 'wheel of business' theory: new companies and new people fill the gap as older, more successful and established ones fade into obscurity. Of course, neither the companies nor the people with the new, fresh approaches have to be young. They just have to keep a youthful attitude.

The converse is also true. Those who fade away are not always old. Neither are they necessarily successful. They merely become tired. Listening to new ideas is too much of a burden for them. Age is merely a state of mind and it can affect companies as much as individuals.

There is another, somewhat more subtle danger in winning all the time. It has to do with expectations. The more you are seen as a winner due to past accomplishments, the less you can afford to take chances in the future. Too much of your reputation is at stake. You and those around you forget that you reached your position by taking a gamble or two back when you were hungry. That's how you built the reputation. But now there's a different set of values and your reactions automatically adjust. Risks become smaller and smaller. As time goes on, it becomes increasingly difficult to recognise opportunity, even when it's staring you in the face.

'The graveyard of business', said some anonymous genius, 'is littered with companies that failed to recognise inevitable change.' It is also filled with those who believed that yesterday's solutions are the only way to achieve tomorrow's objectives. Most, if not all, of the 'graveyard companies' were at one time considered successful in some way or another. So were the people we consign to the graveyard. They stopped looking ahead and, instead, lectured on their past glories. They were seduced into a belief in their own invincibility.

My eyes lit on a phrase from an interview with Bill Gates in a newspaper some time ago. In it he said, 'Success is a lousy teacher.' He's probably right – again. Success may be the best teacher we have, but it is still a lousy one. The room at the top has no space available for those who can only hear echoes from the past. This leads to deafness and, sooner or later, your staff and your customers will become tired of shouting to be heard.

Have I gone overboard? Perhaps. We all know that top business executives are not fools. They wouldn't have made it to the top if they were. And only fools would let their egos run amok. Most at the top have more self-discipline, or so we hope. Nevertheless, it does happen and we see it all the time. I've asked myself why otherwise sane men and women allow this. What follows is the best answer I was able to come up with.

Rule of business life no. 28

You can fool some of the people some of the time – but you can fool yourself all the time

Perhaps I should have stolen a different line from P. T. Barnum. I could have used 'a fool and his reputation are soon parted' and that would have been just as accurate. Both express a form of self-delusion. It becomes worse, however, when you pay people to help you lie to yourself.

Businesses spend large fortunes on public relations. We hire corporate affairs staff, sign contracts with public relations firms, glorify ourselves in our annual reports and do everything possible to get our corporate name in the news. It does not matter if we are a public firm, a private one, a government agency, the military, or even a religious organisation. It also does not matter what we call our PR staff – Corporate Affairs, Internal Communications, Investor Relations or any one of a dozen other high-sounding names. It all comes down to the same thing: telling a controlled message about who we are and how well we perform.

Using this definition, we have to accept that there is more to public relations than the small part controlled by the PR staff. For example, all our advertising is part of our public image. In addition, we have to think about communication with the internal staff. That's another form of PR. We must also consider recruiting advertisements, relations with suppliers, customer surveys, and – well, you get the idea. There's a lot of PR about.

There is nothing wrong with this. Developing and maintaining a positive image with the public, keeping investors satisfied that their money is safely tended, and having your staff believe in the company are absolutely vital activities. We spend a fortune but it is worth every penny – we hope.

Nevertheless, you must be careful. Remember who writes the press releases and controls the flow of information. You do. Even when it's done by outsiders, *you* control the message. You may forget this simple fact. Doing so can become extraordinarily dangerous.

One of the firms I knew a number of years ago had become very well known. It was highly regarded by everyone, especially the analysts on Wall Street. They were cocky, aggressive and everything they touched seemed to turn to gold. The mood at the head office was buoyant and everyone was infected with the optimism of winners.

Then they considered buying another company located in New York City. This was problematical for a couple of reasons. They had never acquired another company before and had no practical experience of how to meld two organisations. They also had no experience in New York City. Personally, I like the city, but the business rules there are foreign to the rest of America, especially for this company's industry. Except for distance, they may as well have purchased a firm on Mars.

There was a heated debate around the conference table as the issue was finally decided. One executive I greatly admired was adamantly opposed to the proposal. He told me he had presented a passionate argument and finished by stating flatly that the company couldn't possibly succeed in that environment.

He said he remembered the president turning to him and saying, 'Of course we can. Didn't you read what *The Wall Street Journal* said about us yesterday? They think we're invincible. We can do anything we damn well please.'

The deal went ahead. They struggled for a few years and finally managed to reach a break-even point with the acquisition, but never any better than that. Finally, they sold out to another firm that knew the city. Their exit was not a failure, but it wasn't a success either. Their aura of invincibility was lost and never regained.

It wasn't *The Wall Street Journal*'s fault. They only reported what the company allowed them to know. It was not the case that the company lied, either. They thought that every word published was the truth and nothing but the truth. They just failed to ask themselves: Was it the whole truth? Did they gloss over some things? Did they write their press releases in a way that favoured their best interest? Did they blindly follow the rules of human nature and paint their picture in the best possible way? Well, of course they did.

That is part of the job, not only of public relations but of each and every one of us. The better our company looks, the better *we* look. What is wrong with that? We want to feel upbeat about ourselves. What is wrong with that? We want our associates in the business to be motivated and proud to be part of the team. What is wrong with that?

Nothing is 'wrong' with it. Just remember who created the image and why. If you forget that it is your job to control the dissemination of information, you can begin to forget what is factual and what is aspirational. Just because some PR person says you are wonderful, don't start believing you are. When the Chair or CFO has his or her picture in the news too often, there may be a point when they believe they are invincible.

It is easy to fall into this trap. We all want that little fifteen-minute dose of fame in our life. Sometimes, it is the only thing that seems to distinguish us from the herd. However, when the separation between image and reality grows, the addiction caused by fame can be more dangerous than the most lethal drug.

To protect yourself from this far too common condition that accompanies fame, make sure the entire staff, including the senior members, recognise there are three forms of truth. First, there is truth in the public domain, which looks backwards and tries to explain past events in a positive manner. You must remember, though, that history is a useful tool for predicting the future only if your version of history is reasonably accurate.

Next, there is the corporate internal truth – the facts we acknowledge and share throughout the firm but which may be too risky to publish widely. Another name for this is aspirational truth. It acknowledges the past accurately but looks forward, emphasising every positive factor and promoting every possible opportunity. This is good as long as you do not commit your company to do too much, too fast. Remember, the danger is subtle. While this is a legitimate form of truth, it is not usually alert to threats, either internal or external.

Finally, there is your personal truth. Regardless of how you have 'dressed up' the facts for the consumption of others, you must always acknowledge things as they really are – whether for yourself, your organisation, or the business as a whole. Avoid, at all costs, the 'Emperor's new clothes' syndrome. This is especially dangerous as it can be nearly impossible to rectify.

In the long run, there is not too much you can do when 'PR' begins distorting your leadership's view of the real world. On a personal level, attempting to remind everyone of the 'true truth' seldom works. Usually, you are seen as a non-believer – someone who is not part of the team. You have two basic choices: leave the firm as quickly as possible; or sit tight through the inevitable crisis that will happen. A harsh dose of reality normally cures these problems and it is always delivered, sooner or later. It hurts a great deal but the pain is short-lived and the company is usually stronger as a result.

Okay, let's stop worrying about the problems with our egos. If you remember these rules, much of the potential trouble will disappear. And, if you don't remember, maybe you will – disappear, that is. Now it's time to look at some of the consequences of not seeing things as they really are. Although there are dangers in what you may do, what is left undone, in the end, incurs the greater liabilities.

Rule of business life no. 29

Dreams are for bedrooms, not boardrooms

> Here we sit in a branchy row,
> thinking of beautiful things we know.
> Dreaming of things we mean to do,
> all complete in a minute or two –
> Something noble, wise and good,
> done by merely wishing we could.
>
> We've forgotten, but – never mind,
> Brother, thy tail hangs down behind!

From the Road Song of the Bandar-Log by Rudyard Kipling

It is said that the road to Hell is paved with good intentions. If so, it must intersect with the street made from daydreaming and wishful thinking. Both certainly end up in the same place. One creates problems by 'do-gooders' over-reacting; the other by 'day dreamers' failing to act at all. It is sometimes difficult to measure which is the more dangerous.

It seems strange, doesn't it? Here we are, business men and women – renowned for being pragmatic and following the gospel of the bottom line, we of all people should not have to worry about wishful thinking. Or so it would seem. However, when you look around, it appears to be an assumption worth challenging.

Look at IBM and the introduction of the personal computer if you need an example. The PC and its related technologies will have, perhaps, the biggest impact on society since the invention of the wheel. For years, IBM told itself and everyone who would listen that the PC was just a distraction. 'Let us show you our newest mainframe,' they said as they tried to draw our attention away.

I've worked for a business in trouble. The chances are you have too. The thing I remember the company doing, first and foremost, was practising denial. 'There really isn't a problem. It's just a minor inconvenience,' they told themselves. This wishful thinking was flagrant by any measure. An 'inconvenience', however minor, can grow to a towering issue merely by pretending it is not important.

The sorry truth is that people, even the most intelligent, hear and see only what they want. When the reality of a situation does not fit their view, they find ways to deny that situation and practise wishful thinking.

In the company I remember suffering the most from this syndrome, the profits were falling and had almost reached zero. Action was urgently needed and the executives started looking for solutions. First, they considered raising the selling price, but decided this couldn't be done. After all, their competitors would take advantage with promotions and kill off their market share, right?

Second, they thought about lowering their cost price for goods. That sounded reasonable. It would have the same effect on the bottom line and would not help their competition. Then they realised that their suppliers would resist this. The suppliers claimed they were already trying to get blood out of a stone and the business relationship wasn't wonderful just then. It was decided they should pass on this solution.

Then the executives decided they should look at reducing expenses. That was all the current rage and still is, with the words downsizing, outsourcing and business process re-engineering on everyone's lips. Unfortunately, this resulted in some corporate in-fighting and a number of executives were upset. 'We'll save this for later', they said.

There was only one thing left, so they decided to go for it. 'Let's hope we get an increase in sales,' they said. 'Yeah, that's the thing to do. It solves all our problems. At least, as long as our customers go along with it. Oh, sure, it might be out of our control, but we really don't have any choice, do we?'

This was another example of wishful thinking at its worst. We always have a choice to make. However, making the one having the least work and with the least real chance of success must not be your favourite solution.

A wishful thinker or daydreamer has another name. He's also known as a 'Wannabe', the one who really wants to be an achiever but somehow never makes it. He's willing to make a commitment and usually does. He also accepts that work only gets done by working, not dreaming. So, you have to wonder where he goes so terribly wrong. Here are a few things that can be done to help your Wannabes, but none are as simple as they seem on the surface.

First, help your firm define and accept what it is now before dreaming of what it wants to become. If your business ignores today's reality and 'planning' is the company watchword, you can hardly condemn your staff for doing the same. It is good to be upbeat and talk about a rosy future but you have to include concrete plans for achieving it. This starts by acknowledging where you stand right now – without fancy words or optimistic projections. If you are tough at the start, it is practical to ease off as progress is made.

Second, cultivate a Company Cynic. Every company needs the person who can see dangers, not just opportunities. The value of the person who demands proof and not optimistic hopes cannot be over-estimated. However, this has some hazards that must be watched. If you want mushrooms in your omelette, take care to avoid toadstools. Likewise, ensure your cynic is kept under tight control, as his pessimism can poison an entire organisation. Listen to your cynic but don't expose him to too many people and, above all, don't let him make the decisions.

Then, try to create a workplace that eliminates the fear of success. That's right – success. The wishful thinker dreams about success but never achieves it. He believes, and he may be right, that success will merely raise the level of expectation higher and higher until the demands become impossible. The one who fears failure worries about getting enough water; the one fearing success knows the next task will be to turn it into wine. Give your winners a little 'down time' and don't expect too much, too fast. That will convert many of your Wannabes into real champions.

If you are a dreamer, take heart. Businesses need dreamers. Without our Wannabes, we merely go along day after day with no excitement, no change and no progress. More than any other endangered species, the Wannabe is the one we have to develop and protect. Just discipline yourself a little. Remember that wishful thinking is our greatest business sin. Make sure your dream is not a useless wish or an excuse for not doing anything proactive. Perhaps most critically, make sure you know what you want to do after your dream comes true.

It's possible we haven't mentioned any of the problems within your company. You have no trouble with corporate arrogance, take fame with a large dose of salt and never spend time dreaming about what could have been. Well, I never said it was probable – only possible. But, if you are that perfect, maybe you should study the following rule very carefully.

Rule of business life no. 30

If you're wreckless today, you'll be reckless tomorrow

How many times have you listened to someone brag about never being in an accident only to hear they had wrecked their car the next day? How many times have you heard someone say, 'It'll never happen to me!' only to see it happen? When it does, do you catch yourself feeling that it is exactly what the self-satisfied, conceited so-and-so deserved? Do you instinctively feel that smugness always gets its just reward?

Life has a way of punishing those who find safety in what hasn't happened and are proud of what they haven't done – yet. This type of 'it-won't-happen-to-me' conceit is a special form of arrogance, special in that it is totally undeserved. Normally, people become arrogant because they are successful, often to a spectacular degree. In achieving this exalted status, they usually took some measured risks and probably had a failure or two along the way. However, there are a few people who do not have a good excuse for their arrogance. Their complacency sets in not because of success but because of lack of failure. You have to question why there were no disasters. Was it due to careful management and good judgement? Possibly, but perhaps it was only because no risks were ever taken, or no opportunities ever recognised.

There was an article in a British trade newspaper some time ago which contained a typographical error that, while subtle, grabbed my attention. In an essay on a particular retail company planning a bold new format, the writer said of the firm, 'Whilst attempting to sell both bed linen and do-it-yourself tools in the same store might seem strange, they have never been wreckless in the past.'

'Hmm,' I thought, 'let me think about this.' While the author obviously wanted to indicate that the company was not known for reckless management, perhaps he was saying more than he intended. Was he pointing out that, because it had never had a large-scale failure – or wreck – in the past, it had become over-confident?

Well, I'm sorry to disappoint those of you who enjoy the aftermath of a good disaster, but that didn't happen here. At least, not yet. The company had had little experience with radical change but possessed a good management team. Naturally, they made errors that caused great consternation and goals changed rapidly, but they must have recognised the danger. They certainly took all the necessary steps to put things right. Whether they will succeed or not is still in doubt. Recovery from this type of over-confidence is never certain. However, this company is the exception to many rules. For every one of its calibre, a dozen or more failures can be found.

Given all this, what did the company do that made it so exceptional? More importantly, what can be done to prevent this kind of complacency?

Perhaps the most important thing is to create a working environment that will allow risks to be taken. This does not mean you reward failures, nor does it mean that ill-advised risks are acceptable. There is a way, though, to encourage healthy innovation without necessarily inviting disaster.

Learn to practise benefit management. There is far too much concentration today on risk management. The basic rule of risk management inevitably is 'Do as little as possible that can cause things to change. After all, change is dangerous.' Benefit management, on the other hand, looks at the same issue or task from a different perspective. It concentrates on achieving the greatest possible gain from an element of investment, whether that investment is in money, work or risk. This is a more aggressive strategy but one that can be controlled with a little common sense.

Start looking for the people who know how to take risks. When hiring, look for prior failures. These are the people who do not trust in luck. If the job candidates claim never to have failed, they are either lying or have consistently failed to react to opportunities throughout their career. Either way, these are not people you want on your team. When promoting someone, do the same. Look for their outstanding successes, not just their ability to survive. For those who have 'failed', find the reasons why. If there were several failures without counterbalancing successes, you can assume poor judgement. Otherwise, it is probably worth taking a chance on the person.

Importantly, avoid impatience. Set your own timetable and do not allow others to do it for you. When experimenting or innovating, create a schedule and then stick to it. Even when you are successful, allow time for the benefits to fully develop. Accelerating a new venture before you understand the dynamics can destroy its full potential.

Finally, keep your arrogance under control. We all tend to be self-confident and a little cocky in business, especially when we're on a winning streak. That's fine. We'll never make progress unless we believe we can do three impossible things before dinner each day. Just make sure that confidence doesn't turn into complacency. It's a sure way to lose your reputation for being wreckless.

I fear I'm beginning to sound too strident. You will soon think I've adopted the morally superior attitude exclusive to cyclists on busy London streets. I don't mean to sound that bad. Honest. I learned these rules the hard way. I broke every single one of them. There is one in particular that has given me trouble. I'm now able to go almost five minutes without breaking it but, then, I've improved a lot recently.

Rule of business life no. 31

Over-simplification is the practice of the lazy

I don't know if it can be proven but it certainly seems to be true that the higher a person is in the management hierarchy, the more they tend to over-simplify. I do it. You do it. Our bosses do it even more. Their bosses are just plain unbelievable.

It can be hard to understand why this happens. There's always a plethora of excuses for it. Some people will tell you it is because their bosses are silly, stupid or both. To quote Mr Spock, this 'does not compute'. Foolish people do not rise to positions of leadership in business today. It's too much of a cut-throat world for that kind or person to survive at the top.

Another favourite excuse is that bosses are too smart. The theory is that they can see the solutions while the rest of us mere mortals are still trying to understand what the problem is. They over-simplify because everything is simple to them, is the way some like to tell it. We could live quite happily with that if it were true. Unfortunately, this doesn't add up either. Really smart people know the consequences of over-simplifying things to those that are less intelligent. They go out of their way to make sure everything is clear and understood. They never over-simplify.

You hear other excuses. There are those who claim they're too busy to explain. Poppycock! The amount of time and money wasted by those who oversimplify could pay the national debt, and I'll even let you pick the country. Of course, there are always those who blame their staff for failing to understand a simple concept. You already know my opinion about that type of leader.

No, you can come to only one conclusion. People who over-simplify are just plain lazy. They don't want to go to the effort required to think things through. They won't accept the burden that goes with complete understanding. They would much rather pass the responsibility for clarity on to people such as you and me. They'll still take the credit for keeping things simple, even though it's the one thing they do not do.

I had a boss who made this his constant practice. Thinking about him brings back one vivid memory. A new president had just been appointed and she wanted to quickly map out a new strategy. All the senior executives were gathered for a five-day strategic planning workshop. I was brought along to help facilitate it.

All went well for the first few days. Then it became apparent that much of the emerging strategy was dependent upon the systems area performing some rather spectacular technical feats. Perhaps miracles would be a better description. Everyone turned to my boss for his reaction.

'Not a problem,' he said. 'It's really quite simple. Terry and his people will take care of it. It's just a question of (waffle, waffle, waffle). Right, Terry?'

'Er, ah, er,' is how I remember beginning my eloquent answer. I was still trying to work out what the first waffle meant. 'Er, I think it could be more difficult that that, Harry. Er, don't get me wrong. I'm not saying it can't be done. It's just that, well, no one has ever done something like this before. I don't think anyone has ever even contemplated doing it. It may take a little longer than everyone is, um, contemplating. Er, maybe we should think about this a little more.'

Of course, Harry explained in some explicit detail later why it was simple. Most of his graphic explanation centred on my lack of intelligence. I came to understand that I should not have embarrassed him in that manner. I won't recount what he said. I doubt if you need or want to learn those particular new words. However, you may appreciate his explanation of simplicity: 'I don't care how you do it. I don't give a damn how hard it is. It's your job to make it simple, Kelley. If you can't do it, find another job.' It should not surprise you to hear that I took his well-timed advice.

One of the biggest problems is that we all think we know what simplicity is. However, when a boss thinks that, it becomes almost irrelevant whether he is right or not. A boss says, 'This is simple. Hey, you. Go and do it for me.' That's when the trouble sets in. What is simple to some may not be so to others, and vice versa.

When your boss tells you that something is simple, don't let him get away with it! He may have crossed the invisible line between simplicity and over-simplification. Make sure you understand why it is simple. It's not enough to understand what needs to be done. If there is any confusion in your mind about why your boss views the problem as simple, you do not share your boss's vision. If that's the case, you will fail, no matter how well you do the job you think needs to be done.

It's more difficult to judge if you are the boss. In addition to the task at hand, you have to look at the people you are delegating it to. For some, it may indeed be simple. For others, it could be a monstrous job. I can only urge you to remember that one directive is too many, while two will never be enough. That's correct. I haven't reversed this statement. If you give only one directive, you'll be expected to give total direction from then onwards. Two will never be sufficient in that case.

Don't tell people what to do. Instead, tell them what you feel needs to be achieved. Then let them ask questions. No, let me make this a stronger statement. *Force* them to ask questions. Continue the pressure until they have a clear vision. Then they will be able to make it simple – for themselves. In the end, that's all it takes to get simplicity that works.

We not only expect more from our leaders; we demand it. Our judgements about them are harsher than those we make about others. If you want to place yourself on the leader's pedestal, be prepared for people to try to knock you off. That is one of the reasons why people in leadership positions seem so aggressive. They know they need power to fight back. The smart ones know when to use their power and when to hold it in reserve.

Rule of business life no. 32

There's no limit to how softly a large hammer can hit

Let's face it, children fight each other. When they are small, kids learn how to hit. As I remember it, some of them could hit darn hard. For most of us, this is something we outgrow. We still remember how to do it, but we just don't do it any more. Instead, we find other ways to acquire and use power. As children, we were satisfied with the mere physical. Adults have more sophisticated needs.

In business, power comes with the position you hold. There's nothing wrong with this; nor is it avoidable. There are few things in business more exhilarating than the exercise of authority. It's one of life's great motivators. We work hard to gain the increasing authority that comes with seniority. We want the big hammer that authority brings, the better to drive issues forward.

It's a funny thing, though. The more authority you have, the more careful you must be when you use it. One day the MD came storming into my office to 'discuss' a problem. He was a large man who had a well-deserved reputation for not suffering fools gladly. When he glared at you, it was as if knives were pinning you against the wall. I can't remember the issue, nor can I recollect my response. I certainly remember the glare, though, and my feeling of relief as he left.

However, that's not the reason why this has stuck in my memory all these years. It was his actions as he left that taught me a lesson. He stopped at my secretary's desk and had a brief word with her. She was new to the firm and had only seen the MD from a distance. Her nervousness was obvious.

'Hello, Marie,' he said with a warm smile. 'I know we haven't met officially but I think it's about time we did. Terry has been telling me what a wonderful job you're doing. I must say you probably have your hands full with him and his mob of uncouth barbarians. If you can hold your sanity intact around this lot, you deserve all the praise he's been giving. At any rate, I just wanted to say hello and welcome you to the company.'

In case you hadn't guessed, I had never mentioned Marie to the MD, much less told him she was doing a great job. I'm not even sure how he knew her name. I was left wondering why he had done it. Was he making some kind of point? Was it merely a political statement I was too thick to understand? I finally reached the conclusion that he had seen how nervous she was and just stopped to calm her down. After all, she had probably heard our none-too-quiet voices earlier.

I then remembered some of the other senior executives I had either known personally or had heard about from friends. I thought about the screamers who took their anger out on everyone, not just those responsible. I remembered those who demanded perfection from everyone but never said thank you when it was delivered. I compared their action to this MD's and realised how smart he really was. He knew when to hit hard and when not to.

Sure, it's important to have authority. There's a limit to the effectiveness of a small hammer when you have something big to drive through. Having a big hammer means you can get more done with less effort. But that's not all there is to the issue. Big hammers can cause big fears.

By now, most of us acknowledge that we have to learn to motivate by mission, not fear. Fear works in some cultures, but unless you want to create a version of the Marines, it doesn't work very well. It can also be useful when you need radical behaviour change. It is just very, very dangerous. It is far better to create goals that everyone can buy into. There are ways other than force to create behaviour change and not maintain the *status quo*. Try bonuses, promotions and just plain talking to people, if you want to know where to start.

Mostly, though, just remember that possessing power doesn't mean you have to use it. Most of the time, that big hammer will be enough without you ever having to swing it.

As you can see, being a business leader is not an easy task. A leader may inspire others and the best ones certainly do. Leadership is not just about inspiration and fancy speeches, however. The management responsibilities of true business leaders are very broad. The social and economic duties are vast and often ill defined.

In addition, the leader has a moral obligation to the company and the staff that a mere manager may not understand.

Still, leaders do have to manage. They have to manage themselves. This is one of the most difficult challenges they could possibly face. Throughout this Part, we have focused on this issue more than on any other. If you want to lead others, you must first control your ego. The moment you decide you are great, others will decide they can do without your services.

We demand a great deal from our leaders, and so we should. Those who want to rise above the rest have to be willing to make sacrifices. It's worth it for them. Leaders are allowed to do something others cannot. We discuss this in the next Part.

Part V
Rules about change

By now, you have figured out that I work with information. There, my dark secret is in the open. Everyone who has got this far but has struggled to understand me now has an excuse. I can hear you saying to yourself, 'Of course – no one can understand any of those techies. It's all his fault.' I started in technology because I thought business would be rational and logical. Hah! But, it's been fun.

One of the primary reasons I love business so much is the pace of change it involves. I tend to become bored quite easily, something that could be very dangerous to those around me. Luckily, working with technology means that every day is different from the one before. It may not necessarily be better, but it will be different. Learning to live with change has taught me a great deal over the years.

Change is a category of work that is so large and so critical that we need to consider it separately. It needs a complete set of rules for itself. This type of work is so weighty that we can't even settle on a name for it. Instead we allow management gurus to become rich and famous by reinventing the topic time and time again with new terminology.

Whether we call it business process re-engineering or business transformation or use the plainer but equally accurate term 'change', we are talking about the same type of work. Since none of us are management gurus, let's just deal with some of the rules about change and leave it at its simplest level.

Before jumping into the rules, however, it might be useful to look at the generic issues concerning change. First we have to accept that some degree of change is necessary. Extinction, after all, is merely failed evolution. Regardless of how wonderful a company is or how successful it is today, the marketplace is constantly evolving. You cannot allow the gap between your company and its market to become too large.

That doesn't mean that all change is for the good. In fact, change can be one of the most dangerous and most difficult things a company can attempt. People who embark on change programmes without care and consideration are fools. If it were possible to prosecute them, we would call them criminal fools. It's not a small problem, is it? On the one hand, if we do not plan and execute change, our organisation can die a slow and sleepy, although not necessarily painless, death. The alternative is not much more attractive. Every act of change runs a risk of mortal injury to the firm.

Of course, the problem does not have to be quite as bad as that. Evolutionary change is a slow process and can take place in reasonable comfort. If your firm has not fallen very far behind, the risk involved in change can be managed without too much danger. It's not as though the need for change isn't visible. A company would have to have myopia to miss some of the signs. There are all types of metrics to tell you when change is necessary: falling sales; loss of market share; increasing employee turnover; erosion of net margin, and so on.

We also have available plenty of advice and help when contemplating change programmes. Whether from the management gurus, large consulting agencies or just highly paid staff specialists, we are typically up to our corporate necks in expensive advice. If only some of the help we are given were consistent, many of the difficulties would be alleviated. Unfortunately, that's not the way things are. No matter where we turn, the suggestions send us scurrying from one business practice to another, wasting enormous time, money and employee goodwill.

Most of our experiences with these advisers, both internal and external, are generally positive. The advice they give us to recognise the need for change and the practical 'how-to' prescriptions to develop and implement change programmes provide excellent models. Even so, most planned changes, especially the large-scale ones, tend to fail. At the very least, they fall considerably short of the intended targets. This, however, should not be laid at the feet of the consultants. We have no one to blame but ourselves. Changes fail because of attitudes.

I hope the following rules will not present additional conflicts for you to resolve. They are intended to complement most of the general advice provided to businesses over the last couple of decades. They are just a few common-sense guidelines that I have found useful through the years.

Before worrying about mundane things such as how to go about changing your business, you must convince the rest of the people you work with that some change is necessary. It's not just your boss that you have to persuade. From the top of the organisation to the bottom, most people have to believe in the programme. Doubters will sabotage you before you can properly begin if you can't bring them to your side. I've found the following rule a useful one to quote whenever people question the need for change. Maybe it will help you too.

Rule of business life no. 33

If you want to be tied to the past, marry a museum curator

Of all the trials we have to suffer in business, working with someone who constantly looks backwards has to be one of the most irritating. I call this type of individual 'the Whenwe'. Their conversations always include the phrases 'When we were ...' or 'In such and such a year, we ...' Like a car alarm sounding in the middle of the night, these phrases send chills down our spines and set our nerves on edge.

The problem is that Whenwes are not nearly as innocuous as we would like to think. They can be dangerous, not because of who they are but because of what they do. Whenwes come in different pedigrees, each with its unique danger. Let's look at two of the more common breeds in this prolific family.

Probably the most disagreeable type of Whenwe is the 'foreigner'. This is the person who comes from another company and never seems to forget it. Regardless of the length of time in his new firm, he still talks of the days 'when we...', although the 'we' has nothing to do with 'us'. The danger here is a double edged sword and it usually cuts both ways. The first cutting edge is that the Whenwe fails to accept ownership of his new responsibilities. The constant chatter about his past company shows he has not succeeded in adapting to his new existence. The second is that his new colleagues may fail to heed his lessons. If he does not try to fit in, why should they pay attention? However, we hired this person for a reason. There is undoubtedly a wealth of knowledge we are failing to take advantage of properly.

If you have ever worked for more than one firm you yourself are probably a bit of a Whenwe. We all call upon our past and attempt to communicate its lessons to others. How you go about conveying the message makes the difference between being an irritating Whenwe or a person who has some critical wisdom to impart. And there is no secret to it. It is so simple! Just stop saying 'When we...' or 'When I...' and say instead 'When they...' In a short time, you will no longer be a foreign Whenwe.

The second type is the 'Old Whenwe' and he is by far the most dangerous. It seems as if the Old Whenwe has been around the company forever. This person has demonstrated their loyalty through thick and thin and knows everything there is to know about the firm. Potentially the most valuable asset the business has, this person can often become the most destructive. The problem is simply that such people know all the reasons something should not be done. They resist change and have the insider knowledge to sabotage any new proposal.

One at a time, Old Whenwes can be managed. But an organisation that can generate the type of loyalty seen in these people usually creates them in large numbers. Firmly tied to the past, their usual response to a new idea is 'Well, we tried that before in such and such a year (or decade) and it did not work then.' When there are too many Old Whenwes, your chances of successful evolution are poor.

Let me give you an example. I was once hired by a firm whose CEO was eager for change. The company had tripled its size over a five-year period but the internal business processes had not progressed in years. The CEO recognised the danger and asked me to address the problem. Within days, I knew I was in trouble.

The first sign was a senior executive from Finance who approached me to take on some project work. She handed me a memo dated five years previously (that's the truth!) and said, 'Until these are completed, I can't possibly devote any time to these so-called process improvements you want us to make.' My objection that any work not done for five years could not possibly be urgent, otherwise something would already have been done, fell on deaf ears. She never did contribute to the programme.

About the same time, I met with a senior manager from the systems department to discuss inventory management. The systems had not been upgraded even though the business was processing three times the original inventory volumes. I felt a fundamental change in this area was absolutely vital. The senior manager's response was interesting. He told me how the original CEO, a person who had left the company four years previously, would object to the proposal. 'After all,' he said, 'the method set up by the old CEO has worked perfectly well so far and there is no proof that we have to change.' He then went on to tell me that 'the new CEO hasn't been with us long enough to form a good judgement on something as "technical" as inventory management' !!! Needless to say, my experiences at this company led to the creation of this rule of business life.

Nothing is quite that simple, of course. There is and always will be a great deal of benefit available from looking backwards. If we ignore the past, we are unlikely to succeed in the future. We also have to avoid making changes merely for the sake of change. Past experience can help us resist that temptation.

But, for crying out loud, don't be married to the past exclusively! Whether your experiences are from prior firms or from many years at your existing one, you have a wealth of knowledge that will be ignored if you become just another boring old Whenwe who lives in the past. Wake up and use your experiences to develop a better future. Remember, you should look backwards every now and again, but you can't see the road ahead by always looking through the rear-view mirror.

Suppose you have convinced everyone that change is needed. They think it's a great idea and are eager to jump right into it. And this is a work of fiction – not a business book. Well, it could happen. The task now is to select the aspects in your organisation that most need change. They could be almost anything. However, there is one type of work that is devilishly hard to recognise and even harder to get others to agree upon. I happen to think it may be the single most important aspect needing change. We all have this problem. Here is a special rule for dealing with it.

Rule of business life no. 34

Sacred cows are full of it

We made a strange pair in the departure lounge at the Philadelphia Airport waiting for our flight to London Heathrow. Dick Andrews and I could not have been more different. You already know something about me so I won't bother with a description. Dick is entirely different. He's a typical British executive of the old school. A Cambridge graduate (he studied ancient Greek literature – in the original, of all silly things), he was the group human resources director and one of the top ten people in a multi-billion-pound firm. Now, I don't respect HR people as a rule, and they seldom fail to reciprocate. Why the two of us became friends neither of us can imagine.

Dick was exercising a great deal of patience as he listened to me complain about the intransigence of the company bureaucracy in respect of some change proposals I was trying to push through. I suppose a disinterested onlooker would have been amused at the spectacle. There I was, my voice rising as I paced back and forth, all the while cursing people who refused to see what was plainly in front of their face. Dick, meanwhile, was making soothing sounds, trying to keep me in check. I imagine he was not looking forward to a seven-hour flight sitting next to me in my current state.

'It's impossible,' I cried. 'No matter how hard we try, they just won't change. However small the change is, they're just going to ignore it. We are going to have to change the whole damn culture and you know how hard that is.'

'Hold on a minute, Terry,' he said in that calm, almost languid way of speaking that the British have when they produce a profound statement, 'I think you might have it backwards. It isn't hard to change culture. It's one of the easier things to do, unless you try to do it in that awful confrontational manner you love to employ. It's really frightfully simple. Just remember, culture is simply the way we do things here.'

He then went on to give me one of the best lectures I have ever received. I wish I could relate it to you word for word, but my memory isn't that good. You'll just have to make do with my watered-down version.

Typically for him, Dick had started with an understatement but then explained more thoroughly. There are few fears that affect business people more than change. All of us resist change, he said, not because we disagree with the need but because we fear the unknown. This is a different type of fear from the ones we experience in the amusement park. This is the fear of walking down into a dark, dank tunnel. I once read a newspaper article which claimed that the five most frightening, stressful things we face are death, divorce, moving house, changing jobs and changing roles within a job. So, it isn't very surprising that people resist when you try to change their job.

It is this fear that makes changing the legacies of a company and modifying its culture so difficult. The effort should not be under-estimated. Any company that has been in business more than three hours begins to develop legacies. These legacies are simply the preserved and accustomed ways of doing things regardless of how important those things are. Over time, people begin seeing these legacies as laws. The more successful the company is, the more rigid these laws become. Pretty soon, we are left with sacred cows that cannot be challenged.

However, there are some tools and methods you can use that will make the job easier. The most basic tactic you can employ to modify the company, or change 'the way we do things here', is to change it in many small ways rather than in one large transition effort. This is actually easier to do than it sounds.

Here are a few quick ways to make minor changes. The first, fastest and least expensive is to change the habits of the secretaries. If you think that's too simplistic to be helpful, you're wrong. Secretaries have an enormous influence on the inner working of each and every company. They have a way of making sure that whatever is important to them becomes important to everyone they come in contact with. And, sooner or later, they come in contact with every employee in the firm. The nice thing about secretaries is that they, as much as anyone in the firm, want to do a good job. While some will resist change like champions, they can be persuaded if you use a little tact.

Another easy, although not quite as inexpensive, way to create cultural change is to modify the computer systems. Almost everyone uses computer systems today. Simple changes in the screens and the computer reports will cause people to react differently. Don't leave the designing of these changes to computer people. Equally important, don't delegate them to a low-level business person. Use the highest-level individual you can to direct these designs. Remember, the real information processor is not the computer, it's the grey cells in the skulls of the company staff. They react to input, the screens and reports, in a very direct and measurable way. So, recognise that when you change the system, you will be changing the culture. Pretend you are Machiavelli and think the process through beforehand.

A third way to implement change must be done exclusively in partnership with your CEO. Every firm has a different set of core business controls and, as you change these controls, you can change the business. This is not about policy and procedure, however. You want to look at what the CEO finds time to read. Sometimes it's as basic as travel expenses. Other CEOs concentrate on capital but not so much on operating expense. No two CEOs think exactly alike, so you will have to find out what yours concentrates on. As the CEO changes focus, the rest of the business executives will follow, and you can start the gradual shift desired.

One of the more difficult things to achieve, but well worth it if you can do it, is to teach the company to practise 'situational' control. This is just an extension of normal business management. It trains you to learn to look at each situation in isolation and make a unique judgement on how it should be addressed. Situational control assumes that no one style or practice is adequate for all situations. Making the transition to this type of control requires a great deal of effort, a necessary improvement in judgement and acceptance of real accountability throughout the business. As noted, it's hard to achieve but will pay enormous dividends.

However, none of the four suggestions above help if you have sacred cows and are not allowed to challenge them. Equally important, you need to be able to recognise a sacred cow when you have one. That is sometimes the most difficult challenge we face. I hate to do it, but I can only offer the standard advice in these circumstances. Hire a top consultant.

While I love consultants as much as I love HR directors, they do have a purpose. They are able to see the sacred cows as they do not suffer from the historical blindness of the rest of us. They can also compare your legacy procedures to those of other firms, helping you develop better, if not the best, practices. Of course, you'll have to find that rare creature, the consultant who will tell you the truth, not just what you want to hear.

There are many firms that think they know how to recognise a sacred cow when they see one. They also think they know how to challenge them when one is discovered. It's in these firms, more than in any other, that you find employees defending themselves by saying 'We do it that way because that's the way we do it.' So, if you don't have a sacred cow, congratulations. But take the time to check. Remember what sacred cows are full of. And if you can't or won't tell your management, give me a call. I will.

At the beginning of this Part, the right attitude was singled out as the most important factor in a successful change programme. If you have followed the last two rules, you have made a start on gaining that attitude. Still, that's not enough. There is a special kind of approach needed for an innovative change programme. And change without innovation is merely copying someone else. The following rule helps when you're looking for that something extra that will make a real difference.

Rule of business life no. 35

Innovation requires no know

This is a strange sort of rule. It almost sounds as if it approves of ignorance, although that is not the case. Rather, as Socrates suggested, it means that recognising how little we know is one of the true signs of wisdom. Let me set the stage by relating a personal experience.

I attended a very useful conference hosted by Wentworth Research in the United Kingdom during the summer of 1995. Stan Davis, a professor at Harvard and author of several books, including *Future Perfect* and *The Monster Under The Bed*, was one of the guest speakers. Talking about the impact of the 'Information Age' on society, he made some very pertinent observations about the information-literate. His comments also covered many general aspects of life. One idea in particular struck me. He said we go through three stages in life. The first stage is infancy when 'we don't know what we don't know'. The second is adolescence when 'we know what we don't know' and begin the process of finding knowledge. Finally, as adults, we believe 'we know'. 'The Information Age', he said, 'is all about gaining knowledge so that "We Know".'

Davis is someone I would never dream of arguing with but something he said struck me as being wrong. During the rebuttal and summing-up session, I raised some objections. 'My fears', I said, 'are simple. Will we come to believe we know so much that we stop asking questions? Are we in danger of creating assumptions of knowledge rather than the reality?' I wish I had listened to myself.

A few weeks later, I was in an executive committee meeting. A new idea was brought up and discussed at some length. During the wrap up, someone said 'We know...', and went on to pontificate about all the things we assumed were true. I just let it happen and the idea died because of our 'knowledge' and my thoughtlessness. The idea was adopted a year later by a competitor and it proved a reasonable success. So much for our 'superior knowledge'.

We can apply Professor Davis's stages of life to our companies. When we do, we must recognise that perhaps the most dangerous phrase in business is 'we know'. Just saying these words, even quietly to yourself, can create a sense of superiority, usually undeserved and always dangerous. Everyone has experienced this in their business life. How many times have you, when reporting to a superior, heard them say, 'Yes, I know', when clearly not only do they not know, but they also don't know they don't know? Worse, they do not even bother to listen. More important, how many times have you destroyed an idea because 'you knew'?

Belief in our own depth of knowledge creates complacency. When we think we know the answers, we stop asking the questions – we stop looking around the corner to see what's coming next. A well-known example of this condition is the story of Charles Duell who resigned as head of the

US Patent Office in 1899 saying, 'Everything that can be invented has been invented,' so he had nothing left to do. He thought he knew.

'I am not another Duell,' you say, 'but maybe we really do know everything necessary to run our business successfully. It is possible. Besides, it has never been wrong to know too much.' Before becoming too optimistic, just remember that most of our knowledge concerns what has happened in the past. Regardless of how brilliant we may be or how spectacular our track record, our knowledge of the future is severely limited.

Throughout life we work hard to increase knowledge. After all, knowledge is a tremendous source of power. However, when we believe we have achieved that goal and know everything, all progress stops. We lose the ability to think ahead, to innovate and control our own environment. Eventually, we can be and often are overtaken by a younger, more 'hungry' organisation. This may, with luck, be a wake-up call, but sometimes it signals nothing more than retirement from the battle.

Have you bought into the idea of change yet? If you have, control your enthusiasm, please. Change may be necessary but the case hasn't been proven, at least not in every situation. Even when it is the right thing to do, there are several dangers associated with change. This rule addresses one of the more subtle problems brought about by change.

Rule of business life no. 36

The pace of change always exceeds the pace of understanding

Here's a quick story to demonstrate how difficult it can be to understand the changes that go on around us. The president of a medium-sized division of a large publishing firm was showing some investors around. He was a smart, well-educated person who had been with the firm for most of his career. Everyone in the company thought highly of him. We even liked him enough to overlook the fact he was a lawyer by training.

As part of the tour, he took his guests into the new computer room. This was back in the early days when the computer rooms were showcases with glass windows and computers were large, bulky boxes with flashing lights. With evident pride, he pointed out the impressive computer his staff had installed and explained how they controlled the entire process with the switches on the control panel.

As far as I know, no one ever told him it was merely the air conditioner.

All of us recognise that the world is changing rapidly. Just look around and see how different things are today compared with only a few years ago. World politics have changed with the demise of the old USSR. New countries seem to spring up overnight, presenting different challenges and opportunities to the rest of the world. Economic conditions are also changing rapidly as China begins to flex its commercial muscles. Technology is still setting the pace for much of the changing social environment, with the Internet growing in importance to everyone, regardless of their position in society.

We see the changes in business, too. New competitors seem to enter the marketplace in the blink of an eye. Some have invented new ways to conduct business, leaving many of the old guard stunned and helpless. Bright young people with fresh new perspectives are entering the workforce. They can literally take our breath away with the skills they have mastered before working a single day. If you were to take a six-month sabbatical, then return to the same function in the same company, you would hardly recognise it.

In other words, it can get pretty confusing out there in the 'new' business jungle. Most of us console ourselves by thinking that everyone has the same problems in adjusting. We tell each other that the world has never before seen as much change and, surely, it will slow down soon. Our parents and grandparents, back through the ages, probably said the same. They were wrong and so are we. The pace of change will continue accelerating. As it does, our understanding of the 'new' world will have to accelerate as well or we will end up making poor decisions and looking foolish in the process. To believe otherwise is simply foolhardy.

There are several key questions. What can we do about the pace of progress, assuming for the moment that all these changes will bring progress? If things won't slow down, how do we speed ourselves up? In this new, confusing business world, can we ever hope to understand the implications of all the changes we see? Or shall we be explaining the complex operation of a future equivalent of 'the computer disguised as an air conditioner' to embarrassed people who know better but are too polite to interrupt?

Chances are that we'll not be able to keep up with everything. Just look around at all the new professions we see in business today. These specialist skills are required just to stay marginally competent. When the needs go beyond that, most firms outsource the work to others even more specialised. However, management is about leading, not abdication. How do we lead what we can't possibly understand?

Here are a few actions worth taking. The first is the most obvious: get good people to help you. Be patient with them. Otherwise, they will not be patient with you and your investment will go to waste. Take the time to listen, even, or perhaps especially, when their message seems to come to you in a foreign language. They're not doing this on purpose to confuse you – just using the words needed to describe these new conditions of business.

Second, reconcile yourself to the need for quick 'good' decisions, not just slow great ones. You don't have time to spare and, besides, the situation will change before your great solution is implemented. Yes, you must try to think far ahead but, more important, you must act now.

Third, don't play with change. We take too many foolish actions when there's no need to do anything at all. We've done so much of this in business that there are common terms to describe it – for example 'automating the quill pen' or 'killing flies with a shotgun'.

Finally, make sure you and the entire team understand the difference between prediction and anticipation. In the first, you assume certain events will occur and you plan your reaction. Take time to learn and understand the issues here. Ignorance will be no excuse. Delay can be harmful.

Anticipation is entirely different. It refers to the range of events that could happen. You generalise possible responses and ensure that someone has a watching brief to detect signs, but you don't have to take any action yet. While it's never safe to be ignorant, perhaps it's acceptable to allow others to gather the necessary knowledge.

The point has been made that change is something you have to live with, like it or not. The alternative to change, like the alternative to growing older, is not very pleasant to contemplate. Knowing that change is dangerous, we still do it because we have to do it. As with any other dangerous activities, we know enough to exercise caution. There is a special kind of rule about this, though, and it may be one you want to be very diligent about.

Rule of business life no. 37

Take care of the baby

There's a great temptation to skip writing this rule. Anything that has to do with quality today has become a highly charged, emotive topic. The whole concept has come to dominate much of what we do in business. The number of books and articles in leading management journals on this topic is simply overwhelming. However, that's not the reason why I hesitate to add to the quantity of literature on the subject.

I simply do not want to be quoted with the message being distorted, though that's what some of you will do. You'll use my words to support a position I would find distasteful and unacceptable. I know. Others have already done it.

Nevertheless, any discussion of change needs to include something about quality. No book of business rules can be complete without it. We all know quality measures are necessary for a healthy, growing business. We also know that, when our business practices change, modifications to the quality formula are vital. Most of us even recognise that the actual programme for change needs to have quality parameters. So, when we talk about change, we are dealing with old quality practices connected to change programme quality practices connected to new quality practices.

Ouch! Quality to quality to quality. Before we know it, we have spent more time and effort, to say nothing about money, on ensuring quality than on the final product. We can reach a situation where, as the doctor said, 'The operation is a success – it's a damned shame the patient died.' Fans of exacting quality control programmes would argue that the patient would have died anyway if the operation *hadn't* been successful. They would be right. However, let's not forget our real goal. We want the operation to be successful but still have a live patient at the end.

Several years ago, my department was leading a large-scale change effort for the company. The process was proceeding quite well and we were somewhat ahead of our most optimistic schedule. There is always tension when undertaking tasks such as this, but my project managers seemed reasonably relaxed and confident.

Quality was a constant topic during our staff meetings. We paid a great deal of attention to the subject and had employed several different types of metrics to measure ourselves. We knew we had to live up to a high set of standards if the change programme was to be accepted. Our self-satisfaction took a turn one day when the quality manager brought a new perspective to the staff meeting.

'It's not sufficient,' he said, 'to have a quality standard. This is something we established for ourselves and it may not be satisfactory to the business. We need to reach a quality agreement with everyone in the company. This agreement needs to formally document all the performance criteria, including the actions and penalties we will employ if the agreed standards are not achieved. I have a sample of an agreement to demonstrate my meaning.'

He proceeded to pass his sample around and we read it with some interest. Service-level agreements are not something new and all of us had some experience with them. We believed that the standards we had set ourselves were sufficiently high that the change in language from 'standards' to 'agreements' was merely that – a change of words. We couldn't have been more mistaken.

The QM's performance agreement would have made a lawyer envious. It had more caveats, excuses and 'gotchas' than my daughters when they came home late from dates. It added little to the quality aspects of the job. In fact, it seemed to put such tight limitations around every deliverable aspect of work that we would be punished even if we exceeded expectations.

'This is just so much bureaucratic mumbo jumbo,' I objected. 'We don't need all of this rubbish. If the business wants higher performance standards, we'll just do it if possible or tell them it ain't possible and why. We have enough lawyers in the company and I don't want to give employment for life to yet another.'

'You're being too cavalier about it, Terry,' he said. 'Delivering quality is like delivering babies – you don't drop babies. These agreements will enforce that. I may trust you to keep the standards up but perhaps someone else will be making the decisions, not you.'

The argument went back and forth for a short while but I was convinced. I had been from the moment he said we couldn't drop the quality baby. As in parenthood, there are some things you just don't argue about. Besides, it made sense. I approved the policy and formal quality agreements were developed with every area of the business affected by our change programme. The project slowed down considerably because of that. We began to fall behind schedule as we went through the negotiations about service levels with the other parts of the business. Rather than negotiations it was more like children squabbling to see which could get the bigger slice of the cake. Actual quality of the product became less and less important as the words we used to describe quality became more and more removed from reality.

Oh, the project was finally completed. It was only a few months late and a few percentage points over budget. That was unsatisfactory considering where we had been, but the real impact was worse. The rest of the business was disappointed in the final delivered product even though it provided more than we originally planned. Why? During the negotiating process, people in the business had undergone a subtle change in their point of view. Rather than looking at the business as a whole, they began looking for specific benefits for their departments. The negotiations led them to believe they were getting less than could be delivered. If that weren't true, they thought, why would we bother to negotiate a settlement? The new process was vastly superior to the old so they could not go back. Nevertheless, it left them disappointed and unhappy. There was nothing left for them to do but complain. My goodness, did they complain! The project was eventually considered a failure even though people continued to use the result and it provided all the benefits we had hoped for.

What's the point behind this story? I believe we took things too far and over-reacted. While it's true that you don't drop babies, that doesn't mean you should put them on a pedestal. If you do, you might be inviting them to fall off on their own. Nor do you isolate babies from their surroundings, or allow them to make important family decisions. Instead, you cherish them, love them and, every once in a while, you change their nappies.

Quality is a tricky subject to debate and an even more difficult one to manage. No one will argue that quality measures are not needed. How you achieve them is another issue. Sometimes, you have to recognise how much you can afford to spend in relation to the sum of goals you are trying to achieve. If you find a spot of mould on a slice of bread at home, you throw it away. Most probably, you throw the whole loaf away. Bread isn't very expensive, after all. That's fine. In business, it's not that simple. We have to recognise that we are not dealing with bread. When there's a little bit of mould on the process, we have to excise it and throw that piece away, not the whole thing.

Quality is an issue that has to be addressed by the senior managers of the organisation. It cannot be delegated. It must not be made an emotional issue. It has to be kept at a pragmatic, rational level of importance. That's the only way true quality will be achieved.

Leading an organisation through a change programme is one of the most difficult tasks we can undertake. It takes the patience of a saint, the cunning of a Machiavelli and the wisdom of Solomon. Unfortunately, those attributes are hard to find. Sometimes the company has to appoint people with lesser talents – such as you and me. The following rule helps if you are stuck with the job.

Rule of business life no. 38

Rowing the boat will cause it to rock

I don't understand some people. They implement programmes of change on a vast scale. They attempt to transform their corporate world and alter the behaviour of their entire staff. They have a vision for the future and the arrogance to force everyone else into accepting it. Given half a chance, they would take over the world.

So far, I understand. If I were smart enough, I might try to do the same thing. My confusion comes when these people pretend that this massive change they are engineering will not affect them personally. They have the audacity, or perhaps just lack of imagination, to assume that their life gets easier as a result of changing the life of others. They just don't understand that moving the boat forward causes it to rock and they're in the boat with the rest of us.

And the people who do this are usually the most senior in the company. You would think they should know better. But grey hair has little to do with grey cells. Let me give you an example.

The president of a fairly large US company was dissatisfied with the manner in which the commercial department performed its role. Having developed some impressive marketing skills early in his career, he had some very definite thoughts on how the job should be done. It seemed that no one in the commercial area wanted to support him, however. After hiring and subsequently firing several executives to run it for him, he decided to use a different strategy. He would employ someone else to do it for him – someone inside the company but not part of the commercial department.

'You don't have to worry about it,' the President said to the young executive he had selected. 'I'll back you all the way. I just want you to study the way the business works from the Commercial people's view. We need an outsider's perspective to see it clearly. Develop the data so that we can understand the performance issues. I'm convinced they can do a better job but I need to be able to prove it to them. I also want you to come up with a series of recommendations. Between us, we'll develop a new process and business strategy that they'll just have to accept.'

So my friend, the young executive, jumped in and did everything he was asked to do. The commercial department was studied as objectively as possible. Performance was measured, showing that the president had been right. Evidence was plentiful that they were both inefficient and ineffectual. Together, he and the president developed a new, dramatically improved strategy for the department. It was implemented with great fanfare and, at first, seemed to work well. Everything was great. Right?

Wrong! 'They're not at all happy,' the President said to the young man. 'All I hear are complaints. The new strategy is causing more unhappiness than I anticipated. It would work if they were more contented. You must have screwed up the implementation. Surely there's something you can do to ease the pain. I don't like all the belly-aching I'm getting from them. Go fix it.'

Of course, the young executive tried. The more he tried, the more the people in the commercial department became aware of their power. The more power they felt they had, the more they complained to enhance the level of influence they had. The more complaints the president received, the more dissatisfied he became with the young executive.

To be frank, no one was surprised when he was fired. It wasn't the first time this particular president had reacted this way. He was a creative individual and had many wonderful ideas. The trouble was that he felt they could be implemented without disturbing the people, procedures and processes already in place. As he could not be wrong, it had to be someone else's fault when these change programmes caused waves.

Of course, you would have to be unlucky to run into someone as difficult to work for as this person. Still, it's worth learning a few lessons from him and his reaction. There is always a risk when making progress. Change upsets the existing order of things. Whenever you do that, there is instability. In other words, the boat will rock.

There will be discomfort in change. Expect it. Accept it. Then get on with the next change programme. It never stops, you know.

Not all the results of change can be counted as beneficial. Change is a risky activity and, as with all risks, there will be some negative results. Just because it may be necessary doesn't mean it's painless. As managers, we are obliged to keep the pain at a tolerable threshold. It may help to remember the following rule.

Rule of business life no. 39

There's a difference between conducting a test and being a guinea pig

Despite what some critics may claim, there is a fair amount of innovation in business today. We may be cynical about change but we are always involved with creating some. Actually, that is not entirely true. There may always be change occurring around us, but we're not necessarily the ones who create it. Others may impose it on us and only then do we really recognise the suffering it entails.

Think about some of the change mechanisms that are constantly happening in businesses. Their names may vary but they have been around for a long time, and will probably stay with us even longer.

There's business process re-engineering, outsourcing and downsizing. We hear about internationalism, centralisation and its mate, decentralisation. We know that some firms are involved with acquisition while, at the same time, others are breaking up to restore shareholder value. For every proponent of one change, there's an equally articulate spokesperson for its opposite.

Of course, there are many other experiments we have to endure. In our own companies, they may not be viewed that way, but that's what they are. There are promotions to test a person in a new, untried role. We create new products, new formats and new services in the attempt to prove our innovative spirit. We build new systems and restructure the organisation to spark a change. We do all this and more, but it is often without proof of benefit and sometimes without any real understanding about how the experiment may turn out.

Still, you may think there is nothing wrong with this. After all, change is generally good, isn't it? Sure it is. Except any change, no matter how small, hurts someone. Some changes hurt everyone. It is important to understand that any change, even when a well-documented success at other companies, is an experiment for yours. Without proper safeguards, experiments can go wrong.

Strangely enough, those companies that really experiment are usually the safest. They know there are risks involved and take steps to mitigate them. While it takes courage to initiate untried techniques, it also takes brains. People who attempt this are smart enough to know where the alligators are likely to be hidden and avoid them. Being on the leading edge doesn't always mean being on the bleeding edge, if you have the intelligence to avoid the sharp parts.

The greater risks come when you attempt to copy others. You hear one firm report how wonderful their results have been with their new process and think this must hold true for you as well. Just think about the number of times you've heard someone say, 'Well, blankety-blank is the right way to go. It's sure worked for so-and-so.' Maybe you were the one who said it.

This is foolish in two distinct ways. First, you have no reason to believe what the other company reports. You have to expect them to say they were successful. If they were to admit otherwise, they would be making a monkey of themselves. The second reason it's foolish is simply because your firm is not theirs. You are unique and your strengths and weaknesses are different. Even if the technique the other company used did work in their case, it may still spell disaster for you.

There is a straightforward solution for all this. Never assume that the results achieved elsewhere are sufficient. There are many plausible theories, but that doesn't mean they are good. Sometimes it only means they are glib. Look at every change as an experiment and then become suspicious. More than that, become downright cynical. It's the best way to protect your company, your staff and, last but not least, yourself. There's nothing wrong with wanting change, but you must never accept it without a thorough challenge and review. Enthusiasm is fine in its place but you want clear eyes when changing your business, not star-filled ones.

Your work doesn't stop with an attitude change, however. You have to test, test, then test again. Even that is not enough. Set up control groups before you test. You must know exactly what you are measuring against or all the tests imaginable are worthless. Make sure you are not producing a Pygmalion effect in your tests and measurements. No matter how much you want it to succeed, make the test fair. There's no useful purpose in stacking the deck. Good ideas will win without your help.

Change is a process that begins with curiosity. You must have the imagination to wonder what will happen when something is changed before you take the first step. You also need the intelligence and strength of character to see the process through each step along the way. Many people have these and think they are enough but success demands one final ingredient.

You have to have some compassion. Ruthlessness has its place and, at times, it is vital. But compassion is much more important if you want to enjoy the change, not just profit by it. Remember, every change is an experiment and someone will get hurt. Try to keep the level of pain as low as possible. Don't treat your people as guinea pigs. After all, some day you might be treated that way yourself.

Being right doesn't necessarily mean you will succeed when you attempt to change something. Change is too emotional an issue for most people to accept without resistance. Nor does this only apply to large issues. All change, whether large or small, will hit a roadblock sooner or later. How you handle this blocking action may spell the difference between long-term success and failure.

Rule of business life no. 40

The first step in training mules is to gain their attention

Some changes are inevitable. Like the proverbial death and taxes, you may dodge or delay them but they will catch up with you sooner or later. In business, we can't afford to disregard signs of change, just as we should never ignore that little brown government envelope that comes once a year. Attempting to avoid change is merely wishful thinking. Unfortunately, many of us indulge in that from time to time.

The president of a major division of a large American conglomerate went to California to make a budget presentation to the chairman. I was part of a small team that went along to support the president and I received a fascinating insight into this type of wishful thinking. After finishing with the numbers and standard action plan we all employ to keep the boss happy, the president brought up the topic that had most concerned him.

'I am absolutely convinced', he stated emphatically, 'that our very future depends on how we address the issue of discounting. It is undoubtedly the wave of the future and we risk being left behind. Wherever our competition is using it, we lose sales and the trend is for even greater impact as time goes by. It is inevitable and we have to recognise it now. I want to trial it as an experiment in one state and, if it works, we should be prepared to execute it nationwide immediately.'

He then went on with detailed plans and projections but received a curious lack of feedback from the conglomerate's executives. Lunchtime came and we all trooped into the executive dining room. This was back in the 1970s but even then it was an anachronism. The china was trimmed with gold, the waiters dressed in tuxedos and the food was exquisite. After the main course, the chairman finally decided to respond to the proposal.

'I do not now, nor will I ever, accept discounting as a tactic within our business,' he said. 'It is neither desirable nor practical. I refuse to believe it is inevitable and reject any proposal to experiment with our corporate style and image. We are a full-line, high-quality business and our customers will gladly pay a premium for the privilege of buying from us. There will be no further discussion on this topic.'

The chairman was no dummy. He had been recruited after building one business from nothing to a highly respected, fairly large firm. After joining, he had then doubled the size of the corporation in less than ten years. He was even well thought of outside the business community and had been selected as a member of the President's Economic Advisory Board.

He was still dead wrong. Any student of business will remember the boom in discounting that occurred in the US during the 1980s. Those that practised it survived. Those that didn't struggled or died. My division, once the star of the corporation, was sold for a pittance in a vain effort to fund the other divisions. It didn't help, and the entire structure folded into ignoble bankruptcy. The chairman had been as stubborn as a mule and we had failed to win his attention.

Stubbornness is not just an affliction of the powerful, however. It can and does affect everyone in the organisation. For example, I had a secretary a few years ago who suffered from this condition. As a secretary, she was neither good nor bad. I had inherited her when I took a new position and she was still trying hard to prove her value to me. One day, I dictated a memo, something I do infrequently. After it was typed, signed and sent off in the internal mail, she brought me a copy for my records.

'I don't need a copy,' I said. 'I wrote it. I don't need to see it again. You have it in the computer and that's all we'll need.'

She seemed confused but, after we talked for a while, she became more comfortable with the idea of not filing paper copies. Or so I thought. Over the next few months, we completed some additional correspondence and repeated the same conversation. Gradually, she stopped giving me unwanted copies and I thought I had finally convinced her.

She went on holiday one week about six months after we started working together. I needed something I knew she kept in her files and went looking for it. What I found, instead, was a complete set of all the correspondence she had typed for me over the six months. She simply wasn't comfortable without some paper to prove to herself that she had done some work.

Because of our relative positions, I was able to gain her attention and the practice I wanted was adopted. Actually, the story made its rounds and almost every secretary in the organisation started following her example. The unnecessary paper storage in the company declined rapidly. Secretaries may be quicker to learn new concepts than senior executives.

Sometimes, you have a big stick and you can use it to get people's attention. Sometimes, you have nothing but instinct. It remains vital that you attempt to make people understand what might happen. Perhaps the changes you anticipate will never take place. The problem remains. As in the case of the discounting policy, you might be right.

When you are the boss, appreciate that people will be trying to gain your attention. Don't be stubborn. Listen and try to understand what is being said. We have enough mule-headed people in business without you adding to the supply.

Motivation for change is another topic that needs to be looked at. While you may be driven by the best intentions, root causes are always worth examination. Attempting to change or, to use the latest buzz word, transform your business is not something done lightly. I find it helps to remember the following rule.

Rule of business life no. 41

Hype springs eternal

Change is addictive. Once it enters the system, it's difficult to control. There's a rush as the adrenaline flows, the pulse quickens and the eyes blaze with fevered intent. You reach a 'high' and never want to come down from it. People tell me it's similar to using drugs. It's difficult to give it up once you're hooked.

There's a network of change-dealers that we must be wary of and watch for. They may not stand on the street corner or look as disreputable as the neighbourhood drug-dealer, but they are every bit as dangerous. Just as their more recognisable cousins, these change-dealers don't care what effect their product will have on their clients – in this case your organisation. They are only interested in making money out of your corporate addiction.

Who are these people? Are they really criminals? Are their products always dangerous? Do we run and hide or call the police when we see them conducting business? Is it acceptable, at least once in a while, to pander to our addiction?

Let's look at the issue more closely to see if we can develop some guide-lines for associating with our local change-dealers. Unlike drug-dealers, the people who peddle change believe in the ultimate goodness of their product. Their products are their thoughts. Whether we are talking about management gurus or consultants, they honestly believe the strategies for change they market are good for our corporate health. Sometimes they are. There is a current and ever-present danger with many of these strategies, however. Just as the drug culture has embraced designer drugs, we have entered the era of fashionable management concepts.

This can be troublesome if it's not kept under control. It's not as if you are dealing with apparel. Businesses, at least internally, should not be part of the fashion industry. Why is it, then, that we seem to follow the dictates of the trend-setters? Every time we do this, we run the risk of losing our focus and diverting energy from what we need to accomplish.

This is not the same as saying that the emerging management philoso-phies and new business practices are wrong. Many of them offer truly exciting potential for our businesses. They show us new ways to perceive reality and encourage original thinking. When we grab hold of the latest and greatest new fad, though, we run the risk of throwing away every-thing we have been working on.

Some changes now being marketed are always dangerous and almost never beneficial. These are the changes based on the FUD factors: fear, uncertainty and doubt. Those who practise this may be external to your organisation. Some are consultants. Others are people marketing their products to you. But the most dangerous are the internal staff who prac-tise FUD. They almost always use it for self-promotion at the expense of the entire organisation, not merely their peers. When a person practising FUD is high in the company, you will find it in deep trouble. The higher in management they are, the deeper the trouble will be. Root such people out, challenge them and force them to change their ways as quickly as possible. Those who practise FUD are full of fear, uncertainty and doubt themselves and, when challenged, can usually be made to stop their destructive tactics.

Far too often, we seem to be governed by laws of Fads, FUDs and Failures. The latest 'practice of the month' is adopted as a reaction to these laws. Bear in mind that those who promote these principles fail in the end. They may receive rapid promotion when they initiate the practice, but they seldom reach the top. Usually, the senior executives in the company recognise the weakness of this approach. If you float from one concept or practice of the month to the next, chances are you'll not last more than the second month.

With all of the wisdom and advice being promoted within industry, how do we keep it under control? The best way is to focus on certain types of work, regardless of your job or your company's industry. There are certain things you have to do. No matter how much you may wish to avoid them, they must be done. First, make sure you are not putting socks on the hippopotamus. After you have eliminated everything unnecessary, the remaining work must be done. Do it.

Then look at other tasks that you should work on. Try to take costs out of the organisation. Every company, whether in the manufacturing or service industry, has a deliverable product. Create ways to make the end product less expensive. This may involve some change but you can be sure that it's worthwhile. It shows on the bottom line. You can prove it's not change just for the sake of change.

Also look at ways to make the end product better without increasing costs in the same proportion. Again, this drive towards greater effectiveness may involve some change. But change itself isn't the focus. You'll see the results everywhere. Your improved product or service will prove itself in the marketplace. You don't need a management consultant to tell you this, or to tell you how to go about doing it. It's inherent in your knowledge of the job.

You are now left with strategic work. This may very well involve a great deal of change. You may look at your corporate infrastructure and decide to change it. You may look at the marketplace and change corporate direction. You may look internally and change the skills and make-up of your staff. Whichever way you turn, strategic work is an area where you can use help. This is where the new management concepts can be applied. This is where external advice is often valuable.

Please remember, though, 'hype springs eternal'. You will be better served and will serve your company better if you listen to what people say and then avoid the commonplace. People are in the habit of using new words to describe yesterday's paradigm. That doesn't mean it's new. It only means someone has found a new way to describe something old.

When you look around, you'll probably see tomorrow's paradigm for yourself. The environment we work in is in a constant state of flux. The definition of work is changing. The way businesses compete is operating according to a new model. The people we hire and the skills we attempt to attract are different from those of the past. Perhaps our new paradigm needs to be based on flexibility, not efficiency or even effectiveness. Perhaps the future belongs to the companies that are nimble, not necessarily those that are strong. Perhaps future business leaders will be those who can anticipate and react quickly. Come to think of it, they have always been like that.

There are plenty of valid management philosophies we can adopt. If the organisation isn't ready for them, however, they are mere hype. Although you shouldn't just put your head down and keep on doing yesterday's work – you have to change – that doesn't mean you should start a change programme without thinking your needs through and sticking to the job till it's done. Work spent on satisfying the latest hype is work that is wasted.

The winds of change bring inevitable resistance. It would be foolish to expect anything less. Regardless of how much common sense an idea for change appears to have or how each individual may benefit, there will always be those who disagree. Some of the changes we will be required to support will be distasteful to us personally. Like it or not, we have no choice. Change will take place. I hope some of these rules will help. There are more rules on this subject but it's time to go on to the next Part. We'll save the others for a later time.

Part VI
Rules about risks

Now, the general who wins makes many computations in his temple before the battle is fought. The general who loses a battle makes but few calculations beforehand.
Sun Tzu, The Art of War

Decisions, decisions, decisions. It sometimes seems as if all we do in business today is make decisions. Sometimes we get them right. Other times, we really screw things up. Generally, we survive and go on to the next decision. Over time, a reputation develops and those people who are right more often than not are called upon to make even more decisions. A certain amount of money, and sometimes a small measure of fame, accompany this reputation. But usually a high price has to be paid as well.

We hear a great deal about executive burn-out these days, and stress is becoming an increasingly important factor in today's business environment. It is now a major concern to most personnel executives and some companies have even taken out insurance policies against stress to protect themselves. It also seems that the problem is becoming more widespread. Where we used to only hear about senior executives being afflicted, today everyone at every level can suffer.

Many reasons are cited. A popular one is that too many people are working too hard. That's nonsense. We're not working any harder today than people did in the past. Besides, most of us enjoy our job and there is little feeling of pressure in it. No, hard work alone is not the explanation. Neither are long hours, paperwork, travel or any of the other reasons most commonly heard.

119

The pressure that causes burn-out must come from the need to make decisions. We seem to be called on to make more of them than ever before, and the need to make them quickly has grown at a phenomenal rate. The most probable cause of this is the vast amount of information each of us has available to process every day. This in turn means we have to form more judgements, make faster decisions and, most importantly, take greater risks than ever before. And we have to do all of this while the pace of business life continues to accelerate.

Let's try to look at the issue rationally and not waste time feeling sorry for ourselves. Businesses don't make investments. People do. Stress comes from making high-risk investments. If you reduce the risk factors, you'll reduce the stress.

Businesses don't exercise judgement, take risks or make decisions. We do. That's what we are paid to do. If there is some pressure involved, that's to be expected. It's also part of what we get paid for. Every time you make a decision, you are taking a risk. So what? You are taking an even bigger risk when you fail to make a decision. When you do that, you're leaving your future open to the whim of others – or in the hands of fate, which may be a heck of a lot worse.

Learning how to make better decisions and to do so with less risk is the best solution to this type of challenge. There are a few general guidelines to help in the decision-making process. They are only general principles, as every decision is unique and must be viewed in the light of existing circumstances. Most of the time, you're on your own and there is little or no help available. Nevertheless, these rules suggest an attitude that keeps problems in perspective.

One of the first things you must understand about risks is that you can't avoid taking some. I'm not referring to simple risks such as driving to work in the morning. I mean the more substantial ones you have to take when building your career. You may not succeed every time but you have to at least try once or twice. Otherwise, you may as well stay home and draw unemployment benefit. When you do fail, try telling your boss the following rule.

Rule of business life no. 42

If you never make a mistake, you'll never make anything

They say opportunity only knocks once. Rubbish! It seems to me that something is knocking on the door every day. At times that knocking may spell trouble but, more often than not, it's a new opportunity. So, we ask ourselves, why aren't we all rich and famous?

For some, it's simply a case of not seeing what's in front of us. We just don't keep our eyes open. Often, that's due to tunnel vision. We're so focused on one objective, we aren't aware of the potential staring us in the face. We often confuse being intelligent with being clever. There are many smart people who are not clever enough to see all the details in front of them. People who suffer from this complaint are usually 'minor' successes. They win the little battles without ever realising that big ones are going on around them.

Others are afflicted by 20/20 hindsight. Most of us experience this to some extent. People suffering from this condition normally see the opportunities too late, usually after someone else has shown them what they already knew but failed to do anything about. Even when they see the opportunity in time, it seldom helps. They forget that an idea has the shelf-life of an over-ripe tomato left out by the sink through the night. They then look back and wonder why someone else was able to take advantage of that opportunity and achieve success, while they were waiting for it to happen to them. Sometimes fairly successful but more often not, people with 20/20 hindsight are always frustrated and easily recognised. Their life story begins with 'I could have been...'

Neither of these shortcomings is the main cause of failing to respond to the opportunities that are thrown at us day in and day out, though. Instead, it's that old nemesis of any progress, the fear of looking foolish. We believe that failure brings nothing but ridicule. If only we could learn that making errors is a necessary part of success. If that makes us look foolish, so be it. It's a price truly successful people are willing to pay.

I am reminded of a man I met briefly when I was quite young. In those days, I was helping my father, a self-employed electrician. One of the places we worked in was a large factory that specialised in plastic moulding. My Dad became a good friend of the owner and so I came to know the story behind this self-made millionaire.

He was a failure.

That's right. He had gone into business for himself three times in the attempt to be a success. Each of these attempts ended in disaster and bankruptcy. The banks had liens on his house, his wife's property and, for all I know, on his children's future. According to him, he became the butt of jokes in the business community. Even his neighbours laughed at his trials and tribulations.

But he never gave up. He knew that making mistakes was no reason to quit. He just kept on answering every opportunity when it knocked, in the knowledge that there was a chance to win if he could only learn from his mistakes. On the fourth attempt, he finally put all his experience together and the rest was history.

What can we learn from his story? Well, he wasn't afraid to lose money, but there's nothing unique about that. Most of us recognise that you have to prime that particular pump to get the water to flow. You have to invest and be willing to take some risk if you want a decent return. No, that's not the primary lesson.

The main lesson is that this man was not afraid to make mistakes – not just one but many. If you think of the successful men and women you know, you'll find that they act the same way. They know that you cannot succeed unless you take a risk now and then. Risks have an implied chance of failure. If you never fail, you are never taking a risk, no matter what you tell yourself. Taking a risk means you must, at times, be prepared to look foolish. Remember, if you are afraid to make a few mistakes, you'll be afraid to make anything.

All right, now that we are all fired up and willing to try to do the impossible, let's not get silly. There is absolutely no excuse for failing on purpose or, just as bad, failing to work hard to avoid failure. You must try to win, and the best way to do that is to prepare. There are several actions you can take as part of your preparation. One that many people forget is covered by the following rule.

Rule of business life no. 43

Listen for the dog that doesn't bark

Have you ever noticed that businesses are noisy? I'm not talking about the manufacturing or plant noises. Nor am I referring to the typical office environment with the clattering of keyboards and the undercurrent of conversation as people talk about their children, the big game last night or the other sundry details that make up our social life. No, the noise I'm talking about is that which comes from the constant clamour as people and companies vie for our attention.

This is true for everyone in the business. Secretaries are constantly contacted by office supply firms which claim that their products are better or cheaper or delivered more quickly and so on. At the other end of the organisation, CEOs are also challenged as they try to sort the wheat from the chaff. Every day, we all suffer as our eardrums are pounded by this loud and persistent clamour. 'Buy from us!' some are shouting. 'Promote me!' another pleads. 'We're the best!' someone else proclaims. The words may be different but the intent is unmistakable.

With all the noise buffeting the air around us, it's a wonder that we can hear at all. The real challenge, however, is hearing what is *not* shouted, sometimes not even whispered. As Sherlock Holmes observed when Inspector Gregory protested that 'The dog did nothing in the night-time', 'That was the curious incident.' Let me give you an example.

The president of a multi-million-dollar service firm made a personal sales call on me. I have worked with several presidents over the years and, while they have been willing to fill many roles, they seldom become involved before the groundwork with the customer is completed. This guy did it in reverse. He called on me, not knowing anything about our business needs or plans, but simply because he knew our reputation. He felt that we were going to be very successful and, as he openly admitted, he wanted to have a share of that success. He knew he would have to work for it and claimed he would. 'We'll knock your socks off, if that's what it takes,' he promised.

Well, he made his presentation. It was effective, perhaps in part because he was not skilled at selling. Whatever the reasons, I felt he genuinely believed in the products and services his firm offered and that he would personally take responsibility for delivering what he promised. This was my kind of executive. I wanted to trust him.

I was somewhat bemused when, as he was leaving, he handed me his business card, explaining, 'I get to the office around six-thirty most days and I can be reached at this number till seven or seven-thirty each night. I'm available after that on my mobile phone until around midnight but, if you need me later than that, my home phone number is also on the card.'

'What of kind of story is this guy telling me?' I wondered. 'People at his level don't go around handing out their home phone number to every Tom, Dick or Terry. After all, I'm not even a customer. Something's fishy here and I had better find out what it is before I spend any money on this.'

As you may have gathered, I like to trust people. However, I don't let that stand in my way, especially where business is concerned. So I checked this guy out. I called him several times, at his office, on his mobile and even at his home over weekends. I invented circumstances with no possible relevance to him and expected him to become involved. Without exception, he was thoughtful, helpful and useful to me. 'Right,' I decided. 'I'm ready to do business.'

I should have listened harder. There was a dog that didn't bark but I never questioned why it was never heard. While I may have listened long and hard to the president of that company, I had failed to listen to the company itself. I never asked why their marketing people had not participated in the sales process. I never queried why their technical people had not supported the presentations.

It was only after the company failed to deliver, not once but several times, that I came to realise that the president was the only competent person in the firm. It was held together by his belief, his energy and his commitment. The rest were a bunch of jackasses. No, that's not fair to jackasses – they have a reputation for hard work, not just stubbornness.

Even that's unfair. In this case I was the jackass. I should have known better. Unlike Sherlock Holmes, I tried to make the facts fit my preconceived notions.

I'll stress this a bit more so that you don't repeat my error. We all have limiting factors that affect our ability to 'hear' what's going on around us. These limiting factors colour our thoughts and determine our perspectives. Most of us jump to the conclusion that others have the same limitations.

Well, that's a silly mistake. We are all different, whether we are talking about companies or individuals. We must be open to the possibility that others are working with different limitations which will affect their performance. Review the example I used above. I know my personal limitations. To compensate, I surround myself with brilliant people who can keep me out of trouble and deliver the commitments I sometimes naïvely make. I had assumed that the president worked on the basis of the same limiting factors. I expected him to have people even better than himself among his staff.

When you listen for the dog that doesn't bark, you will have made a great step forward. However, when you realise that the dog is barking in a way that you are incapable of hearing, and force yourself to recognise other limiting factors, you will have gone much further.

We're all familiar with Murphy's Law and expect that 'if things can go wrong, they will'. Because of that, we have made risk reduction and damage limitation vital to our enterprises. It's not all that difficult. Taking some of the danger out of activities merely requires us to exercise a little common sense. That's all the next rule is – a little common sense. For some unknown reason, though, people seem to go seriously wrong on a regular basis.

Rule of business life no. 44

Time spent on reconnaissance is never wasted

Before taking a decision on anything, you gather as much information as possible. This is one of the few constants in the decision-making process. Other factors may change according to existing circumstances but you always need data. This is no mystery to business leaders. They have known and practised the principle for ages. That doesn't mean they always do it properly.

One of the most popular ways to gather data is to conduct market research. You know how that goes. Some consulting agency is hired by the firm. Usually it's the CEO or the marketing director who manages the engagement. They tell the consultants exactly what they want to know. But sometimes, it's a trick statement.

They don't always say for example, 'I want to know if my customers will like our new product.' Oh, no – that would be too dangerous. Instead, they tell the consultants to find out 'what the customers like about our new product'. The consultants are clever. They want to be hired again. Naturally, they tell the company executives exactly what they want to hear. This often has little to do with the market's view. It has very little to do with true research.

As with gathering information generally, you have to get out and do it yourself. Even if you are a back-office wimp as I am, you must see the customers personally. If you are a very senior executive, it's even more important to do it yourself. It is far too easy to become removed from your basic business. Reading reports created by others will never give you a true feel for the market, nor your company's position within it.

So, get out there and talk to your customers. Find out what they like about your firm. Find out what they dislike. Don't ask questions from some bureaucratic form. Customers may be tempted to tell you only what you want to hear, or worse, what they think you want. Don't write up your notes in front of them. Waving a clipboard in front of people may intimidate some. What you must do is simply talk to them. Try to start an honest dialogue. Listen to them. Make sure they know you are genuinely interested in what they have to say. Most important, try to like them. They will sense it if you don't.

In addition, talk to as many people as possible. Talk to your customers, of course, but try to talk to your competitor's customers as well. Find out why they don't buy from you. Talk to your suppliers. They may be working on new ideas that could revolutionise your industry. Always be aware that a new product or service can create its own market and, if you are too smug to listen, you'll never be part of it. If you're willing to pay attention, your suppliers may share things with you.

Talk and listen to your staff. They have all the information you'll ever need if only you have the patience to sift through it. Finally, talk to your shareholders. For some reason, many business people treat their shareholders as if they have the plague. Don't do this. Your shareholders' expectations are a valuable guide for your firm's future success.

There's more to reconnaissance than this, obviously. But beware the pitfall involved in this rule which is more important than the other features. To be honest, I didn't want to write this rule at all. It's just too dangerous.

Still, you're not children and, even if you were, it's not my job to keep you from being burned if you choose to play with matches. Please, please, please remember that this rule could be hazardous. Taken to extremes, it could land you in jail. That's quite a claim. I think it appropriate to defend this assertion by explaining the negative implications.

Once upon a time, a company was subject to a hostile take-over bid. There were numerous emergency meetings of the board, armies of staff commissioned to perform massive research, and innumerable committees to think up defensive tactics. At one of the committee meetings, the person responsible for corporate security dropped a bombshell. Americans are famous for their cowboys and he typified the breed.

'The other company', he said, 'has access to some of our confidential information. We have been able to isolate the type of reports they are getting. We know they have sales data but we're reasonably sure they do not know our profit margins, yet.'

He then explained at some length how they would be able to use this information in their take-over attempt. When he was questioned about his source of information and how he was able to find out what the opposition company was up to, he suddenly became very reticent. 'I don't know, yet, who I can trust,' he said, with a look that implied he knew far more than the rest of us. 'I'll just keep my sources to myself.'

Well, everyone tried desperately to plug the leak. In all, the defensive manoeuvring took nearly six months and cost an outrageous amount of money. It was successful in the end and normal business resumed. Over though not forgotten, the incident faded into the background. Few of us remember the details and even fewer remember the security officer's comments.

However, the incident raised some searching questions. Which company was the first to engage in this level of spying activity? How did it start? Although the other company had sources of information about us, how did we know they possessed them? In the end, did it do either company any good? Most important, is this the type of behaviour that's appropriate for businesses today?

Western society gives a very emphatic answer. No! Businesses are not to enter into this type of corporate warfare. Special bodies of corporate governance are being established to control businesses. Most of us realise that if we do not provide these controls for our own self-governance, national governments will. If all that is not enough, just bear in mind that this type of corruption can spread throughout your organisation faster than a deadly virus.

By the way, the security expert we were talking about was fired not long after this event. He was detected trying to 'pull a fast one' so, as you can see, even when they provide a benefit, people of this kind do not last long.

In the final analysis, reconnaissance is something you must do. No matter what the cost, it's worth every penny. Spying is something you cannot afford, however cheap it may seem at first.

There is another tactic we all use to minimise risks. We do it at home as well as at work. Almost everyone I talk to seems to think they are good at it. I wish I were as confident as they seem to be. Perhaps it's only the cynic in me trying to express himself, but I have a feeling that most people are not nearly as good at this tactic as they think they are. Or perhaps it's just the coward in me looking for company. Let's look a little deeper.

Rule of business life no. 45

Play it by ear and lose your head

We all recognise the need for planning. Everything good that we do comes from a plan. Every positive action has a plan in the background. Certainly luck has something to do with success and no one would deny that serendipity plays a vital role. All the same, this would come to nought without a plan to take advantage of good fortune. You might wonder why so many companies fail to plan properly if this is the case.

Planning is truly a dilemma for many firms. It is such a pain to go through that some simply don't bother. There's always something more immediate to claim their attention. Besides, they argue, there's always tomorrow, and that's soon enough. Of course, we all know that tomorrow never comes, but when has that ever stopped us from procrastinating?

Even those firms that go through the planning effort are often just fooling themselves. That strategic plan they worked on for so long and at such great expense just sits on a shelf in the CEO's office, gathering dust. Oh, it may be referred to several times during its first six months or so of life, but that soon becomes boring. Someone may even decide to look at it once a year to ensure it will still satisfy the board, who usually do not care how good the plan is as long as there is one. In the end, though, many plans turn out to be merely another pointless exercise that adds no value and satisfies no need.

Of course, there are those who disagree. They smile sanctimoniously at the rest of us and claim that they have a plan and use it every day. We might forgive them if only they were telling the truth. But most of the time these people confuse a plan with a budget. They work out a series of numbers and then, come what may, that's what they live by. The rest of the world may be turning backwards on its axis but they'll never realise it. They have their budget, after all, and that's what counts.

The problem is not one of effort. We are all willing to work hard at developing plans. Nor is there a problem with understanding how to go about creating one. There are tools and methodologies to help if the necessary experience is lacking. When all else fails, we can always hire consultants who are only too eager to help. We cannot blame funding either. There will always be enough money available if only we can prove the results are worth the expense.

In the end, most efforts at planning probably fail for the same reason that many firms do not even attempt to plan. There is simply no confidence that the effort is worthwhile. People know, at least instinctively, that planning has severe limitations. As the old military axiom expresses it, no battle plan ever survives first contact with the enemy.

As far as excuses are concerned, this one about limitations is particularly weak. Just because your plan may have to change does not mean you can forgo developing it. There is no benefit in complaining that your plan needs a degree of built-in flexibility. Everything in business has some limitations. We simply have to live with them and do the best we can.

I think the easiest way to deal with planning is to separate it into three distinct activities. I call them the budget plan, the predictive plan and the anticipation plan. Each has a unique purpose and each needs to be approached in a different manner.

We are all familiar with the budgeting process so I can add little to that.

Go ahead and create your budget. Do it formally at least twice a year. The world around your company changes far too rapidly to depend on an annual cycle. If you can, try to institute a monthly review, or short-term forecast, that adjusts your spending patterns to match current events. The important thing, however, is not the cycle you use. It is flexibility and acceptance of rapid change that will make the difference here. Remember, your budget is just a bunch of numbers that balance. The balance is important but the numbers themselves are only a means of achieving it.

The second type of planning is called predictive because all you have to do is make predictions. These forecast the events you feel fairly confident will happen. Once you have decided what they are, you can create a series of initiatives to respond to them. It is not necessary to put the initiatives into practice until the prediction comes true, but don't forget that a cause and effect relationship is involved. If you predict that something will happen, prepare for it and react to it early; the odds are that it will occur.

This is what most companies understand by planning. They do their research, find out what others are doing, and then assume the same conditions will apply for them if they follow what the other firms are doing. Such planning is not as immediate as budgetary planning but, because it is dealing with known concepts and activities, it does not have a very long life. Most firms accept this and limit the lifespan of their plan to three years. Even that is optimistic; the actual duration of many plans is less than two years.

True long-range planning is much more difficult and requires a totally different approach. Whether you call it anticipation or scenario planning, it is the technique of looking at all possible events, regardless of how unlikely they may be. The purpose is not to create planned responses. Instead, you are making it possible to recognise the unexpected when it does happen. Once you have recognised it, you can fall back into the more traditional 'predictive' planning mode.

I once organised this type of planning session. We contacted several well-known gurus who were versed in looking ahead at social, economic and technical change. We also arranged for several customers, suppliers and employees to be part of the exercise. It was an eclectic mix of people from the super-intelligent to the average 'person in the street'. The only people I would not allow to participate were my own staff responsible for planning.

Unfortunately, the boss thought it would take too much time and money for too few results. We never did try anticipation planning. Naturally, we were later hit hard by something we never thought could happen. I'll never know if that aborted session would have helped. Perhaps, if you try this some day, you'll let me know how it worked.

Planning will never solve all your problems. If you think it will, you may be letting yourself in for even greater ones. You must keep things in perspective. If an event is planned for, maybe that's all that will happen. Still, there is no substitute for planning. Sometimes if an event is not planned, it can't happen. If it does, you may not be able to recognise it. The solution is to keep plans flexible and adapt them as needed.

Whatever you do, keep your priorities straight. Concentrating on the wrong issues will increase the risks, not reduce them. The one tool that everyone in business uses to maintain a handle on priorities is money – and so they should. Money is the dominating factor in all risk assessment. It's odd how often very smart people confuse the issue even when they think they are measuring money.

Rule of business life no. 46

Money talks – don't let yours say goodbye

Joseph Stalin, that quaint old Soviet philosopher, had a peculiar way of looking at things. He once said that a single death is a tragedy, but a million is merely a statistic. Sometimes, you might easily believe that he taught at a famous business school. It seems that half the business leaders in the world think that the loss of a single dollar is a sin, but the loss of a million or more is only normal business procedure.

I was called into the president's office a number of years ago for a budget review. At least, that was what I expected. My department was seriously over-spent and the situation was likely to become worse before it would get better. I expected to be chewed out at best. I didn't even want to think about what would happen at worst.

'Listen, Terry,' he began, 'you have to do something about these expense claims. They are outrageous. You approved them so I assume you don't think these kinds of errors are important. Well, I won't tolerate it. I want you to get it sorted out.'

'Er, okay, boss,' I stammered. 'I'll take care of it right now. Uh, what exactly is the problem, by the way?'

'It's these damn mileage claims,' he answered, as he passed some expense forms across to me. 'One of them states it is 46 miles to the warehouse and the other says it's 50. Your people are travelling there several times each week now that the new system is being installed. It adds up over time.'

My lower jaw dropped and I stared at him for several seconds. We paid our staff $0.25 per mile for travel. The total discrepancy was a dollar. Assuming the lower mileage was correct, the most we were losing was $10 per week. Meanwhile, this same president had several large-scale projects in the multi-million-dollar category that needed to be guided through the perils of the bureaucracy. Some of them, including one I was responsible for, were in trouble.

'Don't you want to discuss the Raven Project?' I asked. I crossed my fingers and went on, 'I think we have a handle on it now and I'm fairly confident we can predict the end date and final costs.'

'No, I haven't any time for that now,' he said, as he stood up to indicate that the meeting was over. 'Just get your department's travel expenses to balance.'

I went back to my office and spoke to my secretary. I explained that I didn't really care which was the correct mileage but would appreciate it if she would just reconcile all the forms from then onwards. I never even tried to find out what the actual mileage was. It simply wasn't that important to me. It still isn't.

That doesn't mean I disagree with every aspect of the president's conduct. I know exactly what he was trying to achieve. He felt, with some justification, that if you prove to people that the little expenses are important, they will pay more attention to all expenses. It's the same principle articulated by Xenophon, an ancient Greek warrior, when he stated that, if ordered to move a mountain, you must start with a single stone. Everything is important, not just the big, highly visible issues.

Still, the president was wrong in these circumstances. He spent no time on the large points and far too much on little things. You must keep a sense of perspective when dealing with risks. When the danger is large and the penalty for failure expensive, you must devote sufficient attention to keep it under control. If you have any energy left over to spend on minor topics, treat it as a gift. It's satisfying but not always important.

The danger grows as the size of the company increases and its management begins to feel it is sophisticated. Just as some US senator was reported to have said that 'a billion dollars here and a billion dollars there, and pretty soon you're talking real money', large companies tend to trivialise large sums of money. They are very good at mathematics but forget their simple arithmetic. They may use exotic formulas to determine returns on shareholders' equity or gross margin return on investment but fail to add two plus two correctly.

The problem is simple, and this is a simple rule to control it. Money is critical to every company, and that means to each and every employee. Any action we take can make us money, otherwise we would not bother. It can also lose us a lot. All investments involve risk, and, further, all risks involve a potential for monetary loss.

The bigger your investment, the more you should monitor it. Small investments and small risks deserve only a small amount of your attention. Any self-employed person knows this. They have to pay the bills out of their own equity. You'll never see them waste their time or their money on things that give little return. Yet many of us in larger businesses seem to forget this simple truth and carry on with little thought as to the consequences.

Some people go to extraordinary lengths to reduce risks. Sometimes this works. Just as often, they achieve little more than shooting themselves in the foot. Usually, the efforts that end in failure have not been very creative. Such an attitude has more in common with an ostrich burying its head in the sand than with dynamic business leadership, and it can have catastrophic consequences.

If you stand in the middle of the road, you can be hit from both directions

We do everything possible to reduce risks when making decisions. We gather as much data as we can, analyse them as thoroughly as possible and make our decision only when the issues are clearly understood. At least, that's what we try to do. As far as correct business behaviour goes, this is perfectly acceptable. No one will object. Indeed, you'll probably be praised for keeping the level of risk down.

But there are times when this behaviour goes horribly wrong. Instead of reducing risks, we merely delay them. We lie to ourselves, saying that we are making decisions, when the truth is that we are avoiding them. In our efforts to make everything right, we manage to make everything wrong. In other words, we attempt to dodge bullets by running straight into a minefield.

This type of disaster is all too common. It is due to one single cause – one we all succumb to from time to time. It's that old trap of trying to keep everyone happy. To paraphrase President Lincoln, you can keep some of the people happy all of the time, all of the people happy some of the time, but you can't keep all of the people happy all of the time. In business, it's quite hard to keep one person happy once in a while. When you stretch it further than that, you're heading for trouble.

The president of a major division of a fairly large corporation in the US found this out the hard way. This happened a number of years ago when the newest fad in business was to 'practise consumerism'. People were not yet saying things like 'customers for life', but that was soon to follow.

The chairman of the corporation was very astute and thought he could see what was going to happen. He was convinced that firms which established a reputation for great service early would earn a high level of loyalty from their customers. Those that came in late would be locked out. He passed the word on to all his divisions that 'customer service' was the password for the future. He warned them against trying to fake it. He would be watching carefully.

Naturally, the divisional president created a new customer service policy statement and a new programme was started. The company made an honest attempt to listen to its customers and learn what they wanted. New products were developed and introduced. New pricing policies were implemented. Above all, customer complaints were reacted to quickly and without hassle. The chairman was pleased. The president felt relieved.

Three months went by and the climate in the divisional office started to change. The mechanism put in place to track complaints showed that customers were happy but sales had not improved noticeably. Meanwhile, the cost of the new programmes was very high. The Finance people were screaming and demanding curbs unless some other way could be found to improve profits. Even more pronounced was the attitude of the field managers. They felt that the company was being disloyal to them. They did not like having to give in to customer demands and tried hard to prove that complaints were the customer's fault, not theirs. Pressure began to build up for the president.

The president 'decided' this was unacceptable, of course. He couldn't have his own staff in revolt. The policies were toned down and field personnel were given more discretion to handle customer complaints in the way they felt was appropriate. Customers may not have been as happy, but employee morale began to rise again. The situation seemed to stabilise over the next few months.

But the chairman was still reviewing the reports about customer complaints. He didn't like what he saw. He made a telephone call and later that day the president called a staff meeting. He explained that he had 'decided' that the previous programme of high customer service was the right one after all, and that it would be re-implemented with immediate effect.

Six months later, the programme changed again to the less accommodating policy. And then again to high service standards. And finally, one more time back to the original. In just over two years, the policy was changed six times. The cost of the constant policy changes was higher than even the most expensive choice if the company had just kept to it. Of course, the customers were totally confused by this time and more and more of them were taking their custom elsewhere.

The divisional president was finally asked to 'pursue his interests outside the firm', but it was too late. The damage was done. As the chairman had foreseen, the first company to establish high service standards gained a dominant position. Unfortunately for him, it was another firm that achieved it.

This is not a story about consumerism, however. It doesn't matter which of the policies the company used was the better one. The story shows what happens if you are wishy-washy in your decisions. This doesn't mean you have to be dogmatic or pig-headed. You may change your decision from time to time. New facts become known and you would be unwise to ignore them.

No, this is simply about making up your own mind, not letting someone else do your thinking for you. In the final analysis, you can't straddle the road. You must never play one side against the other to avoid making choices. People who stand in the middle of the street are very, very exposed.

Whenever you take risks, one of the biggest dangers comes from over-extending yourself and your department. Sometimes, this is caused by arrogance and a feeling of personal invincibility, but this isn't the usual case. Mostly, people go too far because they simply do not stop and think about the consequences. It may be that intellectual laziness is a bigger problem than arrogance. There's an ancient rule that warns against this age-old problem.

Rule of business life no. 48

Never fight a foreign war when your own soil is not secure

It is not often that we praise the military. But we must always be willing to learn lessons from those who might know better than us, whoever they are. Perhaps this is one occasion when we can learn from military men.

The military has known and followed for centuries the axiom that one should not fight foreign wars when one's own soil is not secure. Alexander the Great certainly knew it. He made sure that Greece was consolidated and under control before he attempted to conquer the rest of the world. Caesar knew it. When he was threatened at home, he returned to sort things out before carrying on with his conquests. Even Napoleon and Hitler knew it, at least when they started. America probably forgot it during their 'adventure' in Vietnam. As people at home did not support the war, the resulting débâcle was predictable.

In business, and sometimes in our personal life, we frequently over-extend ourselves. Prudence, we feel, is necessary, but there comes a time when, to be great, we must dare to do great things. Perhaps John Paul Jones stated it best when he said 'it seems to be a law inflexible and inexorable that he who will not risk cannot win'. Thus we accept new positions, grow into new markets, open new businesses, develop new product lines and generally feel that growth at any cost is worthwhile.

Usually, we are able to keep the risks under control but there are times when colossal failures happen. As you read the business press, you have to think this happens more frequently than it should. Too many businesses seem to start new ventures when their foundations are poor. Too many are failing to take care of today's business and instead are focused solely on some future dream. The string of profit warnings and bankruptcy proceedings give ample testimony to this. Now, if we see news about such failures at the corporate level, just think how much more frequent it is at the department and individual level.

For the most part, the cause is the same. Our greed and ambition outweigh our prudence. The military cannot afford this type of wishful thinking. Successful armies never over-extend themselves. Why do we in business not understand this? It seems simple enough. Perhaps it is because lives are not in danger. Perhaps it is because there is seldom a clear-cut enemy. Military leaders almost always know whom they are fighting, even when it's their commanding officers. Businesses usually have multiple competitors and it is sometimes difficult to know which is the most dangerous.

Let's look at some of the reasons for failure. Maybe we can find profitable ways to use the principle of securing our own soil first. Oh, by the way, we in business *do* have to worry about our own soil. At the corporate level, we call it market share. The way we defend it is to have an infrastructure in place that supports our day-to-day business activities in an easily sustainable manner. At the personal level, we call our soil 'the job' and we keep it by being capable of doing everything the boss demands.

One of the strongest reasons for failure during growth is having ambitions bigger than we can support. This once happened to me. At the time, I was a young supervisor of a small team involved in some very tricky work. It was enjoyable but it absorbed almost all my time to keep things on schedule. Because of a reorganisation, I was offered the job of managing the entire department. It was my first big chance to move up the management ladder and I jumped at it. I almost missed the rung.

In my eagerness to take on the new venture, I forgot about my old section. I was still responsible for them but was giving no help. As I said, the job they were doing was difficult enough when I was there. Now they were alone. The entire work almost collapsed and I was lucky that my staff had the courage to reprimand me for my neglect. We patched the work together and I was able to accept running the new territory, but it was a close call.

There is nothing wrong with thinking on a large and ambitious scale. Indeed, there is much to admire about it. But keep reminding yourself that it is necessary to plan, not just dream. Most failures occur not because the ambition is too large, but because the preparation is too little. Strategic planning is more than just deciding what you want to do. You must define in detail how you will do it if you are to have a chance to succeed.

Another useful tactic is to practise survival before expansion. The old adage about learning to walk before attempting to run is worth remembering. Growth can distract the management team of any organisation. Will your commercial enemies at home take advantage of that distraction? Have you allowed enough support to remain on the 'home front'? Bear in mind that you are committing your 'forces' to 'combat' on two fronts, something which is always hazardous. Turn the situation around. One of your competitors is expanding into untried territories. What are you doing about it? Well, if you are astute enough to take advantage of their situation, expect them to have the same killer instinct.

Before leaving this topic, let's clarify one thing. Growth does not always mean new territories, nor do threats always come from outside the organisation. Internal expansion, including taking on further responsibility individually or for your division, implies specific issues that must also follow our military maxim.

In summary, the biggest danger of expansion is not ambition or lack of planning, or even failure to practise survival. It is the same phenomenon that, in the end, destroyed almost all the conquering leaders in history. Hitler was secure in Germany before World War II just as Napoleon was in France before he, too, tried to rule all of Europe. Unlike Genghis Khan, they forgot, or more likely their arrogance prevented them from recognising, that each territory conquered needs to be made secure before continued expansion is possible. In business, this means we have to secure our infrastructure and ensure that it can support us as we plan our new ventures.

Sometimes there is nothing you can do. No matter what actions you take, things will go wrong. You can berate yourself later. You can listen to those who say 'You should have . . .', at some other time. Right now you have a disaster on your hands and you must react. There's one thing you cannot afford to do.

Rule of business life no. 49

Don't freeze in the headlights

Safety through inaction is the safety of a rabbit that freezes in the headlights of an oncoming car. Lack of movement is the habit of prey, and people who freeze will always be at the mercy of a predator. Success that comes by default – from not taking action yourself, but as the result of the action of others – is not true success. Business has created a technical term for it. We call it luck. Now, there is nothing wrong with luck. We just have to remember that some day it may run out.

Mine ran out once and, I'm sorry to say, I froze. I don't particularly want to tell this story but, embarrassing though it is, it may help you understand this rule better. It all starts with a boss I had many years ago. Now, I've had a fair number of bosses. I've respected almost all of them and even liked a few, but I truly loathed this one. That's okay – the feeling was mutual. It wasn't his fault or, at least, not entirely. Nor was it mine, although I expect I wasn't entirely blameless. We simply didn't like each other one little bit. But he was the boss.

At any rate, the situation deteriorated and I could see the proverbial writing on the wall. So could my friends in the company. I knew I had to do something and if I hadn't known, their continued haranguing was enough to wake the dead. But it was our busy period, so I made excuses to myself and took no action. I didn't try to bury the hatchet; didn't ask for a transfer; didn't even try to look for a new job.

I simply froze and told myself that everything was all right. I was working hard and that would be appreciated. Wouldn't it? Although I thought I was pretty good at recognising trends, and I've been known to develop elegant strategic plans, it didn't do me any good. As Father Brown, G.K. Chesterton's protagonist, said, 'It doesn't take a strategist to get out of the way of a motor-bus' – but you still have to move. I just pretended that one day would follow the next with no change and no action needed from me.

Fat chance. The busy period and my employment ended the same day. I was given two weeks' severance pay and escorted out of the front door. I had a wife and three small children. They needed food, clothing and the other necessities of life. I was finally ready to make the move but it was too late. The headlights were huge and I couldn't dodge the path of this particular bus.

I really wanted to get even with him. It was all the boss's fault – or was it? It took a while before I woke up. Then I realised I had no one to blame but myself. After that, it became easier and I got my life back on track. And kept food on the table and clothes on the kids in the process. I also began to understand that survival in business is largely about personal attitudes.

Understand this: there is no one to blame but yourself. You have total responsibility for what happens to you. Don't blame the boss. Don't say your subordinates let you down. Don't claim that circumstances were against you. It's all up to you. If you don't like something that's going on around you, do something about it or leave.

There's one additional attitude that can help. On a deep, personal level, don't allow yourself to feel too comfortable. You lose your capacity for survival if you are not constantly alert for danger. In addition, as the old Chinese proverb says, 'Progress is not made by a contented person.' It is perhaps best always to feel on the verge of failure. You then work twice as hard to avoid it.

You can't afford to take your eyes off the road or your brain off the activity around you. Yes, that pair of headlights in the road ahead may be a pair of motorcycles and perhaps they'll pass on either side of you. Then again, maybe it's a big old London bus.

There is little more to be said about risks. You have to take them whether you like it or not. Neither you nor your firm will go anywhere without some risk being taken along the way. Pretending otherwise is the height of foolishness. But never take poor risks. Nor should you fail to take as many precautions as possible. Be bold but be careful. That's the best you can do. Let's move on to a different subject.

Part VII
Rules about organisations

We trained hard ... but every time we were beginning to form up into teams, we would be reorganised. I was to learn later in life that we tend to meet any new situation by reorganising ... and a wonderful method it can be for creating the illusion of progress while producing inefficiency and demoralisation.
Petronius

Organisations are curious creatures. They act the same as any living thing and they share many features in common with humanity: they are born, grow up through various stages of (im)maturity, become senile and eventually die of old age. Of course, that's only if they're lucky. Some organisations have a shorter and much more unpleasant fate. Come to think of it, the same is true of many of us.

There are other similarities between humanity and business organisations. Before studying some of the rules needed for working within organisational structures, it's worth looking at a few of these similarities. If nothing else, it may prove that companies are living organisms that require the same consideration and safety barriers as people do.

Start with proto-man at the dawn of evolution. What allowed man to develop his superior intelligence? Was it his opposable thumb? Maybe, but other animals have that. The ability to stand upright? Again, man was not alone in possessing this ability. He was a formidable fighter, at least in packs. But there were other creatures much fiercer. He was adept at

143

running away, but there were others much faster and more agile. By themselves, these reasons seem inadequate as the explanation for humanity winning the race for intelligence.

Perhaps it was the combination of traits that made the difference. Man was big enough to fight and win – sometimes. He was fast enough to run to safety – again, sometimes. This meant he had to exercise judgement to survive. Over time, this need for judgement may be what led to his superior brain capacity.

Now, let's look at organisations, not necessarily companies. We can use the military, the church, a government body, a charity, or whatever you prefer. Whenever more than two people group together, they form an organisation. As was the case with ancient man, the organisation may be strong enough to fight and win. If not, it may be clever enough to hide while the larger predators are on the loose. It has to exercise judgement.

But what happens when these conditions are not present? Perhaps the company becomes so large that it doesn't need to fear anything. Then the ability to use judgement atrophies. Slowly but inevitably, corporate intelligence dies, or at least goes into decline. Consider IBM in the 1980s, for example. The same probably holds for some small companies. If their answer is always to run and hide, they will never develop the skills that competitive judgement brings.

As with any other living thing, each organisation reacts differently to various factors. Each will be unique in its approach to either success or failure, problem or opportunity. How you interact with organisations can, at times, be a revealing test.

Since we started this section talking about ancient man, the following rule seems an appropriate place to begin. For at least that long, one half of the world's population has been giving the other half hope by proclaiming its truth. Of course, neither half really believes it, but that's beside the point. It sounds good and it's comforting, even if we're not convinced. Let's see how well this old saying applies to business.

Rule of business life no. 50

Size doesn't matter – it's how you use it that counts

The issue of size is a real dilemma for businesses. Talk to some business leaders. If you ask them what their objectives are, they'll all respond with the same answer. They want to grow their firm in both size and profit. This is how they measure themselves against their peers. It's how they will know they have succeeded. Given a choice, every leader would want to run a company as big as General Motors and then try to make it bigger.

At the same time, they will all acknowledge that decisions are made more quickly in small organisations. They look with envy at smaller, more mobile firms, and fondly remember when they could respond to new conditions as quickly. You'll hear them mumble analogies about race boats and the *Queen Mary* and you'll wonder if they really want their company to grow larger. They will all say it used to be more fun 'in the good old days' when things were far simpler – and far smaller.

This doesn't just apply to the heads of large companies. It affects us all. Whether we are talking about a small team, a medium to large department or a huge division, the issue is the same as that faced by the chief executive. For every benefit gained by growth, we lose an equal amount of flexibility because of it.

Have you ever noticed, though, that some people don't have this problem? They can manage large departments, even very large companies, without any need to look back. For some reason, they seem to keep all the benefits of a small, compact organisation even when it's huge. Let's overlook all the personal characteristics of these leaders. We don't care if they are charming, dynamic, brilliant or whatever. We just want to know what they have in common that allows them to do this. Is there any one thing they all do that we could emulate?

There certainly is! Books have been written about it and companies all over the world attempt to practise the technique. It's called 'empowerment' and, without doubt, it is one of the best ways to enable big organisations to act with the speed and urgency of small ones. It also is one of the key elements in allowing small organisations to grow into big ones. Why don't we all use it? Because so many companies and managers muck it up, that's why.

Empowerment is simple. At least, it's supposed to be simple. It merely means that we allow, or 'empower', if you prefer, capable people to make decisions at the lowest possible level in the organisation. If they have the facts necessary, the experience, and, more important, if they are given the accountability, they should do it. If everyone is making decisions at their own level without bureaucratic delays, their organisation can react quickly to any situation. Of course mistakes will be made now and then, but your nimble reactions will more than compensate for them.

But empowerment doesn't often work that way, does it? In most firms, it has exactly the opposite effect. There are several reasons for this, including the tendency of poor managers to use it to cover their own inadequacies. It's someone else's fault – the person they empowered to make the decision. However, the focus here is not on the failures of management but on organisational rules. We need to understand how empowerment must be structured if it is to produce the desired result. If we examine why we sometimes do exactly the reverse of what we intend, maybe we can then see how to do it right.

I once knew a man who had recently been appointed president and had many ideas for making the company better. Most of his ideas were straight out of the latest management books and they were good. Everyone knew it. He told them so. He was sharp – so sharp he was in danger of cutting himself. On the issue of empowerment, he cut everyone.

'You are all empowered,' he told his staff, 'and I want that concept to go all the way down the line. Everyone should make the decisions they are capable of making. Decisions should only come up to us at the executive level when they are beyond the limits of the people we delegate to. We'll review all the decisions and use the result to teach our staff how to make better ones when they are wrong.'

It sounded wonderful and the concept was rapidly put into practice. Results were pretty decent in the beginning and there was a great deal of enthusiasm. Very slowly, however, the structure started to crumble. More and more decisions were passed up the line for judgement. More staff than ever were avoiding their accountabilities, and that included most of the senior executives. Soon, the president was making all the decisions, not only the key ones, himself. He was not just the top of the pyramid; he was the entire pyramid.

Strangely, the concept of empowerment was never blamed. If the decision to be made reached his level, he assumed he was the only one capable of making it. To be honest, he never became aware that there was a problem. He merely knew that, for some reason, the organisation was not as nimble as it had to be. It was just too top-heavy, he thought, so some of the senior managers were dismissed, followed by yet more staff. To use popular terminology, the company was downsized. This affected not only the size of the organisation but also the scope of its ambition.

If you were to ask why this happened, the answer would be both complex and simple at the same time. The problem started with the decision review process. Any decision can be improved with hindsight, so every decision reviewed was judged to be inferior. The president always knew better and did not hesitate to tell his people that he was disappointed with their performance. Knowing that every decision they made would be the subject of a formal review, people tended to take the safe route. It was always easier and safer to say 'no' to any change or exceptional request than to face the public censure that was certain to accompany agreement.

Nimble, flexible organisations are the result of so-called flat structures. In these everyone accepts the responsibility they have been given and makes the decisions they should make. This does not mean eliminating most of the management structure. You can have as many senior executives, or as few, as the firm needs to cope with its market circumstances. Flat structures come from the freedom to say 'yes' to new proposals and changes, not from the number of people involved, or from the way you arrange them. Top-heavy structures exist when the only power delegated is the power to say 'no'. Even if there is only one person considered as an executive, the structure is still top-heavy and bureaucratic when that is the way things are decided.

When people are genuinely empowered to agree to something beyond the *status quo*, you are on your way to an effective organisation, regardless of its size. That's when large or small makes no difference and the skill involved is the only critical factor.

Leadership is one of the most important factors you have to consider when building an organisation. Usually, we think of this only when looking at the company as a whole, but it's equally important in any component part of the company, however small. We all think we know the right things to look for when we make decisions. We also think we know the rules that are necessary for leaders. The following is one rule that is sometimes overlooked.

Rule of business life no. 51

If you're putting two bulls together, build a bigger pen

As with many of the rules, this one is easy to misunderstand. People will tell you 'don't put two bulls in the same pen', instead. What a load of, if you'll excuse the pun, bull. We're not farm animals and we shouldn't limit ourselves to the rules that apply to them.

Okay, whenever leadership is changing, it is important to have only one boss. The higher the leadership position, the truer this becomes. If you are promoted or take on a new position, make sure the rules are explicit if you are expected to share command with the incumbent. This isn't a question of power and control, or at least not entirely. It is just practical necessity and the consideration of human nature. The person you're replacing is being asked to 'give up' an authority that has become second nature. The normal ego, even when commanded by a conscious will, fights this 'surrender' and develops obstacles for everyone.

But that doesn't mean you can't work with people. In one company a few years ago, a unique management transition occurred. The CEO/president was a hands-on person who gave a great deal of attention to detail. He notified the board that the job was beginning to be an obsession and he wanted to leave. They objected but finally bowed to his wishes. A *five-year* programme was put in place, a successor found and training started.

For five years, these two people, both dominant personalities, worked together. How did they both fit comfortably in the same pen? Simple. They just expanded the firm sixfold (!) over the five years. They made it big enough for any number of bulls. For a good part of that time, it was the fastest-growing company in the US.

This doesn't just apply to those at the top level, though. During my early years, I worked with a woman who was – well, let's just put it this way – neither of us was a shy, retiring sort of person. She would have been a great Marine. Formidable. The things we were able to accomplish together were amazing. Of course, in the process, we had to expand the department just to make room for both of us, but the company was happy. So were we, once we learned to accommodate each other.

This concept won't work if you don't give it a chance and that may cost your organisation a great deal. Take, for example, the case in which the president of a medium-sized firm wanted to leave in order to take care of his sick wife and child. Because the firm had been very good to him, he agreed to stay on until a replacement was found and trained. In due course, the future president was hired and put on an induction programme.

As often happens in these cases, other matters needed attention and the new man's efforts were diverted into other areas of the business. A year went by and he seemed to have less and less time to spend with his future team, and almost none at all with the old president. At least, that was the general belief. Finally, the incumbent said enough was enough. He left, and the new individual took over.

'I know I haven't spent much time with you,' he said at his first management meeting, 'but I didn't want to be here under the old regime. It never works when you have two bulls in the same pen, so I found other things to do while I was waiting.'

And thus the firm lost all the knowledge of the old president. It lost a year's development time. It lost the teamwork that could have grown during that time. It simply lost.

Before we leave this subject, let's discuss how you can make a success of this situation. If you have two or more dominant people working for you, don't be afraid to put them together. The results may astound you. Of course, they could astound you in a negative way if you're not careful. The main feature of strong people is that their results are – well – strong. There are a few actions you can take to ensure that objectives are met in a positive manner and that the risk is minimised.

First, provide tough controls. If it's not possible to make one dominant person the boss and have the other accept it, you'll have to be the boss yourself. This isn't usually recommended in good management guides, nor should you do it in normal conditions. But, when dealing with two or more strong personalities, you must make sure you can control the conflicts that will, inevitably, occur.

Second, make sure they have plenty of room. Let them build a bigger pen for themselves. Be careful that, in your attempt to control, you don't limit their scope. Otherwise, you not only end up with average results, but also some very dissatisfied people.

Finally, don't be afraid to allow yourself to be put in this position. Be willing to share control with another. If you're a dominant person, you won't like this. You will suspect the other person is as strong, and possibly (horrors!) stronger than you. Few of us who are 'bulls' like to be in this situation, but the results can be worth it.

This rule applies to assertive people. They are not only able to exercise power; they like it. No company can have too many of them. Just allow them to expand their 'pen' enough to avoid charging into each other.

The last rule recommended sharing responsibility. The next warns about the dangers of doing so. Is there a conflict? Certainly. Who ever said life was simple and everything would add up into neat little columns? You must look at your circumstances, judge the conditions and then decide which course is best.

Rule of business life no. 52

Duelling speakers ruin the music

Stereo music is wonderful. You can hear the harmony better, appreciate the quality, and every note is clear and uncluttered. Our ears not only cope with these distinct sounds; we want more. Music systems now employ quadraphonic or surround-sound speakers. In fact, the more sound there is, the better most of us like it. Stereo management, or matrix management as it's more commonly called, is a different story altogether.

The issue of matrix management was summed up for me one day during an operations board meeting. Of course, I was aware of the theories. I had also, to some extent, practised matrix management, just as most of us have. However, until that day I had always believed matrix management could actually work. One innocent statement destroyed that belief.

We were embarking on a new product introduction and the responsibility for developing the programme had been assigned jointly to Marketing and Merchandising. As in most firms, these two departments were more accustomed to competing than cooperating with each other. Executives from the two areas were brought into the boardroom to make a presentation on progress. After each praised the cooperation received from the other, they showed their first presentation slide entitled, 'Managing our duel responsibilities'.

The board roared with laughter. After all, we saw it as just a simple but hilarious Freudian slip. The two young people responsible didn't understand at first and were, to say the least, embarrassed when they did. I'm afraid the presentation didn't go very far after that. Nor did the enforced partnership between the two departments. Progress was slow and became worse. In the end the project was disbanded.

I spent some time wondering if this was a normal event or not. As we all know, many new business ventures are investigated but never acted on. But I was troubled. This was one project that should have worked. I kept asking myself if the matrix management structure was the underlying cause of its demise. Over time, I became convinced it was the prime reason for the project's failure.

So, does matrix management work or is it an experiment in management that is doomed? First, we have to understand what it is. Forget all the definitions and different types of matrix organisations described in the management books and the *Harvard Business Review*. The only way to understand it is to look at examples. Take Finance. For argument's sake, assume an operating division of a larger company has a finance executive reporting to the head of the division. Let's also assume that there is a corporate executive responsible for the overall financial performance and that the divisional finance function has to satisfy this person as well as the division head. This is a classic example of matrix management, with one person reporting to two different individuals.

The next step is to take our attention away from the divisional finance person, who is relatively unimportant to the question of whether the matrix style of management works or not. Certainly this person will get hurt when it doesn't work but he still doesn't count. He has little power to really affect the outcome. He's not going to be upset when you try matrix management, so don't worry about that. We all have at least two bosses (remember, the customer is always the ultimate boss) so he'll probably be able to cope with the situation – that is, if the two bosses don't make a mess of it.

And that, in a nutshell, is the basic problem in any matrix organisation. The bosses all too often screw up. There's no excuse for it either. Matrix management is a very simple technique that can work if the bosses would only let it.

In our example, there is only one boss – the divisional executive. In any structure that has any sort of dual accountability, the primary power must always remain with the nearest line manager. Any other choice is fool-hardy and dangerous. The corporate executive, while powerful in a political sense, may attempt to influence how the job should be done but has zero authority for the content of the job. He may set standards and measure competence, but he must never give direct orders. We may all have multiple bosses but only one *boss*, if you understand the difference.

Matrix management works for the individual with the two bosses. When push comes to shove, he knows whom he must satisfy. It's good to be able to eliminate a little confusion, and he'll appreciate it. It works for the direct superior, as well. No one wants, nor should they accept, a situa-tion where they are responsible for the actions of others when they cannot command those actions. Finally, it also works for the indirect or corporate influence person, although they don't always see it that way. It's hard to manage someone you don't see every day. It's even harder to take direct responsibility for their actions.

The implication of this is that the responsibilities of the two (or more) superiors in the matrix structure must be absolutely clear and distinct. One directs and the other, at most, exerts influence. They cannot have the same level of authority.

The trouble is that people don't see it that way. We become managers because we are comfortable with exercising authority. Some of us take it a step further and are uncomfortable when others have authority over us. When a peer or someone in another branch of the management structure can change our directives, we are no longer masters of our destiny. We won't agree to that.

That's when matrix theory becomes stereo reality. Management is not like music. When two people in management try to sing exactly the same song of power, they create disharmony and confusion.

As the last rule raised the issue of who controls what in an organisation, we should explore the rule related to this. After all, organisations are made up of various components and, at times, the controls for one part will conflict with those for another. To keep the fighting at a civilised level, remember the following.

Rule of business life no. 53

It's hard to go exploring when you're defending the castle

In many ways, organisations resemble feudal England. Then, the barons and lords paid tribute to the king. At the same time they ran their own fiefdoms with an iron hand and allowed no incursion from outside their borders. They built their castles and defended their territories vigorously. Today's organisations have become structures with walls as thick as any of the ancient castles, and just as jealously guarded.

Most modern business organisations have, with a few, very rare exceptions, been compartmentalised. Most are organised by functions and, within the functions, they may be broken down by geographical territories. Others have reversed the formula and a few have taken more original approaches. Whatever the case, the managers of these departments defend them as if they were an old-style fiefdom. They pay homage to the chief executive and the chairman, but God help the peer who attempts to interfere.

It doesn't happen in your company, does it? Curious thing, that. No matter whom I talk to, they insist that their people are above those petty power politics. 'We wouldn't tolerate that kind of attitude here,' they tell me. Some of them may even believe it.

Whenever I hear such claims, memories of past conversations I have overheard cross my mind. A recent one was between two senior executives seated at the end of the conference table while waiting for a meeting to start.

'Why didn't your department process the paperwork?' one department manager cried in exasperation. 'The whole thing's been set back by weeks! Even if we win the contract, it'll cost us thousands more than it should.'

The other department head shrugged his shoulders. 'We developed a new procedure and a new set of forms for this type of work weeks ago. Your department was notified. If you want our cooperation, you have to follow the rules.'

Oh yes, there speaks a team player! Does he remind you of anyone in your firm? Are you sure? He'll play any game you want as long as you play by his rules. You might not call this power politics, but thousands would.

Here's another overheard conversation that may be familiar to you. The words may be slightly different but this has been replayed countless times around the world.

'Why aren't you helping us on this one?' said one executive to another. 'You know how important this project is. Your department has always jumped in to help in the past. What's changed?'

Without the least bit of shame, the other executive looked him in the eye and said, 'Your people didn't ask.'

And, lest we forget, there's the most famous quotation of all – 'It isn't my job.'

Just as I am sure you have, I've heard these kinds of exchanges countless times, and repetition doesn't make me any calmer. The whole topic makes me so upset I could swear, but that wouldn't be helpful. Try this. To describe the situation, take a blank piece of paper. Lay it sideways on your desk and draw a circle half-way down on the left-hand side. Label that circle 'chief executive'. Now draw another circle on the right-hand side of the paper. Label that one 'staff and employees'. Draw two parallel lines between the two circles. Put an arrow on one showing the direction of communication from the chief executive to the staff and employees. Now draw an arrow on the other line showing communication in the opposite direction.

You have just drawn the best organisation structure possible. Unfortunately, the chief executive doesn't have time to talk to each employee on every occasion that it would be useful. So, the chief executive compromises this perfect organisation chart. The new invention is called 'the department'. Draw several smaller circles on one of the communication lines. Label these department circles with the titles you prefer. Now draw the same circles on the other line. After all, departments must boost the signals in both directions.

Well, it's not laid out in a typical hierarchical manner but that's the situation. And, it should work. This type of structure should do the job. But sometimes it doesn't. Why? Let me show you.

Take a pair of scissors. Cut the paper between two of the departmental circles. Choose two departments that you know seldom work together in concert. Make sure you cut through both communication lines. When two departments won't talk with each other honestly, they also will not talk with either the chief executive or their own people. Go ahead and cut all the way through the paper. Now take each half, crumple them up and throw both pieces in the waste bin. You have just created the typical organisation structure.

Now you see why I become so upset, along with every chief executive I've ever met. Departments are supposed to boost the communications of the company. When departments don't work together with full and open partnership, we end up terminating the signal instead.

I once was lucky enough to be present at a discussion on this issue between some of the world's leading business visionaries. They were debating the possibility that the hierarchical business structure is about to die. They gave several logical reasons for this conclusion. One is the move towards more independent contractors who work outside the hierarchy on a project-by-project basis. Another reason is the massive imminent improvement in communications capability, which will allow the chief executive to communicate easily and, more important, personally with his or her staff. Perhaps the strongest argument they made is that today's organisation simply does not work well enough for today's business world. We must invent something better, they insisted.

I regret to say they identified me as an old dinosaur. While I will not lament the passing of hierarchical management structures if they should die, I do not yet see an alternative approach. Someone has to accept accountability. Someone has to make decisions. That person will always rise to a greater level of authority than those who do not accept the burdens. Authority, especially when exercised, is just another term for hierarchy. In many, many ways, I wish these visionaries were right. However, I fear they are being overly optimistic about finding another means of managing a business. Wanting something unrealistic may make it possible but will never make it probable.

Whether they are correct or my gloomy prediction is more accurate is irrelevant. We have to do better *today*. The only way we can achieve better results within today's typical hierarchical business structure is to solve the department problem. We cannot break down the walls from the outside. Only the department managers can achieve that. We have to support them when they start boosting the signal, and chastise them when they spend their efforts in cutting it. We have to encourage them to go exploring and learn about the rest of the company. All of us, from the boss to the most junior employee, must help kick them out of their castles. We don't want them defending their departmental walls.

Ah-ha, I know what you're thinking. You probably believe you've worked the next rule out just by reading the title. What's the use in going any further? you wonder. It'll probably be just another senseless diatribe against one particular function of the business. The guy's prejudiced, you're thinking, and, whatever the message is, it won't be balanced. Finance people are rubbing their hands together, getting ready to prove me wrong before I begin.

Well, yes. No? Maybe. Read it anyway and see what you think.

Rule of business life no. 54

Accountants should be on tap – not on top

This isn't really about accountants. It's about you and your position within your organisation, regardless of function, level or department. I use this rule because it's easy to remember. Besides, it never hurts to poke fun at accountants. It's an enjoyable perk.

Let's start with a simple supposition: accountants should not be on top. No, not even in an accounting firm. All the same, I have known some financial officers who became chief executives and their performance was terrific. Let's expand the scope of this premise. Marketing people should not be on top. Again, I've known several chief executives that came from a marketing discipline and they too have a marvellous track record. All right, let's expand our assumption all the way. Operations people should not be on top. Sales people should not be there either. Nor should Personnel or manufacturing executives run the company. In fact, even technology people should not have the top job.

The next question is obvious and you already know the answer. Who should be in the top position of the organisation? Why, anyone who can put their background and credentials behind them so that they can represent the entire enterprise, not just their old area. If you're an accountant today, don't give up hope. You can still reach the top of the company. You just can't be an accountant once you are there.

This rule doesn't apply only to the top layers of the organisation. Regardless of how senior or junior you are, whether you are responsible for ten thousand people or work on a two-person team, this rule applies to you personally. You must understand and follow it. Failure to do so may have a severely negative impact on your organisation – and, ultimately, on your career.

For example, suppose you are a manager in the personnel department responsible for recruitment. You are promoted. Now you are the head of the entire personnel department. Your responsibilities include labour negotiations, training, wages and compensation, health and safety, and so on. If you continue to concentrate on recruitment, what will happen?

First, the person who follows you as the recruitment manager will never be given the freedom to make a mistake. She will become dependent on your judgement and will fail to develop the skills needed. In the end, you will get rid of her, but it will be your fault, not hers.

Second, and even more profound, all your new responsibilities will suffer. You will not have the time to learn how to manage them or make decisions about them if you try to continue to do your old job. Now, the performance of your entire department will fall short. If I'm your boss, I'll probably dismiss you.

One additional aspect is worth mentioning. In the long term, it may be the most significant problem of all when the new boss keeps doing his old job. When you have a job, you want nothing more than the freedom to do it. That's impossible when your boss attempts to tell you how it should be done, or worse, tries to do it for you. I know about this because it has happened to me.

It's a sad story but all too common. I won't bore you with all the details. Suffice it to say that I worked for someone who had the same skills and background as I do. Now, there are not many I'll give ground to when it comes to professional competence. If it weren't for this person, I would admit to no one being better. Unfortunately for my pride, he *was* better – and he let me know it.

There was, in the end, no room for me. I felt no ownership for the people, the problems or for the department I was supposed to run. Indeed, I felt little for the company. Without ownership, there was no interest. Without interest, there was no great performance. I could feel my competence deteriorating. I left, as anyone would. I don't think the company was better for my departure, nor was my boss in a better position. He failed to give up his old function, hurting himself, his company and me.

This holds true for any position within any department. If you're still doing your old job after you've been given a new one, failure is right around the corner. It's even more profound than that. If you still define yourself by your old function or title, it's as bad as if you are doing the old job. That's why accountants can't be on top. When they're the chief executive, that's *all* they are. That's all they can be. The same is true for everyone.

Organisations depend on their myths and legends. These are part of the corporate 'state of mind' which helps create and maintain the culture of the organisation. If they are not based on the complete truth, that doesn't matter. We need them to help us to be unique from the rest of the herd, and accuracy isn't too important in this context. There is one myth that we all share and this one, unfortunately, can hurt us. This is one occasion when we cannot lie to ourselves.

Rule of business life no. 55

Teamwork: an illusion searching for a delusion

The concept of teamwork in business seems absolutely fundamental. We have management teams, project teams, strategy and planning teams and 'you name it, we have it' teams for every conceivable purpose. We spend a small fortune on training courses with titles such as 'team development', 'team leading' and 'general teamwork'. We put posters on the wall that tell us 'There is no "I" in team' and 'Together, we can move mountains'. We write mission statements to give us all the same objectives and business drivers. Then, at the end of all that, we have a meeting and we are a team. Or are we?

It may be heretical to challenge teamwork, but it is usually more image than reality. True team spirit seems to be very rare indeed. Calling a group of individuals a team does not make them one. Merely calling them that may do more harm than good. Saying 'we' instead of 'I' or 'us' rather than 'me' helps, but again you must be very careful. People are smart enough to recognise insincerity. Like mirages, the illusion of teamwork may lead you far astray.

What is it, then, that makes team building so difficult? We start by trying to understand team personality and identity. Each team develops a distinct nature very early after being formed. This is not merely the sum of the team members – it is often quite different from the nature of any individual. For each team, there is a totally different set of characteristics that has more to do with the tasks and urgencies than the people involved. New people join and old ones leave, including the 'leader', but the team continues to maintain that unique personality.

To be effective, this team temperament must supersede the members' individual personalities and take precedence over their identities. Now, you might ask how often this happens in practice. Most successful people have a strong core of individualism that they are unwilling, except in the most dire circumstances, to sacrifice. The biggest oxymoron in business circles is undoubtedly 'management team' and it is easy to see why. Most people who rise to management levels do so because their personalities are stronger and more independent than those around them. They do not give that up willingly.

Another problem we have in business relates to the number of 'teams' we attempt to support. Someone gathers a group of people together and a 'team' is formed. Each member is given an assignment and the team leader is satisfied. Then the members go back to their area, gather their own team together and repeat the process. Depending on the size of the organisation, this 'big team breeding little teams' effect can resemble a rabbit farm. The question we need to ask is 'Which team do people associate themselves with?' The one someone else is leading or their own? A cynic might feel justified in believing that teams only exist in the team leaders' mind.

159

Well, the cynic would be wrong. Teamwork does exist and effective teams can be created. The spirit and warmth portrayed in the television series M*A*S*H is not a dramatic fiction. History, including the history of business, is replete with examples of this condition. But there is a price to pay. Think of the times you have seen or experienced real teamwork and remember the closeness of the people concerned. Now think of the conditions that existed before this evolved.

With few exceptions, the people in these 'teams' have had to endure some hard experiences. You can see it in the 'gallows humour' that they practise and the 'Let's get it done, no matter what it takes!' attitude they have. Good morale and teamwork usually come from these shared hardships – 'shared' is the key word. You have to experience the hardship with them, not just create it for them.

There are very few ways to form teams without this kind of pain. Although they are not as certain to succeed, let's examine two or three of them.

The 'project team' is reasonably common and works well, at least to an extent. This type of team has a defined task and, more important, a scheduled finish. Good project teams establish the date they will dissolve the team as the first item on the agenda of their first meeting. Successful team leaders view themselves more as strike force commanders than managers. This is an effective ploy as the other members recognise the task-driven nature of the role and accept this kind of leadership when they might resist a more individualised type. People are always more willing to subordinate themselves to a team if they know it will be for a limited time. The project team requires multi-disciplinary skills to complete the job and, in theory, members can be drawn from the entire organisation. The danger is that once people demonstrate they can work in this type of team and meet objectives, they are constantly 'volunteered' to be on project teams.

There is another type of team, but it is very unusual. Many great managers try to surround themselves with a special bunch of people. They may not have a group name, they may not all be at the same level or rank, and they may have different reporting structures. Nevertheless, these are the people, almost never called a 'team', who help make the difference when the manager tries something new.

If you don't have this type of team, try creating one. Keep it unofficial to avoid hubris and, perhaps, don't even let members know they are part of your private 'skunk works'. At least one of them should be naïve, one a true maverick, one a cynic, one the doer, another the visionary and one who is the glue to hold the others together. Above all, don't forget to include the jester to make sure the boss and the other strong personalities do not become too overweening. Try to avoid acting as their team leader. They will produce more for you if they believe they are independent.

If that was unusual, what about something truly outlandish? We have all heard about the global village and have probably experienced the use of the Internet or some other form of electronics to accomplish 'informal' communications. Put these two concepts together and create 'electronic teams'. No one objects to being on a team (they may even enjoy it) when there are no social, business or peer pressures involved. If you allow contributions to be anonymous, people won't feel the burden of 'performing' for the team; nor do you see the posturing which is sometimes a feature of face-to- face meetings.

You can form and dissolve teams as needed and conduct meetings remotely to avoid the hassle of gathering in the same place. You can even set up an extended 'meeting' that allows people to contribute whenever they want to. Before you write this off as futuristic nonsense, I must tell you I have tried it and it works! I promise!

One final word before we leave this subject: teamwork is absolutely vital and none of us can afford to allow it to fail. Remember, charisma has no role in teams or team leadership. If you, or those you work for, believe they are creating a team spirit because of their 'winning personality', you will struggle. Bland leadership will have a better chance at success. The team *must* be seen as more important than any of the individuals involved. Otherwise, it is merely a bunch of employees doing what the boss demands.

Organisations don't destroy themselves. It takes us, the people who make up the company, to do that. Sometimes, the destruction from within is the result of indifference, sometimes arrogance. Infrequently, it's caused by problems with skills. There's a bigger killer, though. It's called politics. The next rule shows how destructive this is, and suggests ways to avoid it in your organisation.

Rule of business life no. 56

There's no such thing as friendly fire

The military is often accused of not being very creative. Of course, they'll deny it. They'll claim they are representative of society as a whole and have the same creativity, or lack of it, as any other cross-section. There is one area where the military has come into its own *vis-à-vis* creativity. As you may have guessed, the area is terminology.

It's easy to believe that the most important military job is to invent new words. And military people seem to do this to confuse issues, not clarify them. At least, that's how it seems to civilians. The military motto appears to be 'always hide the true meaning from the uninitiated'.

Perhaps the worst example of this is the military expression 'friendly fire'. Using this term makes it sound as if the troops were out on a picnic when it happened. When you finally realise the ugly truth of what they are referring to, you'll still find some trying to minimise the effect. They'll tell you that it has been going on since the days when men hid in caves and were swinging wooden clubs. It just cannot be avoided, they'll claim.

Rubbish! I would use stronger words but my wife won't allow it. I have been on the receiving end of 'friendly fire' and it's not fun. When you're being shot at, you don't care who's doing the shooting. You just put your head down and hope you'll have a chance to shoot back some day.

Does this happen in business? You bet it does. I have been on the receiving end of friendly fire in business, as well. Again, it's not a pleasant experience. This time, however, I knew it was going to happen. Whenever a conversation begins with 'I say this out of friendship and with the highest respect, but...', you know what's coming next.

The chairman had brought in one of the better-known consulting firms to provide an independent view of the company's effectiveness. Although they were to look at the entire firm, they were particularly renowned for skills in two areas. I knew they would be looking hardest at my area and at another managed by a friend. The review took several months while we tried to continue running the business.

At last, their report was finished and presented to the board. Surprisingly, both my department and the one managed by my friend survived with only mild criticism. Instead, the consultants identified a different area of the business as the main inhibitor of progress.

That wasn't good enough for my friend. Assuming his area would be castigated, he had stocked up with plenty of ammunition. After all, the best defence is offence. As my area, so he thought, was the easiest target, most of his ammunition was pointed my way. Like the military, who give medals to the people who expend the most ammunition, regardless of where it's pointed, he couldn't resist using up his stockpile. I and the rest of the people in my area were shot and injured quite badly by him, not the consultants.

People become accustomed to this kind of situation in business and I was not overly upset. However, the impact on the rest of the company was terrible. All the other department heads saw the results of these shots in the dark. If I couldn't trust my friend, whom could they trust? Naturally, they started becoming defensive to ensure their survival. More ammunition was gathered and expended. In the end, they seldom cared who the targets were. It took more than six months to bring the situation under control and I hate to think how much time, effort and goodwill were lost.

What can we learn from this? I think there are a few clear lessons. The first is obvious. Avoid departmental in-fighting. The company cannot afford it. The company is, after all, merely the sum of its parts and if those parts are fighting each other, the sum is greatly reduced. Make peace with your peers, regardless of cost in pride or ego. The company will benefit and so will all of you.

The second lesson is pertinent when you are the boss. You can't afford to allow situations to develop which encourage this type of behaviour. It doesn't 'toughen' your staff to fight each other. It only destroys them. Your job is to teach them how to win, not to put them in a situation where they can learn to lose.

Finally, there's always the question of whether you should retaliate or not. Generally speaking, it's not recommended. Sometimes it may be necessary. Some people will never learn the lesson unless they are taught the hard way that it's dangerous to attack friends. You run a danger in doing this, however. The threat is an internal one which most people overlook. You may learn how to retaliate too well. This inevitably leads to a state of mind called 'getting your retaliation in first', and the result of this is deadly to both you and your firm.

The military are trying as hard as they can to eliminate conditions that result in friendly fire. They know that dead is dead, regardless of who is blamed. The least we business people can do is recognise the wisdom in this and try to emulate it.

The problem with attempting to define rules for organisations is that they are chaotic and – well – disorganised. There are as many rules as there are organisations and each rule has another that states the opposite. We try matrix management, flat structures, separation of core activities and all the latest fads. Then we recognise that the balloons of organisational theory are held down by the lead weights of practical reality – people. Organisations either work or they fail and it's up to us. Something that can make a huge difference is covered in the next Part.

Part VIII
Rules about communications

Man has such a predilection for systems and abstract deductions that he is ready to distort truth intentionally, he is ready to deny the evidence of his senses in order to justify his logic.
Fyodor Dostoyevsky,
Notes from Underground

One thing is for sure – no one could ever accuse a business person of not trying to communicate. Think about it for a moment. When was the last time you were not involved in some type of communication? Sometimes it seems as if we spend all our time in talking or writing. Whether we allow ourselves the time to think before we do so is another story.

There are so many people we have to contact. They range from our own staff to customers, suppliers, investors and every other stakeholder in the business. Sometimes, we even have to communicate with friends. And the types of people or even the sheer number of people are not the only issues. We also have to worry about the way we contact them. Think of the choices. We can meet face to face, call on the telephone, write a letter or memo, leave messages, have our secretary contact their secretary – the list goes on and on.

We need to think about the objectives of our communications as well. If we're trying to sell something or persuade someone to favour us, that must be handled differently from a more formal, functional style of communication. Marketing is another special type of message transmission. It has to appeal to a broad audience but it goes beyond the normal speech and text approach. Again, the number of objectives and how we try to achieve them is almost limitless.

Because of this variety, we have had to improve on the ways we communicate. No longer do we depend solely on the traditional secretary. Today we have all kinds of special tools and devices to help us. We used to be satisfied with an office telephone but now we use portable phones so that we are always in contact with the rest of the world. We use computers, especially electronic mail, to keep in touch. We have voice-mailboxes so that messages are never lost. We use television and image-projection devices. We have pagers. We have . . . far too much, maybe.

We also have the English language, one of the most versatile tools imaginable. There is little that a business person cannot articulate to everyone's satisfaction. And, if we can't, we just invent a new word. It happens all the time. Finally, we have external help. There are countless consultants, gurus and experts ready to help us improve our communication skills. There are books, white papers and policy documents to prescribe how we can do everything better.

Why then are business communications so unintelligible? Are we being obtuse? Do we intend to confuse rather than clarify? Are people trying to hide things or deliberately mislead us? When you look around at the everyday efforts to communicate, you have to judge the efforts as failing, no matter what standards you choose to use.

So far, this book has proved that I am a systems development person, not someone skilled in the art of communications. I can't improve on the advice given by experts. Nor do I intend to try. However, there are a few rules most of the textbooks and experts overlook. They are, for the most part, the basic, common-sense rules that are fundamental for any type of communications. They are also useful reminders that you may not see in the more common guides available on this subject.

The key requirement of all communications is to convey our intended meaning to others without distortion. Sounds simple, doesn't it? But it seldom turns out to be. Somewhere in the process, the message becomes corrupted. We usually find someone to blame and go on to the next step, only to repeat the exercise. It doesn't matter – there's always someone to blame. It's a shame we seldom look to ourselves as the source of the adulterated meaning.

Rule of business life no. 57

Lapses in language lead to lamentable lies

When businesses discover a big falsehood, there is an immediate reaction. We can no longer tolerate fraud, distortion or flagrant lies. We do not accept cover-ups nor, in most cases, scapegoats. We know that, if tolerated, this type of cheating becomes part of the company culture and can infect every area of the business. Our customers inevitably discover this, and whatever loyalties we had previously earned now disappear. In this way we business folk have learned, often through painful experience, that the truth is important when dealing with big issues.

Strange as it may seem, it is the innocent prevarication that is the most dangerous. Our little lies, which we may not even recognise, can kill our business without us realising the hazard. Now, before you start telling yourself that you do not tolerate lies of any kind, so this rule does not apply to you, we'll examine this to find out if there is, just possibly, a little weakness in your belief.

We all practise self-delusion to some extent. We cannot help ourselves. It is built into our language. Perhaps one of the following examples of how our use of language does, indeed, distort the truth will ring a bell.

'Empowerment' is one of the buzz words that has blazed its trail through the business community. We all know what it was supposed to mean. We're encouraged to give people the power and the tools to make decisions at the appropriate level. Instead, look at what has happened in many of the companies that have attempted to empower their staff. It seems that the correct interpretation when someone says 'I will empower you' is 'I will hold you responsible and you will take the blame.'

Still not convinced? Try this example. Retailers, along with a few other industries, have decided that they must follow the advice of a leading consultant and become 'customer intimate'. Now, they explain this in many different ways and use various phrases. Many firms use the term 'intimate' when they really mean 'intrusive'. They want to know things about their customers but what does the individual get in return? Damned little, in the opinion of most customers.

This is fun. Perhaps we can interpret some other common phrases. When your boss says, 'Of course, the decision is yours,' doesn't he really mean, 'I have indicated what I want you to decide – don't you dare to be independent.' And then there is the boss who always claims 'You are not listening to me,' when he really means, 'I will not listen to you.' Of course, we all dread to hear our boss say 'You don't have to worry about your job,' as we know the true meaning may be 'You'd better brush up your job-finding skills.' Are there still doubters among you?

Perhaps the most worrying of these little lies are the ones we tell ourselves. Here's an example which I swear is a true story. A senior vice-president of a well-known and successful firm attended a seminar given by Tom Peters on the concepts detailed in his book, *In Search of Excellence*. He returned to work bubbling with enthusiasm about what he had heard.

'Actually, I didn't learn much that was new,' he confessed, 'but it was good to know I have been doing things right. It turns out that I have instinctively followed his most vital principles, such as "managing by walking about", all my life.'

Now, he was quite a good executive. Much that he did *was* right and he had a very good track record of accomplishments. However, one thing he did *not* do was manage by walking about. Whenever he showed his face outside his office, fear and panic set in among his staff. This was a truly unfriendly person who never had a pleasant comment to make and never went out of his way to see others. He was looking at himself through rose-coloured glasses, a special form of lying. Because he did this, he never gave himself a chance to improve.

There are far too many examples. The trouble is that these little lies add up and create enormous problems. Then we compound the issue by telling ourselves, in ever so sensible terms, that there isn't really a problem after all. Even when we accept that there is something that needs fixing, we often have difficulty getting others to see it as well because of language.

The first step, then, is to work on your corporate language. Stop trying to make unpleasant things sound nice. Learn that clarity is more important than salvaged feelings. We don't 'downsize'. We shrink our ambitions because we are not good enough at today's level of work. We are 'not letting people go'; we are firing them. We must not expect or think we have created a better way of doing things when we merely put a new name on an old process.

Second, we must simplify the language. We must use common words but they often have too many meanings. Stress and enforce the one exclusive definition you want for internal business use so that it is not subject to misinterpretation. If that is not possible, go to the extra effort of giving definitions. Repeat those definitions until they become part of your company culture. Do not, under any circumstances, allow new words to be invented to describe something that already exists.

Beware making reasonable-sounding statements that have little to do with the situation. This is too much like our politicians who say things like, 'All my friends are voters,' and try to make it seem as if all voters are their friends. Politicians are paid for hiding the truth while keeping people satisfied. We are not.

Last, we must stop lying to ourselves. This means learning to accept criticism, both internal and external. When negative comments are made, stop making excuses. Don't allow your team to say 'But they don't understand,' regardless of who 'they' are or what they 'don't understand'. Avoid using selective memory, by which you remember the one time you did something correctly but forget the many times you screwed it up. We cannot afford this level of self-delusion and expect our business to survive. Remember, failure and self-destruction begin not with a gamble but a lie.

Language isn't the only tool that changes meaning, nor is it the only way we lie to ourselves. Sometimes boredom is a factor. We seem to need to make things more dramatic than they are. This can, as you will see, present big problems to business people.

Rule of business life no. 58

Don't distort, just report

Businesses can experience exciting moments but, let's face it, this is the exception rather than the rule. One day can be very much like the day before. We try to keep the excitement in measured doses. Too much all at once is not good for our corporate health. The older, greyer and sometimes wiser heads prefer it that way. They know it's better to be bored than bombed.

Not everyone feels the same way. Some crave excitement as addicts crave their drugs. When business life becomes too tedious, they look for ways to escape. They want drama and excitement in their business life. Sometimes, this desire can be taken too far. In some circumstances, this damages everyone in the company, not just the thrill-seekers.

When the truth becomes too boring, the excitement addicts attempt to twist it. They add a little exaggeration, a touch of innuendo and a small dose of inappropriate anecdote. The resulting concoction stimulates new action and gives them new mountains to climb. They don't care if it's the wrong mountain. They don't see the problems when all the energy is diverted to their make-believe projects; nor do they understand how it could be put to better use somewhere else. Although I've seen several small-scale instances of this, the story a friend once told me is a prime example.

Shortly after my friend accepted a position as the information services director with a new company, a young business analyst was assigned to his department. As he described her, she was bright, articulate and full of energy. Previously, she had worked directly for the president on a number of special projects and had developed an excellent reputation for her work. One project in particular, the last she had completed, was very influential.

'The president told me', he explained, 'that her work was terrific. He wanted me to read her latest analysis without delay. He assured me it was dynamite. Because of it, he said, all our plans would have to be reviewed. I was really excited because the old work priorities had meant we would be spending our time fixing old systems, not developing new ones.

'So I read her report,' he went on. 'It described one of the main foundation systems for the company. It went through all the features and functions and showed what the systems did for the people using it. I couldn't see anything else that might be needed and wondered why the department heads using the systems were complaining. I sent them a copy of her report and then we started getting ready to tackle the exciting new projects we all wanted to do. Priorities were changed, new people were hired and everyone started on a new training programme. We were going full steam ahead when we were hit from the blind side.

'Her report was all a lie. She knew what the president wanted so she wrote the report as if everything needed already existed. The truth about the old system was just too boring to waste time on.'

In the end, my friend's company lost more than six months' work in correcting a major defect. Forget the thousands of dollars wasted in recruiting fees and personnel training. Just think of the lost income from working at a competitive disadvantage. My friend lost his job, which was unfortunate for the firm. I rated him quite highly. As far as I know, the young analyst is still there. I don't know whether she learned her lesson or whether she still makes up stories whenever life becomes boring.

This is a simple rule. Just be honest. In the immortal words of Sgt Joe Friday from the old television programme *Dragnet*, 'Just the facts, Ma'am.' That's all you need to do. It may be fun to make mountains out of molehills but it's also stupid. A robin may be bigger than a fly but there's no need to describe it as an eagle.

Your business needs facts. Its leaders need to hear the truth, especially when they don't want to listen. Even when the truth destroys elegant strategies and organisational theories, the truth is always worthwhile. Don't twist it just because it's tedious. Don't distort it for entertainment. It's simply not worth it.

Assume for the moment that we have these issues under control. We tell the truth and nothing but the truth – without exaggeration, no distortion, no self-delusions. Is this all we have to worry about? Can we now communicate with others in relative safety? Maybe. But we still have to maintain some control.

Rule of business life no. 59

You can't see through a blizzard of paper

'To be or not to be?' was the question posed by Hamlet. Interesting though it may be, we're not much interested in existentialism in business. We're too pragmatic for that. Still, there is a rather important question the commercial world has to ask itself. Our dilemma, to borrow from Shakespeare, is 'To write or not to write?' Perhaps it should be 'too right, not to write'.

The written word is important to us. It must be. There's simply too much of it for us to claim otherwise. Just look around. Most offices look as if they have been buried in an avalanche of paper. It flows over the top of most desks. Filing cabinets creak with the weight of it. Whether it's stacked on the floors or stored in archives is irrelevant. The printed word is everywhere throughout the office.

And the situation is getting worse, not better. Technology, which promised to deliver the paperless office, has done the opposite. Today, nearly everyone has a personal computer, from chief executives to clerks. Attached to these computers is a laser printer. Instead of struggling to produce that neat one-page analysis, we now generate volumes of paper with masses of statistics and complicated graphs to do the same thing.

Then, to make a bad situation worse, we lie to ourselves about it. I even had one senior executive explain to me that her team no longer produced paperwork. 'We do it all by electronic mail,' she said, not realising that the words displayed on a computer screen are even more dangerous than those printed on paper.

Let's not be too hasty to condemn the written word, though. It's not only at the heart of any communication strategy, it's also a critical component of our corporate culture. It helps keeps our traditions and legends alive. More than that, the written word is our bond. It's our commitment to people inside the organisation as well as our customers, suppliers and other stakeholders. If you go to the trouble to write something down, you will not change it because of some whim. You'll need very substantial reasons indeed.

There are other good reasons for writing. Used correctly, the written word can enhance clarity or, at the very least, control ambiguity. This may be more important than you think. A young technician who worked for another company had a conversation with me on this topic one day. I felt she articulated the need for written communications quite well.

'I stopped doing anything unless they put it in writing,' she explained. 'When I first joined the firm, I thought it was my fault. They would tell me their requirements and I would complete the design. But it never seemed to be what they wanted. I thought it was just because I didn't know the company well enough to understand them. I'm not so sure now. Maybe they were being ambiguous so they could change their minds later.'

She might have had a valid point. I've certainly known bosses who never dream of giving clear and complete directions. It's one way to make sure you always have someone else to blame.

There's one final reason for writing things down on paper. If it were not so dangerous and subject to abuse, I would be tempted to make this a separate rule of business life. Quite simply, if it's not written, it's forgotten. Let's face it, no one has a perfect memory, especially for details. Writing not only preserves the memory but makes it a public one, in which others share the responsibility for remembering commitments.

If only there were no other reasons for writing things down on paper, there would be no problems. But business life is neither fair nor simple. Even if it were, people would still go out of their way to make life more difficult than it has to be. It's not just that most written communications are wasted. It's much worse than that. A great deal of it simply muddies the water. Rather than clarify, it causes more confusion. Even when the communication absolutely must be read, it becomes buried under the blizzard of paper descending on our offices.

If the confusion isn't bad enough, think of the additional wasted time and effort. These amount to a substantial overhead cost that no company can afford. We have managers who spend their entire life writing memos that no one needs and few people read.

Why do we do this to ourselves? Mostly it comes from people's need for security. If they are busy, their jobs won't be threatened, and the best way to prove that you're busy is to have plenty of paperwork to do.

The dilemma we face in business when we ask whether to write or not to write is severe. Nor can we ignore the impact of electronic mail. Because of its ease and simplicity, the amount of correspondence is increasing at an exponential rate.

The only solution is to review who needs to read what, rather than concentrating on who is writing what. Entry-level people need clearly written directions in full. So too do technicians and similar staff where precision in specifying features is vital.

Senior executives neither want nor need to see detailed writing. As a rule of thumb, if you have to make a written report for them, never exceed one written page. If you can't manage it in one page, try harder. You can always provide appendices with the required details if necessary but still summarise everything on one page.

Our problem comes with middle management levels. These people should not need detailed documents or directions but often desire them. It's their way of protecting themselves. Besides, they feel, if their staff have the security of detailed directions, they should have it from their bosses too. You need to explain to them gently that if you have to treat them as juniors, you will feel free to pay them accordingly.

It will be difficult, but try to persuade people to follow these guidelines. Never, never write something unless you are absolutely sure that someone needs to read it. Never make extra copies 'for information' unless the receiving person requests it repeatedly. Always write responses to memos in handwriting on the originals and send them back. That way it will be obvious that you are not keeping a copy. Reduce the number of filing cabinets to the barest minimum – then halve it. Now throw away 90 per cent of all that remains. Finally, if you have the courage, never let anyone in middle management write anything – no matter how important they think it is – unless under the instruction of a director.

It's my experience that most people try to be truthful. Even so, they often distort facts and end up hiding the truth. They think they are being honest and they don't distort on purpose. But we all see things differently, and that colours our thoughts and expressions, so that it is sometimes difficult to tell what is the truth. Most people probably obey the following rule instinctively. You may find it useful, however, to think it through and use it as a deliberate tactic.

Rule of business life no. 60

Listen with your eyes

'Actions speak louder than words,' they say. 'A picture is worth a thousand words,' they go on. Great stuff. It simply means that what people say has relatively little worth. What they do is far more valuable.

We business folk seem to forget this simple fact time and time again, partly from conceit and partly from wishful thinking. The moment a flattering word is spoken, we immediately assume that the speaker is absolutely correct. It may also be due to our trust in our associates. After all, this person talking to us would never lie, would they? Well, probably not.

We have to remember that others do not see themselves as either flatterers or liars. They usually view themselves as honest people simply telling you what they believe. The problem exists because their beliefs are not necessarily well founded. As individuals, we all have a view of ourselves which becomes the basis of our career objectives. Although this is a subjective observation, experience indicates this personal view is often distorted.

The only way to appreciate the reality of any situation is to look at the actions going on around you, not just listen to the chatter. This works at both the individual as well as at the corporate level. Here are a couple of examples.

A young woman worked for me many years ago as a supervisor on the company's 'help desk'. She, along with four other clerks, took phone calls from the staff at remote locations and helped resolve their problems. Joining the firm straight out of college, she had held the same position for nearly ten years. According to her, she had no further ambitions.

At the same time, I was extremely impressed with her ability to get the job done, regardless of how difficult or foreign to her background. She was both smart and practical, but more important, she had more leadership in her little finger than most of the rest of us will ever develop. It took months to persuade her to transfer to another area of the business.

'I don't think I'm capable of doing this new job,' she kept saying. 'I don't like giving orders to people.' Actually, she was a very polite, quiet person who phrased everything as a request. Nevertheless, without realising it, she was making command decisions. She also made sure the decisions were followed. As is so often the case, what she thought she was capable of doing merely reflected the style she used. Her real actions were very different. Today, she's a vice-president of one of America's larger, more successful firms.

I was incredibly lucky. I almost accepted her modesty as an honest self-assessment. I almost forgot to use my eyes to see what she was capable of achieving. It would have been a miserable blot on my score sheet if I had failed that way. I was very fortunate to remember that we can 'hear' with senses other than our ears.

It's possible to use this same technique on a broader level. Companies are little more than the sum of the ambitions and fears of the people employed. In the same way as you make judgements about people by what they do and not what they say, you must also judge firms. The common way to do this is to review the track record. The annual report for public firms is the standard route, although there are a few others. However, the typical methods have one failing. They all show how the company has performed in the past, not how they are doing today nor, more important, how they will do in the future.

Here is an unusual suggestion. If you want to 'see' how a company is really performing, watch how the people in the business walk. This is particularly useful if you are looking for a new job. The 'bosses' interviewing you will paint an attractive picture of their company, one they probably believe. But, of course, they can afford to make a mistake. You'll be one of many, many employees. You do not have that luxury. Each firm you work for will become part of your history and you will be judged by the 'companies you kept'.

If there is too little motivation or if the company's prospects are weak, the walk will be casual with many hallway conversations and little apparent urgency. If the future is bleak, there may be fear or panic; movements will seem jerky, and there will be little or no interaction between people. The right mix is seen when there is a measured pace indicating a clear destination but evidence of some casual banter or conversation. Incidentally, this is a useful way for 'bosses' to measure the morale in their own organisations. It will be at least as accurate as the information produced from job satisfaction surveys conducted by their personnel departments.

Another idea is to watch people's actions before and after attending a meeting. Now, no 'real people' like meetings, so don't look for eagerness on their part. Look instead at their preparation. Have they loaded themselves down with paper just in case they need it? Are they prepared, in other words, to 'cover their butts' and, if so, why? Conversely, are they attending with no preparation at all? Is the meeting just for form's sake with no tangible results meant to come out of it?

How you choose to interpret action is up to you. But bear in mind that actions really do speak louder than words. Use your eyes and try to see what is going on around you. Remember to include yourself in this analysis. Determine what work you enjoy and what you don't. Don't lie to yourself, and don't allow others to lie to you. This requires that you listen with *all* your senses, not just your ears.

There is one aspect of communications that is seldom mentioned but which is vital to every firm. We all know about it and we can all appreciate the need for it. Of course, we are talking security and confidentiality. Some things must not be communicated. Most of us have no problem accepting and following this precept. However, it is necessary to expand the definition of communication beyond the written or spoken word, as you will see.

Rule of business life no. 61

Milk in the cow never turns sour

Today, we live in a very open society. There are few restrictions on us when it comes to obtaining information. The latest news, whether from the press, radio or television, provides a deluge of facts that can seem to swamp us at times. It seems that little remains confidential, even things that should. This seems to hold true in business as well. More and more firms are practising openness with their staff, suppliers and investors. Fewer and fewer issues are kept secret.

Well, there's nothing wrong with that, is there? We all prefer to be open, honest and totally above board in our dealings, don't we? That's what modern life, including business life, is all about, after all. Right? Well, maybe. Then again, maybe not all the time.

There are times in life when you should simply keep your mouth shut. That doesn't mean you should practise deceit. Lies are absolutely wrong. But sometimes too much openness causes all kinds of trouble. Anyone in business for a while can tell stories about this. Whether it is about new products, a planned merger, an organisation change or any one of a dozen or more sensitive issues, the stories all repeat the same message – premature disclosure hurts everyone involved.

Sometimes, it's not just talk that has to be controlled. Twenty years ago, one large conglomerate wanted to take control of another. Over several years, there had been informal contacts between the two chairmen. They had been friendly rivals for the affections and the custom of their target market. It was hard to see how a merger would provide any benefit to either set of shareholders. Nevertheless, some phone calls were made and both began seeing how, at least in a personal, ego-stroking way, each could benefit. After some time, they decided that it was appropriate to get together to discuss the 'friendly' take-over in more detail.

Now, the chairman of one firm thought he was pretty hot stuff. A private jet was chartered for the flight to Chicago and limousines were hired to take the entire entourage of fourteen or fifteen people to the hotel. Naturally, the hotel was the best in town. Of course, the Chicago-based firm which was in the process of being acquired had its own entourage. To keep things 'secret', they too had to be housed in one of Chicago's superb hotels. They too needed limousine services. As you can imagine, the initial dinner between the two groups that evening was in the best restaurant available.

You can easily see what inevitably occurred. A miracle was needed for this 'secret' meeting to escape public notice. What I could never understand was why everyone was so surprised when the newspapers the next day reported that the two firms were talking. When the financial analysts of several Wall Street firms found out what was going on, the reports turned very negative. They could see that the only ones to benefit from the merger would be the two chairmen, not the shareholders and certainly not the customers.

We're not talking here about the ethics or lack thereof of the two men involved. We are concerned with the need to keep some things confidential. Before you dismiss these two chairmen as stupid, remember that they are not exceptional. Similar events take place all the time. People forget that businesses need to protect certain information, and protection comes in many different formats. Actions can spell out your intentions as if they were printed on billboards. You must control your actions as carefully as you control confidential memos and letters.

The point has already been made several times in this book and in innumerable others that good businesses never lie. That does not mean that they should talk about everything publicly. There are some issues that simply must be kept in the dark. Like a full roll of film, your entire business can be destroyed through over-exposure.

There are a few obvious measures to take to prevent this. First, remember that knowledge is one of the most important sources of power. In situations where information is critical, never disclose it to those who don't need it. As Benjamin Franklin once said, 'Three people can keep a secret as long as two of them are dead.' A secret known to more than two isn't a secret. You might as well write up your press release and publish it in a tabloid if too many insiders know about it. Similarly, never attempt to become one of the people who know a secret. If you should know it, then someone will tell you. Otherwise, your knowledge can hurt both you and your company.

Manipulate the circumstances so that you are never questioned about a secret, whether you know it or not. If you're not clever enough to do this, you probably shouldn't be party to any. Sometimes, though, you may be questioned about events outside your control. The best way to handle this is the way adopted by almost every business known. It's called 'no comment'. For this to be effective, you must use it whether there is truth behind the question or not. If you only exercise 'no comment' when you wish to hide a subject, people will realise that very quickly.

Finally, bear in mind that here too actions speak louder than words. I have known senior people who twitched with repressed excitement when confidential information was shared with them. The people they worked with were quickly able to guess at the background. Even if they hadn't, the rumours and guesses would have been just as damaging. You must do more than simply lock the papers away and keep your mouth shut. You have to control your emotions and your body language as well – it's not only milk that goes sour when left out in the open.

While we are on the subject of non-communications, there's still one of this type yet to be discussed. It comes in several different styles but each has the same aim. It's the listening half of the communication that you must pay the greatest attention to – and sometimes listening is difficult to achieve.

Rule of business life no. 62

A rattled sabre makes noise – a drawn one doesn't

Of all the skills required for good communications, the one most over-looked is the art of listening. This is not to say that people don't try. While there are a few who only pretend, most people work hard at listening. It's not their fault that they fail. Well, not entirely.

There are several reasons for failure. Some people have hearing problems. Whether officially hearing-impaired or merely suffering a minor deficiency, they have to work harder than others to hear what is going on around them. I know. I'm one of them. Sometimes, we miss important points. Okay, we have a legitimate problem, but this is still no excuse. It can be overcome.

Another common obstacle is what I'll call 'here-ing' problems. From time to time, all of us suffer from this. It's the old 'been there, done that' syndrome. We may be physically present, but mentally we are miles away. Our daydreams keep us from being aware of the here and now. It is tempting to classify this as a mere lack of self-discipline. It's not that simple, though. Nothing to do with self-discipline ever is. This obstacle can be overcome but you have to work hard at it.

The third type of failure to hear is even more common but the most difficult to overcome. It occurs when you hear part of the statement or argument being given, then you allow your mind to begin forming a rebuttal. While you're busy thinking about what you will say, you have stopped listening to what the other person is trying to communicate. Your counter-argument may seem logical and strong but it could be wildly off target. By the way, this also holds true if you are thinking about comments that support the other's view. Keep your mind on what the other person is saying until they have made their point. Then, and only then, is it proper to form and give your opinion.

So far, none of these problems has anything to do with sabres – rattled, drawn or otherwise. I use this rule to cover a special type of listening – the art of hearing what hasn't been said but what should nevertheless be obvious. There is always more information available than what is actually spoken or spelled out in black and white. While there may not always be a sabre involved, there is usually something that can cut severely if you're not paying attention. I thought of several stories to demonstrate this point and had, in fact, selected one. But then my wife received a chain letter through her Internet mailbox which, I believe, provides a good example. Listen carefully and perhaps you'll hear that unspoken statement as the sabre cuts.

A woman and her daughter were shopping at a famous department store in Texas and took a lunch break in the store's café. After finishing their salads, they decided to have dessert. Both being cookie lovers, they each ordered the 'Famous Department Store Cookie.' It was excellent and the woman asked if she could have the recipe. The waitress frowned and said, 'I'm afraid not.'

'Well,' the woman asked, 'will you let me buy the recipe?' With a sweet smile, the waitress responded, 'Yes.' When asked how much it would cost, she continued, 'It's only two-fifty. It's a great deal!'

The woman agreed, thinking it was indeed a good bargain, and told the waitress to add it to her tab. She didn't pay too much attention when she signed the bill. After all, this was not just another famous department store. It was 'The Famous Department Store.' Then, one month later, the credit card statement caused her to change her mind.

At the bottom, it said, 'Cookie Recipe – $250.00'. 'Outrageous!' she thought, and called the accounting department of The Famous Department Store. Explaining that the waitress had said it was two-fifty, 'which clearly does not mean two hundred and fifty by any *possible* interpretation of the phrase', (her emphasis, not mine), she asked for a refund.

The Famous Department Store refused to budge. According to the woman, they said, 'What the waitress told you is your problem, not ours. You have already seen the recipe. We absolutely will not refund your money at this point.'

Threatening didn't help. Nor did pleading. She finally left it, telling the people at The Famous Department Store, 'Okay, you folks got my $250, and now I'm going to have $250 worth of fun.'

Her final comment on the E-mail message we received in England was, 'So, here it is!!! Please, please please pass it on to everyone you can possibly think of. I paid $250 for this: I don't want [The Famous Department Store] to *ever* get another penny off this recipe.'

I don't know how many thousands of people now have that recipe filed away. It must be a considerable number. By the way, the cookies are delicious.

But what can we learn from this story of misadventure and revenge? While some of us find it amusing, I'm sure neither the store nor the woman involved were happy about what happened.

There are a couple of obvious answers. First, the woman was careless. She didn't hear the sound of danger from the waitress. Well, perhaps it wasn't a sabre, but it certainly cut her. She should have listened more closely.

But the real deafness occurred at The Famous Department Store. They were so busy rattling their own sabre, they failed to hear when another was quietly drawn from its scabbard. They weren't listening because they did not think it was necessary. They were a large firm, after all, and the woman was only a single individual.

Communications can fail. That's what happened in this case. Both parties were trying to say something, but neither was listening to the other. Sometimes it is when there is the least noise that you have to listen hardest.

Here's a rule we're all familiar with. They don't teach it in schools and I've never read about it any business publication, but we all know it anyway. We usually learn it from hard and sometimes bitter experience. Any communications can be difficult, but there's a special predicament that makes business writing especially frustrating. It doesn't matter whether you are compiling a policy document, working on advertising copy or just writing a simple memo. See if the next rule hits a note you recognise.

Rule of business life no. 63

There's always some kid with a crayon

Most of our written communications benefit from external editing. We've all experienced this. We are so close to what we write that we can't judge it properly. We know what we mean to say and that's what our eyes see. We can't pick up the missing words, the improper grammar or the confusing phrases that destroy the meaning we are trying to convey. If you have to write a great deal, find someone you work with who can help by editing. This is a rare person to be treasured. It's not often you can find someone who will be brutally honest, which is what your 'editor' must be.

But there's another type of editing which can become destructive, rather than helpful. The strange thing is that it almost always occurs on the most important documents you produce. It's when you're preparing policy documents, strategic plans and, heaven forbid, mission statements that everyone tries to have a hand in the process. Absurd though it seems, the higher in the organisation the people are and the more important the meeting is, the more apparent this is. Acting like children with crayons, they all want to make their mark.

A young woman who worked for me encountered a situation of this kind. To understand her story, you'll need to know something about her. She was the manager of strategic planning for an international company and was well suited for her role. She spoke five or six European languages and knew many of the national cultures intimately. She was a certified accountant in one of them but had received her MBA in another. More than merely one of the most brilliant people I have ever met, she was by far the most competent in using language to impart meaning accurately.

All the senior directors of the company were gathered for a special meeting on the draft strategic plan. She and I, along with the rest of the team, had put a tremendous amount of effort into it and were pleased with the result. While not radical, the plan proposed several innovative directions the company could take. We also felt it addressed several of the more significant problems the firm would face over the next few years. We took a great deal of care in the presentation of our ideas and allowed six hours for the meeting. We felt that was more than sufficient time.

Were we ever wrong! The meeting started with a planned brief introduction. The manager reminded the directors of the company's mission statement. This, as you might expect from a company with American roots, had been articulated long before and was part of the company's culture. She also reviewed the company's values and philosophy. None of these were new. They had all been accepted for years and were only intended to set the scene for the new strategic plan.

Unfortunately, the meeting never went any further. Arguments raged for the next six hours over the use of language in the mission statement. That's right – six hours: one paragraph, three sentences, 38 words. All for something that had been accepted years previously. At the end of the meeting, three words were changed.

'What was the matter with those jerks?' she asked me later. 'We changed a few words to a few different ones that mean exactly the same thing. How did that help anything? No progress in understanding the strategic plan was achieved. No advance of any kind was made. I just wasted a day of my life and for what? Three words! And you know what else? We'll be blamed for not making any progress on the strategic plan. It'll be our fault they played little boys' games!'

Two days later, the chairman called to say he did not like the changes to the mission statement and wanted everything put back to its original phrasing.

Why is it that people need to show off their education when good communication requires simplicity? Why do they feel the need to change the way things are expressed when there is no need? Many years ago I worked with a person who, more than any other I've met, always wanted to play with words. Once, he substituted the word 'fungible' in a proposal at every conceivable opportunity. I couldn't understand what fungus had to do with our product descriptions and had to look it up in a dictionary. If you don't know what it means but want to, look it up for yourself but make sure you have a big dictionary. An abbreviated version won't list it.

I hope you will understand that there are limits to the editing that should be performed. By all means, use others to review what you have created. Listen carefully to their suggestions and comments. Pay attention when they disagree. If they're not worth listening to, you shouldn't have asked them in the first place. But don't let them control what you have to say. It's your decision, not theirs.

Remember that lesson, then apply it when it's your turn to edit someone else's work. Don't make needless suggestions. Don't change someone's words just because you might have power over them. Don't be another kid with a crayon destroying someone else's art.

We've nearly finished this Part. However, we can't leave a discussion about communications without at least a brief visit to the next topic. There may be many times when you shouldn't communicate, but one in particular stands out. It's strange how often we forget to follow the next rule.

Rule of business life no. 64

The best excuses are silent

We won't spend much time on this. All of you know this rule as well as you know the back of your hand. Excuses are not allowed. Not ever. When someone who works for you tries to make an excuse, you jump all over them. Even your peers and superiors in the organisation are not exempt. Nor are your spouse and children. Nor the members of your church or club. No one is allowed to do it. Excuses are not acceptable and you'll preach that message till the cows come home.

So why do *you* try to get away with it? That's right. Stop trying to look so innocent. Search your memory for a moment. Try to be honest. The only one you'll lie to is yourself. If we were to gather enough people to fill the largest stadium we could find and ask those who never make excuses to raise their hands, how many do you think we would see? If everyone were truthful, the answer would probably be zero.

Let's look at some of the more common excuses we hear in business. Perhaps you've never used these. It's possible. I once had an American friend who swore he heard a pig whistle in the backwoods of West Virginia. I told him the same thing. It's possible. I give them both about the same odds.

Of course, everybody's favourite excuse is, 'Oh, I wasn't the one who did that. It was the guy who left.' When you reach a certain level, naturally, those words won't do. You become more sophisticated and say things such as, 'That policy was formulated by the prior incumbent.' Fancy words, though, do not make this acceptable. It's still an excuse.

This is really the coward's way out. There are few things more contemptible than this. It's putting the blame on someone who is no longer there to defend themselves. It will not bring you much long-term admiration, at least not from the people who count. Of course the problem, or whatever may indeed have been the fault of the person who's no longer there. The bosses will know that. To be honest, though, they don't care. They just want to see things fixed.

'It wasn't my job,' is the next most popular excuse given. Again, the words may change from time to time but the meaning is the same. The one who claims 'It wasn't part of my remit' or 'It didn't happen on my shift' is merely saying that he doesn't want to accept any responsibility. I don't know about you, but I am happy to accommodate him. Permanently.

If you know something is going wrong, take action. Even if it's nothing more than letting others know something needs to be done, at least do that. If the action you take is wrong, you can always apologise afterwards. Your responsibility may not mean your action is necessary, but your moral duty is different. You owe it to those you work with and, more importantly, to yourself. You must try.

There is one excuse I absolutely detest. I cannot tolerate it when someone tells me that he told his staff to do something and it was they who failed, not him. If you are not willing to accept the responsibility for your people, you don't deserve to have them. If I'm given a chance, I'll make sure you don't keep them long.

There are all sorts of excuses. Some are simple ones such as 'I wasn't there. I was ill or on holiday or at another office.' Others are slightly more clever and the blame is less targeted, making it harder to refute. These usually go something like, 'I was never trained for this – it's the company's fault for not sending me on a development course.' Well, if you make this type of excuse to me, I'll send you back to class with the six-year-olds where you belong.

Almost all excuses are based around an individual. They are there to protect one person at the expense of another. There is one exception to this and it's particularly distressing. It is when the executives of a firm tell their board 'The situation is out of our control. It wasn't our fault. It was our competitors, or our supplier, or our customer, or...' – well, you get the idea. The collective excuse is probably the worst of all because it is only made when everyone lacks the courage to accept any accountability. I can't think of a sadder situation.

We all make excuses at some time or another, and they amount to the same thing. We say 'It's not my fault. Here's somebody else you can blame.' No matter how hard we try to avoid it, it is human nature. Whenever there is danger, we take steps to protect ourselves. If bullets are flying, we duck. If criticism is rampant, we try to avoid it. An excuse is just an instinctive reaction for self-protection.

Even so, this is one time when instinct is *not* good for us. Most of us have bosses who have heard all the excuses before. They can smell an excuse as if it were an open cesspool and they find all of them equally distasteful.

Sometimes we have a legitimate reason for the things we do, even when it results in failure. It still doesn't make any difference. Remember, the distinction between an excuse and a good reason is made by the listener, not the speaker. It doesn't take very long for most listeners to get tired of the story. This is one time to practise silence.

Of course, there is a great deal more to good communications than the rules outlined in this Part. There are more rules and skills for the serious student. This has been only a primer.

It is impossible to over-estimate the value of good communications. When good people gather together and have a clear, uninhibited exchange of ideas, the impossible can suddenly become an accomplished fact. Communications are also vital as you establish relationships, both within and outside your company. As we move on to the next category of rules, keep the rules on language and communications in mind.

Part IX
Rules about people and relationships

Mule, horse, elephant, or bullock, he obeys his driver, and the driver his sergeant, and the sergeant his lieutenant, and the lieutenant his captain, and the captain his major, and the major his colonel, and the colonel his brigadier commanding three regiments, and the brigadier the general who obeys the Viceroy, who is servant to the Empress. Thus it is done.
Rudyard Kipling,
Servants of the Queen

Of course, that's how it was in Kipling's time. Then, the key word in most relationships between people was 'obey', whether the situation concerned an empire or just a small corner-shop. Someone gave an order and those below obeyed. Thus it was done.

It's very different today. While a few people in management still attempt to be autocrats, we live in an era unlike that of Kipling. Business executives no longer enjoy the luxury of giving direct orders as they did in the past. Moreover, they can't expect their orders to be obeyed without question. Today, business people are guided by an entirely different doctrine and it is practised by everyone, not just those in management. We can call this the 'influence principle'.

The use of influence is not something new. Throughout history, the best leaders have been ardent students and practitioners of influence. People at the top have almost always realised that it is better to convince others of the rightness of an action rather than simply order them to do it. From Alexander the Great to Winston Churchill, and from Henry Ford to Thomas Watson, great leaders know that work performed because of belief, not obedience, is always work done better.

If the influence principle is not new, its acceptance and use in business is certainly more pronounced now than in the past. Giving orders without explanation has always been the refuge of the mediocre. Today, even these poor relatives of good leadership are learning new skills. The bullies and dictators are, if not gone, going fast. Influence is the newest password to success.

Nor is the principle restricted to management staff. Influence has to do with relationships between people, regardless of level. It is something that must be and is practised by everyone. We all want to sway decisions and, if our logic has value, chances are good that the boss will listen to our opinions.

How you go about exerting influence remains an issue of your personal style. You can be direct about it. You can attempt to be subtle and try to emulate Machiavelli. You can use logic or offer emotional arguments. There are as many ways to cause a desired effect as there are people. The one thing you must remember is that influence follows certain laws. The more you influence others, the more you are influenced by them. The way you treat them is, in turn, the way you are treated by them. If you expect to succeed by manipulation without suffering the same in return, you will pay a steep price one of these days.

The rules for influence are innumerable. Every time you meet a new person or establish a new business relationship, you are following one of the rules. Maybe it will be one you have always known. Perhaps you'll invent a new one. Those I have listed in this Part are the ones I find that people in business tend to forget or overlook.

Your ability to influence others and the basis for all your relationships is built on your personal credibility. People want to know if they can trust you and accept your personal word as an iron-clad guarantee. We all understand this and work hard to secure credibility. I wonder, however, if everyone realises just how easily all their hard work can be thrown away. Here's an example of how one moment's indiscretion or one little bad habit can destroy a career.

Rule of business life no. 65

Say what you'll do – do what you say

In the end, we really depend on very few things. Most of us are willing to stand squarely on our abilities and face the business world alone and unafraid. We have the skills we worked so hard to develop which allow us to do our jobs. We have whatever intellect and capabilities we were born with. We have, or so we hope, a certain strength of character. We also have instincts to see us through difficult periods. Once these abilities are cultivated, they last us throughout our business life.

Of course, there are a few more weapons in our armoury. But those mentioned are the ones we need the most. Or so we tell ourselves. The truth is that we really don't want to face the world alone, we're not unafraid. Most of us seek the comfort of others. That's why we treasure all the friends we have made during our careers. They are important to us not just for what they can do for us but simply because they are there. We all need someone and the friends at work are nearly as important as at home.

It's surprising, then, how negligent some people are when it comes to keeping up their business friendships, especially when it's so easy to do. Friendship in business is built on your personal credibility, not on any other characteristic. The most important attribute you can develop is dependability. In business, being friendly is fine, but it doesn't mean very much. No one cares a great deal about friendliness. They just want to know that your word is good and they can trust you.

The problem is that your credibility can be destroyed far too easily. Your reputation is only as good as your last performance, and no one is perfect all the time. Well, *you* may be, but the rest of us are not. We err from time to time and our reputations suffer. It's part of being in business and we learn to live with it. Sometimes, however, we throw all credibility away for no reason.

This is a story about two senior executives in two different firms. They both had the same positions within their firms and they were both involved, among other issues, in setting and maintaining the moral fabric of their organisations. I respected both of them. Not only that; I liked them. The differences between them finally became apparent on the golf course.

I like golf. I can't play it but love to try. Both of my friends were also keen and I played with each of them at different times. The first was a happy, boisterous individual with a constant smile on his face and a joke at his lips. He usually played outrageously, claiming a 'mulligan' at every bad shot. If a putt didn't go in when he felt it should, he would keep trying until it dropped, then count it as only one putt.

It didn't matter. I never objected; nor did anyone else. You see, he always told us exactly what he was going to do. He used these games as practice to improve his ability, not something serious. There was never any money or prestige involved when he did it. If we were playing seriously, he would change his entire approach and follow the rules the same as the rest of us.

It was different with the other executive. He was an intense person and always played the game seriously. He also made sure everyone else did as well. He looked for infractions of the rules of golf and never accepted excuses. His conduct on the golf course, he used to claim, was the same as in the office. Everything was 'by the book' and no exceptions were permitted.

I didn't see it myself. Even worse, a young person who worked for him noticed it one day. It was simple and foolish and a truly stupid way to lose a reputation. He always 'marked' his ball on the green by placing a marker in front of it. Then, when replacing the ball to putt, he would put it in front of the marker. It only saved two inches on the putt but it lost him a great deal of respect in the business world as well as in the club-house. From then on, no one who knew about it trusted him. It was surprising how often he was caught practising deception away from the golf course once people started looking.

In business, few surprises are allowed. Each of us must develop a personal credibility that only comes from 'delivering our promise' every time. This means you cannot say you will do something and then fail. You cannot be seen as the boy who cried wolf. Most of all, you cannot develop an impression among those you work with and then turn out to be someone different.

The moral of this is simple. Actions and words must be aligned. False images and phoney façades can never replace true character. Saying what you'll do is almost as important as doing what you say you will. Being the person people think you are is vital to your credibility.

When discussing relationships in the business environment, people auto-matically refer to those they work with every day. That is entirely understand-able. Your close associates are more important to you than the ones you see infrequently. Nevertheless, sometimes you can learn a great deal about issues when you look at them from a different perspective. Let's review a rule for sup-plier relationships and, as we do so, think about ways to apply it in relationships with your everyday workmates.

Rule of business life no. 66

A sword in the hand doesn't allow for handshakes

It is often said that business is another form of warfare. It's not too sur-prising, then, to find some belligerence in our semi-civilised version of a combat zone. What is surprising is that you see people being belligerent time after time when they can tell from the results that it doesn't do any good. Sometimes, we seem to have so much fun proving how tough we are that we forget that the purpose behind our meetings with others is monetary, not physical.

This is especially true when negotiating terms with other companies. We all have a responsibility to win the best deal we can for our firm, but we must look at the overall conditions. Often the best price is not the best deal. When you are constantly fighting with the people you have to do business with, it's hard to remember that.

I ran into a situation once where the fighting had got out of hand. I was new at a large, international firm. My company had been using a particu-lar service provider for several years. While the original contract had been negotiated in good faith by the heads of the two groups involved, both the principal players had subsequently departed. The aftermath of their leaving was nasty. The two organisations were at each other's throat constantly – but I didn't know that.

At my new firm I was still learning how to put both feet on the floor without tripping over them. Meanwhile, I needed to expand vastly the scope of services under the contract. I sent for the manager responsible and explained what I wanted, expecting him to renegotiate the contract. I might as well have sent Genghis Khan to make peace with the Roman

Empire. A proposal was made and forwarded for me to review. 'Horrified' doesn't come close to describing my reaction. They wanted $27 million over five years! That may not seem like a lot to you, but back in those days it was a huge sum for what I wanted.

'We beat them over the head with a big stick, Terry,' the manager explained. 'They made all kind of sacrifices and we still wouldn't ease off. They're really hurting now. You can't get a better deal in a million years.'

I had my hands full with other issues and was tempted to sign the deal and forget it. I had never worked with this type of contract service before and did not really know what would be a reasonable expense. Nevertheless, something didn't seem right. I decided to visit the service company myself to find out more. An appointment was made and I met their sales director the following week. Immediately after we were introduced, he started swinging his sword.

'Your people are messing with us,' he told me. 'They never take our word on anything and are always complaining. The deals your people demand are simply unreasonable. I'd just as soon give up the business as give further ground.'

That sounded good to me. I have never liked being attacked and I certainly wasn't prepared to take it from a stranger. I asked him to put into writing his willingness to break the contract early. Of course, he realised his error and tried to back off. In the end, we decided to start afresh. In return, the contract was up for grabs and his firm would have to compete with others on a more open tender basis.

I took aside the young manager who had been negotiating for us. I explained that he would catch more flies with honey than with vinegar and I wanted him to stop conducting himself the way he had been. I went on to let him know that it was still his job and I would not try to do it for him. Then I made a few suggestions about how to build better deals from the basis of better relationships.

To make the story shorter, a deal was finally made, but with another firm. We structured the services very differently from the original plan and at a total cost of just $9 million for the same level of functionality. I never involved myself in the negotiations except at the very end. Our manager, who had not been so fondly regarded as the company's pit bull terrier, was a reformed character. He had learned to shake hands with the people we would do business with, not automatically take an adversarial position.

As for the sales director I met, he lost his job a short while later. I never felt sorry for him or guilty for what happened. He should have known better than to try to conduct negotiations with a sword in his hand. After all, the other person might have been armed with an AK-47.

Most of us develop the ability to influence others to some degree, if only for survival. There are a few people who are expert in the skill and they have taken it to a level that most of us can't begin to emulate. While we struggle to develop one-to-one relationships, they can influence large groups with just a few simple phrases. They are artists while we are still learning to draw a straight line. The danger is that most of us do not recognise our limitations. We think we can practise influence without seeing the problems. Here's one that I see more frequently than any other.

Rule of business life no. 67

If you're doing all the talking, no one is doing the thinking

Business managers love to talk. Oh, how they love to talk! Put two business managers in the same room, but with no other single thing in common, and time how long the silence lasts. Maybe it will be up to fifteen seconds but that will be lucky.

Actually, this is a pretty good thing. Businesses are successful to the same degree as they are able to communicate. If managers were not in love with talking, the ability to exchange and nurture ideas would be severely limited.

Talking is one thing. Giving talks is another. At least when you are engaged in the former, you have to listen once in a while. But people giving talks expect to be listened to. They seldom see the need to listen themselves. Instead, they just keep on talking until we succumb to their arguments out of boredom. Of course, it's not boring to them. They love the sound of their own voices.

Now, we have to recognise that we all suffer from this to some degree. We have wonderful ideas and valid, worthwhile opinions which others would easily share if we only had the opportunity to convince them.

Listen in on any conversation – in a business office, a church or your local pub – and you'll see the proof. Everyone expects others to listen, but few are willing to return the courtesy.

Once, there was a new president of a reasonably successful company. The previous incumbent had retired several months before the new one was recruited, but a good management team had been left in place. The company had some problems because of the gap in leadership, but most were easily solved. Besides, what company doesn't have some problems? The president called a meeting of all his senior executives to 'get to know each other' and draft some initial direction statements and plans.

'Before we start,' he said, 'I think I should tell you a little bit about my management style.'

'This should be good,' most of them thought. It was 8:00 a.m. and many of the executives were still hiding their yawns. 'At least we'll have a few minutes to wake up before we get to the substantive issues.'

Then a morning of unrelieved torture began. It wasn't that he was a bad speaker. In fact, he was quite eloquent. He had even prepared overhead slides to help with his presentation. No, the problem wasn't his presentation. It was his subject. While it may have been a fascinating topic in his own mind, he rapidly bored the rest of the people to tears as he talked about himself.

He described in excruciating detail what he meant when he used the word 'dynamic'. The topic of his ethics and moral standards took three quarters of an hour. 'Detailed' and 'focused' were two more favourite themes. So were 'hard-working' and 'committed'. There was no doubt about it. He was absolutely wonderful. Everyone knew it because he told them so.

Meanwhile, the management team lost track of the monologue. Their thoughts drifted. Some spent their time thinking about the strategic issues they wanted to bring up later. Others worried about work they should be doing instead of listening to this inflated ego talking. Most simply daydreamed, thinking about dinner that evening or the last argument with their spouse or even the TV programme they wanted to watch later that day. The one thing no one was doing was paying any attention to the president's comments.

At 10:30 a.m., the meeting was interrupted for a brief coffee break. The executives gathered in small groups as far away from their president as possible. The most common comment was, 'What the hell was all that about?' They reconvened fifteen minutes later, most of them hoping that something could be salvaged from the morning. They were sadly disappointed when they found that the president was only half-way through the synopsis of his style. No real progress was made during the day. No direction was adopted, no strategies discussed.

This is a warning to the boss who likes to hear himself speak. We're not stupid. We may be your subordinates but that doesn't mean we don't have something to contribute. If all you want is an audience, all you will get are the 'yes-men' and 'brown-nosers'. We don't want or need leaders with love-bites on their mirrors.

That doesn't mean we're not sympathetic. Most of us are bosses too, though in a lesser position. We fall into the same trap of practising eloquence even when we know it destroys intellect. We allow ourselves the indulgence of lecturing our staff, knowing that it means they may stop thinking in the false assumption that we will do it for them.

As bosses, we have to practise something I call stealth management. This simply means that we have to maintain the lowest profile possible. We must allow our staff to do as much independent thinking as they are capable of. When we have a particular idea or policy we want them to adopt, we should 'whisper in their ear' and let them make the idea their own. If they are asked merely to execute our plans without input, they're not thinking, merely reacting.

Sometimes stealth management can't be used. There are circumstances where you have to stand in front of everyone and cry 'Charge!' but this is less frequent than most of us like to admit. Even when you have to do it that way, remember that conversation is a two-way street. If you want to be heard, you must be prepared to listen.

That president was actually a very pleasant person and had many good ideas. Some of them were used but a few of the outstanding ones were lost. They were his, and never became owned by his management team

There's no escaping the influence principle if you want to be in management. Still, there are many different interpretations of it. The following rule describes one of the more obscure meanings. In the old days, most managers (and all leaders) understood this. Perhaps they would not express it as I do, but they all practised this rule constantly. Today, with the men and women in grey suits commanding most boardrooms, many company executives forget this aspect.

Rule of business life no. 68

If they snooze, you lose

I have always said that if you're not enjoying it, stop doing it. Since I'm still in the 'management game' myself, I suppose I must enjoy it – at least most of the time. Work doesn't have to be boring and managers don't have to be stuffed shirts. No, let's make that statement stronger. Work *cannot afford* to be boring and managers *must not* be stuffed shirts.

If you want to be in management, one of your primary jobs is to make work entertaining for the people you lead. You and your business cannot accept the expense associated with a turned-off, disgruntled staff. If they fall asleep on the job, everyone loses. It's our role as managers to ensure that this doesn't happen.

The way to do this, as we are all told, is to inject some passion into the business. Try to make everyone love their work, the company and their peers. Well, 'love' may not be the right word, but it's close. A manager achieves this by being passionate about these things first, knowing the others will follow.

It's not quite that simple, though, is it? Investors and stockholders aren't really interested in passion. They want solid, dependable people at the top who can analyse situations and make decisions dispassionately. When you show them passion, they become worried. Yet without enthusiasm, you can't inspire loyalty in the rest of the company's members. And your business will only run successfully if you do everything yourself, as your lack of passion will kill off the potential for others to develop any.

There's a flip side that complicates things even more. If you show too much passion, you leave no room for your staff. It becomes *your* company, not theirs. You can actually achieve the opposite of your aims. You exclude them from the process. You run the risk of confusing yourself as their lack of response incites you to even further passion.

So, how do we balance the need for analysis and passion while still making the work entertaining? I once worked for someone who was a world-class master of this art. At times, he would bully people. At other times, he would sweet-talk and cajole them. He was wonderful when telling a funny joke but a moment later he would throw a temper tantrum that had everyone shaking in their boots. He was shocking. He was audacious. He was unique. Many loved him. Even more hated him. No one was indifferent. When he was near, no one was bored. They didn't dare to be.

I was having lunch with him one day and steeled my nerve to ask him about his actions. 'I don't understand you,' I said, 'I've never met anyone with a management style like yours. You don't seem to give a damn whether you're loved or hated. You are the most outrageous person I have ever known. Yet, you get away with it. You're the head of one of the largest companies I've ever been associated with. Come on – be honest. Why do you do it?'

He glared at me for a moment and I feared I had triggered a fresh display of temper. Then he slowly relaxed, sat back in his seat and gave me a sly grin. 'Okay, young fellow,' he said. 'Pay attention. I'll let you in on one of the more important secrets of leadership.

'I have more than 25 000 people working for me. They work in over 1 600 locations and, as if that isn't bad enough, the Atlantic Ocean separates two of my largest divisions. Now, just think about the mathematics behind that. If I spent every day doing what I would like to do, visiting locations, meeting people and being a leader, it would take me almost eight years to call upon the whole group. That's only if I spend just one day apiece with them, which is far too little to give meaningful leadership. And it doesn't consider travel time or those other, fairly important days I have to spend as the CEO.

'All in all, it's an impossible task. The best I can hope for is to visit any given location once every ten to twelve years. By that time, the staff has undergone at least one cycle of turnover and every lesson I have tried to impart is lost. Some would say I shouldn't even bother. But then we would have no leadership from the top, only bureaucracy and memos.

'So, I've learned to practise something I call 'management by theatre'. It keeps the show interesting. Three quarters of the people who work for me have never met me but each and every one knows about me. I'm more than just a picture in the management reports. Why? I've gone about my job so that they have created legends about me. Most of the time they use the same words you did – they think I'm outrageous. That's okay. The legends all have a purpose. Each one contains a lesson. The more often they tell the story, the better the lesson is learned.'

Let's think about this concept: management by theatre. Business can be boring and people do fall asleep at their desks. Managers and leaders need to give some type of wake-up call. Perhaps we do have to stage-manage the business show and keep it interesting. Whether the business is large or small, management by theatre seems to solve many of the problems.

Besides, it sounds like fun. And managers are allowed to have some fun, too.

Some of the older, greyer readers are waiting for one rule in particular. If I omit it, they'll know I have made a big mistake. You can apply this rule in every aspect of your business life. It is so important and so relevant that it could have easily been placed in any of the Parts so far. We'll see how it fits in with influence and relationships, but think of all the other applications it has.

Rule of business life no. 69

Doing nothing is often the best thing to do

Modern life brings us a challenge greater than our forebears had to face. Today's challenge is one of choice. Each time we choose, we are forced to make a decision. We make choices from the first moment of awakening each morning. Shall we go to work or stay at home? Which route shall we use today as we journey to work? What's the first task – what's the second? And so on and so on all day long. This constant decision-making adds a great deal of stress to our life. We can see the result of that all around us. We have even coined a special phrase, 'burn out', to encapsulate the effects of this stressful decision-making process. Well, I hate to do this, but I am going to make it worse.

There is another choice. It's one we often overlook but we shouldn't. It can be damned useful. It's the decision to do nothing at all. It's especially pertinent when putting a new programme into operation or attempting to change an existing one.

There is, however, a danger that must be pointed out. Doing nothing must be the result of a proactive decision. You cannot simply do it through abdication, laziness or lack of thought. It is just another one of the tough choices you must make every minute of every day.

Gamblers do this all the time. They call it 'standing pat' and use this option whenever the odds of improving their hand by exchanging a card are not appreciably greater than leaving things alone. Like the gambler, we should look at the consequences of acting, but remember, *not* acting is one of the alternatives. Perhaps the odds are in our favour by leaving things alone.

Many years ago, I was the manager of quite a large department. A fairly substantial part of the staff was involved in clerical activities. In itself, this was not an issue and I rarely had a problem with them. Mary, their supervisor, had been in charge of the area for more than eight years. She knew the job well and seldom needed my help or advice.

One day, as I was preparing for a week-long trip to our parent company on the other coast of the US, a minor personality clash occurred. One of Mary's staff objected to her abrupt and somewhat dictatorial manner. I suppose I should explain that Mary would have made a perfectly adequate drill instructor in the Marines. Nevertheless, the complaint was made to Personnel so Mary, her subordinate and one of the personnel managers joined me in my office to discuss the issue.

I took the actions I felt were appropriate and believed the matter was settled, at least for the time being. I spoke briefly with Mary and asked her to be a little bit more patient with her subordinates. I then stepped into Personnel on my way to the airport and instructed them to keep a very low profile until I returned.

It was only a week later, but what a difference I encountered when I returned! Five people had resigned, another fourteen were threatening to leave and there were even rumours going round that the clerical staff wanted to form a union. Meanwhile, the department had divided into two bitterly opposed groups, one backing their supervisor and the other attacking her. I don't normally use words like 'aghast' but I cannot think of a better one to describe my feelings. As you can imagine, my first act was to find out what on earth had happened.

Mary was at home, ill, probably from stress. I called to find out what had happened. She was adamant that she had taken no action, had been very low-keyed while I was away, and blamed the entire problem on 'those stupid idiots in Personnel'.

So I walked over to Personnel to find out what had happened from their perspective. The personnel director told me that his team had just implemented a new programme. He was trying to involve his department more in the day-to-day running of the business. Because a complaint had been made, they had decided that the situation merited further investigation. Without taking counsel from my boss, they had developed a questionnaire and circulated it to all members of Mary's staff to determine if she was doing an adequate job as a manager. Remember, she had been doing it for eight years.

To cut a long story short, the questionnaire made every employee think of every time they had had a grievance. It didn't always have to do with Mary. It could have been a grievance against anyone in the company. However, one fact was obvious to them. If it was important enough to cause the company to conduct an investigation, something was obviously wrong with Mary. The molehill had become a mountain in their eyes and every slight, every disciplinary act, every non-sympathetic word spoken for the previous eight years was dragged from their memory.

Well, I could not afford to lose almost 20 per cent of the staff, so I managed to persuade everyone to turn the clock back to the previous week. With Mary's help, I was even able to persuade the people who had resigned to rejoin us for a trial period. Things gradually went back to normal and we could all breathe again.

This was a case where doing nothing would have been appropriate. Instead, a bureaucratic policy caused a series of poor decisions to be made when none were required. The company's hand was not improved by bringing yet another level of management into the equation. The personnel director's programme to influence behaviour added no value to the operation of the company.

Of course, there are several ways to use this rule. One benefit of it is that it helps you remember that organisations can become weary (and wary) of too much change. So can people. You have to stage work and influence behaviour in phases so that it is digestible. Bear in mind, you eat three meals a day. You don't try to take it all in at once.

When the company has gone through a period of change, give it time to rest. This is when doing nothing is the best option. Farmers give their fields time to lie fallow, mountain climbers rest when they've reached a plateau and your firm needs a break between transformations.

Most organisations are prone to over-react to challenges presented. I suppose that also applies to people. When an organisation over-reacts, however, events seem to gain their own momentum and there's no one in control, with a foot on the brake. One of the challenges we constantly face is the never-ending drive for greater and greater efficiency. Even something as seemingly good and worthwhile as this can be taken too far unless someone stops to think, as the next rule tries to point out.

Rule of business life no. 70

Don't throw rocks when you need hand grenades

All businesses thrive on competition. Without it, we become fat and bloated, unable to provide the necessary drive and passion that marks a truly successful firm. Look at most state-run organisations if you need an example. They become institutions rather than businesses. There is no way, in the long term, for a business to succeed unless there are at least two others fighting for the same dollar of profit.

However, there is more to it than that. We enjoy a good fight, especially when it's for customer approval. The military stockpiles weapons. We in business stockpile people skills. Every once in a while, the military feels the need to flex its muscles. It wants to try out all their fancy new weapon systems and prove their worth. We do the same. We jump into new markets, develop new products or programmes and try like hell to beat our competition into the ground. It's fun.

Sometimes, though, there is a need to reduce the level of combat. We may get in over our heads with too much competition and too little chance of winning. The military calls this a retreat. We have rather more creative names for it, but most of us in business have experienced the same conditions. Whether we call it restructuring, downsizing, outsourcing or 'adjusting our profile to respond to current market conditions', we must sometimes cut back.

Generally, this tactic works and the company becomes much stronger as a result. As with all changes of direction, however, it can be dangerous when the execution is wrong. The soldier knows that retreats are the most hazardous manoeuvre possible. While it may be necessary to move into a defensible position, he worries about getting there alive. Sometimes we business folk, especially management, forget about survival. In that regard, we have a great deal in common with some of the back office military leadership.

In the early days of the Vietnam conflict, we were told that the 'brass' did not want the fighting to escalate. Now, I don't know if it applied to everyone or just the small unit I was attached to, but orders came down from on high to 'retaliate in kind'. This was explained by our platoon leader (I've cleaned up the language) in the following way.

'If we see the enemy, we do nothing. If they shoot at us, we're allowed to fire back. If they pitch grenades at us, we can throw some back at them. But, if they only throw rocks, that's all we can toss at them.' We looked at each other and nodded to show our mutual understanding. That was one order that would be 'misunderstood'. Even dumb Marines know you don't throw rocks when you need hand grenades.

Sometimes the 'brass' in business seem to forget that survival is more important than policy, that people are more important than an extra dollar or two of profit. In the continual effort to squeeze just a little more efficiency out of the organisation, cuts are sometimes made too deeply. Our remaining armoury can be cut to nothing more than a pile of rocks.

Important as being efficient undoubtedly is, overdoing efficiency drives can be dangerous. You run the risk of spreading the company resources out too much and, as your grandmother may have told you, when you spread the butter too thinly, you can't taste it any more. It's better to reduce the work needed than stretch the staff beyond the point where they lose effectiveness.

The reason these efficiency drives are so readily accepted by business leaders is that most firms are in need of reform programmes. Remember that cuts are not the same as reforms. Reforms may cut, but don't be tempted to lie to yourself and think you are succeeding just because you have cut some expenses. If you only deal with the cost side of issues, you'll be like a dog chasing a car – making a lot of noise but never catching up.

When you are involved in a cost-cutting exercise, there are three things to remember. The first is don't be ill-equipped to do today's job. It is very difficult to heal the wound if you cut too deep. It is much, much easier to make subsequent small cuts if needed.

Second, don't limit your ability to respond to changing conditions. Your competitors may recognise your self-imposed limitations. If they do, they can change the nature of the battle for market share and take the lead away from you far too easily. Knowing that you are limited in your response capability gives them far too many options. Think about how they might react to your cut-backs. Make sure they cannot keep you down for long.

Third, remember that business success is mostly about good people. Just as a military unit can become ineffective if the combat losses are too high, businesses will suffer if the attrition rate climbs too much. For us, however, it is not merely a numbers game. The hidden danger is that the best people will resign just before things go sour, leaving only the dead wood. Recovery may then be impossible.

Keep a focus on your operational efficiency, but be aware that there is more to business life than today's results in financial terms. We have to remember that business is just a form of combat. It may be more civilised than warfare (sometimes!) but we are always fighting for our corporate life. Copy the military. Keep something in reserve. You never know with accuracy who your enemy will be tomorrow or when you may need a few hand grenades to fight them off.

No discussion about relationships and exerting influence can be complete without some comment on customer contact. Far too many people delegate this to the marketing department and assume their responsibilities are over. Wrong! Every company has a customer of some kind. And every worker has to think about that customer, regardless of the nature of their job. Whether you see them every day or you are a back-room specialist, influencing customers is vital for all of us.

Rule of business life no. 71

Every contact may be your last chance

Here is an old joke: what do you get when you cross a Mafia godfather with a marketing executive? Answer: an offer you can't refuse but still don't understand. It seems that many customers may suffer from this condition far too often.

This isn't intended to be a diatribe against marketing, or even marketing people. The truth is that people in my field have a great deal in common with Marketing. We both have to take big risks. When we succeed, the results are magic. When we fail, it's a disaster. And, sadly, there are too few good people in either profession.

I've been lucky. While I don't understand marketing myself, I have been privileged to work with a couple of outstanding marketing people. I was also fortunate enough to hear a senior marketing executive talk to our board one day, describing Marketing's role in influencing customer decisions. I wasn't smart enough to take notes. It wasn't until after he had finished that I realised just how privileged I was to hear his thoughts. I have attempted to organise my understanding of the issues under this general heading, largely based on his views. I hope I have not distorted them too much.

One of the most important aspects of influencing customers is to tell people about your values in order to build brand equity. Most firms have only one brand or name, and must do everything possible to protect it. A way to look at this is to understand the difference between marketing themes and marketing schemes. The first asks who we want our customers to believe we are, while the second asks what products or services we offer today. We need to answer both of these but must do so in a complementary way.

Second, the message must be consistent. It must reflect both today's reality and tomorrow's aspirations. For example, Ford used a slogan, 'Quality is job 1', long before they achieved recognition for quality automobiles. This message would have been lost, both internally and externally, had they not been consistent.

Next, you must listen to your customers. Communication is, after all, a two-way process. To do this you must take heed of the actual process the customer goes through, not what you imagine or wish it to be. This should include everything from their understanding of what is being offered through using the final delivered product. In the end, you can only succeed if you understand how your customers view your brand name. This perception must be without the bias that may come from an operational interface.

This means you have to be sensitive to your customer's needs. It is more important to understand who your customer 'thinks' he is than who *you* think he is. Somehow, you have to touch a nerve. You need to force the customer to make an emotional choice to buy from you – now.

You must also make the customer feel good about the experience of buying and, to do that, you have to enhance the reality of buying. Sometimes this means you will have to be politically correct. For example, some companies must be seen as part of the green or environmental movement. At other times, you will have to be known as a class organisation. Making a customer feel good requires you to understand their emotional make-up and appeal to it.

You can't just rely on communications to do all this for you, however. You must test, test, and test again. And, after that, conduct research using both internal and external resources. If it moves, measure it. If it doesn't move, measure it twice. It is a strange thing about customers, but just when you believe you understand their perception, everything changes. Just because a campaign works today does not mean it will work tomorrow. For marketing to be proactive, it must measure itself in terms of customer-perceived value.

When you mention marketing or customer communications, many people automatically think 'Oh, he's talking about advertising'. While it's true that advertising is an important part of the marketing function, it's not the whole picture. The truth is that if the other activities are done well, advertising is not only a much more straightforward proposition, it can also cost significantly less.

As all advertising people will tell you, 'presence' is paramount. To survive, every company must seek constant visibility. This is especially true when the customer begins looking. In the past, this requirement was generally filled through the national press and flyers. Over the past few decades, the possibilities have expanded, with economically viable TV and radio becoming available. It is inevitable that no single medium will provide the presence needed; some combination of advertising will always be required. In addition, the mix of media will be a moving target.

If you look at the advertising we see every day, whatever the medium, you'll notice another guideline that everyone tries to follow. They must be different. That's good, but only if it's done in a positive way. The key is to concentrate on those aspects that distinguish your company from the competition. This can take some creativity. When there is little to distinguish you, you have to develop new ways to attract more customers. Don't copy others; develop your own unique message.

Note, too, that advertising has to sell. There is no other reason for it. To do this, your advertising must rise above all others, not just your direct competition. You must develop new, breakthrough offers that are not a mere repetition of yesterday's advertising campaign.

The last of the guidelines is the most important but you mustn't restrict it to marketing people. This is one for everyone in the company. This is the 'golden rule' for all companies and all marketing programmes. It's simple. Never, ever, tell a lie. There's no sense screaming about something being 'new and improved' if it isn't both new and improved. An empty box with snazzy packaging is still just a box. There's no benefit in claiming your products or services are better than the competition's if they're not better. No use of language, however clever, can disguise a lie for long. Eventually, your customers will realise you have lied and they may never trust you again. No company can afford to lose their customers' trust for a short-term pick-up in sales.

Competition for customer approval is a battle. Sometimes in combat you only get one chance. Failure to take advantage may be the difference between life and death. It may not be as dramatic in business, but there still may only be that one opportunity. We have to assume that one chance is all we'll get and we must anticipate and plan for needs ahead of time. This attitude is what makes some companies great and others just bit part players.

Some of these rules are more useful than others. When it comes to your career, this next one may very well be the most important rule you will ever learn. It's the 'Golden Rule' and it deserves your full attention.

Rule of business life no. 72

Make your boss a partner

If you manage to practise this rule, everything about your business career becomes twice as easy. Mistakes become reasonable and thoughtful experiments. Successes go twice as far and the credit you may share doubles and redoubles to your benefit. And it's all so simple. Just make your boss a partner. The trouble is, the practice is not as easy as the concept. I know. I found out the hard way.

It all started with a typical bureaucratic exercise from the human resources department. They wanted us to write new job descriptions for everyone in the business. In those days, I was a newly promoted vice-president of a fairly large American business and I wanted to keep everyone happy by following the company line, so I went along with it. New descriptions were written and turned in on schedule and I thought it was over. Unfortunately, they wanted *my* job description as well.

So, I wrote one that was two or three pages long and went to see my boss, the CEO. Before going further, I must tell you about him. I admired this man, and still do, as much as anyone I have ever met, in or out of business. He's as dynamic and charismatic as you can imagine, deeply concerned about the people who work for him, innovative in everything he does, and so damned smart it bruises the ego to even think about it. To give you an idea of his capability, he started his own business and sold it for millions before he was thirty. He then joined the firm I'm talking about, which was in a totally different field, as a VP, and rose to CEO within four years. In other words, he is about the best there is.

He quickly glanced through the job description, all the while muttering quietly. I heard words like 'nonsense, bullshit' and various other obscenities and then he turned and glared at me. 'Listen, Terry,' he said. 'We don't need all this crap. You've only got one job – keep your boss happy. I'm your boss. Engrave that on your forehead and forget the rest of this shit. Now, get out of here and go do something useful.'

'Okay,' I thought.' If that's what he wants, by God, that's what he'll get.' I admired the man too much to even think about disappointing him. For the next few years, I did my damnedest to keep him happy.

Of course it didn't work. The more I tried, the less I succeeded. Finally I left the company just before, I suspect, my time ran out. What had gone so terribly wrong? As focused as I was, how could I have failed when others seemed to find it easy? It took me a while, but I finally came to understand my error.

You see, I didn't try to make him my partner. That's what he really wanted. That's all it would have taken to 'keep my boss happy'. Instead, I had tried to shelter him from my work. Where he had wanted to contribute to the solutions, I had cut him out. Rather than ask him to share the risks of extending the boundaries of my operations, I had simply minimised the risks. I innocently prevented a meaningful dialogue between us with my naïve attempts to save him some time.

Don't make the mistake of thinking that this is a rule limited to vice-presidents or directors or even CEOs. This is the Golden Rule for everyone, and it works in both directions. Whether you're the boss or the subordinate, you must form a partnership with everyone around you. This has nothing to do with personal survival or promotion, although it helps with both. It's not even about you as an individual. It is, instead, the best way possible to manage risks.

Successful businesses can be measured by the risks they take. Those that never take a chance seldom take any substantial reward. Those that take risks foolishly are normally punished, sometimes quite severely. However, it's not just the number of risks taken but the manner in which they are handled that marks the really successful business person.

Picture yourself in a business situation where it's necessary to break a rule or act in a way contrary to normal procedure. It makes sense to talk to your boss about it. Even when it's within your scope to break the rule, it still makes sense. Perhaps your boss will have some insights that will modify the actions you may take. If nothing else, it's a courtesy to let your boss know what you're doing.

On the other side, picture yourself as a boss. Your most important job is to help your staff develop. That's different from protecting them. If you're going to help them, you must know what's going on. If they're breaking rules, you need to understand why. If necessary, you can change the rules to make their jobs easier.

Making your boss a partner sounds easy, but it may be one of the most difficult things we have to do. No one likes sharing with others. The best employees usually want to show the boss what they have accomplished, not what they have to do to get there. There are others who will use this rule to make sure the boss makes every decision and takes every risk. Bosses don't want to give up control or power, yet that is exactly what they must do if they are to encourage their subordinates to be partners.

Okay, so it's not easy. What of real value ever is? You'll have to struggle to make it happen. So what? They won't teach this in school. Big deal; much of what you learn there is wasted anyway. This is still the single most important skill you can learn to help your career go forward. Work at it. You'll find it will reward every effort by an order of magnitude.

Nothing you experience during your business career is more important than the relationships you develop. The people you come to know and the alliances you build can last your entire life, but only if you treat them with respect. In a similar fashion, you will succeed or not based on your ability to influence the people with whom you have created relationships. Again, this must be accomplished with respect, not back-stabbing.

So far, we have reviewed rules that cover most of the aspects of our business lives. They haven't covered much in detail but have, I hope, introduced a few of the issues far too often overlooked in business. There's one other aspect that is very appropriate for this book and we must cover it before we can call it a day. Don't despair. It won't take long.

Part X
Rules about rules

As the entire book has been about rules, we'll finish by talking about the nature of rules and their impact on us in our everyday business life. First, we have to define what a rule is. My dictionary states that it is 'an authoritative regulation or direction concerning method or procedure'. That's all right as far as it goes, but it begs almost as many questions as it answers.

Initially, you can think of rules as falling into two main categories. The first tells you what you must do. The second defines what you are prohibited from doing. That seems simple – but it's a little more complicated than that. Some rules are good and should be followed diligently. Some are absolutely stupid and following them defines you in the same way. Most are neither fully good nor fully bad. They just exist and are useful to varying degrees, depending on the circumstances.

A further complication comes from the ways a rule is presented. It can be given in an authoritarian manner: 'You *will* do it this way – or else!' Alternatively, it may be expressed as a rather mild suggestion: 'I think you probably shouldn't do it that way.' The trouble is that the presentation tells you much more about the person defining the rule than it does about the rule itself. It never tells you if the rule is hard-and-fast or not.

In other words, judgement is always involved and sometimes a great deal of risk. You can either do exactly what the rule demands, ignore it or break it. With apologies to George Orwell, some rules, just as some animals, are more equal than others. The trouble is that no two people view any rule in the same way. The choice is yours, but remember – you'll always be wrong in someone's eyes.

In theory, you usually have a fairly simple choice to make. Just because it's simple, don't assume your choice will be easy. For general advice, I can think of no better words than those penned by William Blake when he wrote, 'The errors of a wise man make your rule, rather than the perfections of a fool.'

We condemn the petty bureaucrat. We make fun of the 'old colonel' who does everything by the book. We cast aspersions on the poor underling who merely tries to follow orders and obey the rules. Why? Rules are there for a reason. Much of the time, only a fool would disagree with a modern rule. We'll start by looking at the issue from a perspective that assumes most rules have a role to play.

Rule of business life no. 73

Some rules are made to be followed

Rules are our friends. They tell us what is safe and what isn't. They provide us with a condensed form of wisdom that has been handed down, sometimes from generation to generation. From gentle guidelines to rigid laws, rules cover the entire spectrum of human behaviour.

Some rules you follow because they make good sense. You don't walk across a motorway during the rush-hour. You don't play Russian roulette. Think about it for a moment and you'll see there are plenty of rules you follow because you know that failure to do so will adversely affect your life. Other rules you follow simply because they're fun or at least enjoyable.

There's one special reason, often forgotten, why rules are helpful to us. If you want to claim that you are making intelligent decisions, rules must first be established. Then, when you break the rules (and you should, at least once in a while), you are forced to make a decision to do so consciously. Let's look at the alternatives to prove the point.

Having too many rules and following them too rigidly stifles all creativity. While we want some control, we have to mix it with a little chaos to achieve the right blend. Cutting back on the number of rules is not sufficient, either. Even when the count is low, unyielding adherence to the rules allows the same situation to develop. Let the bureaucrats take control, and they inhibit improvement.

A young bureaucrat in the making once worked for me and caused me a great deal of concern. He always followed the rules and I could never fault him. While he never did anything wrong, he never really did anything right, either. I thought he had potential but I didn't like the way he was developing.

I decided it was time to do something sneaky and underhand. I called him into my office one day to review the department's rules and procedures. After discussing the top dozen or so, I raised my hand to stop the conversation and pretended to ponder for several moments.

'You know,' I said, 'one of these standards is absolute garbage. It causes more trouble than I can possibly accept. One of your biggest problems is that you think it's great. Well, I can't allow that to continue. You're smart enough. Work out which one I'm taking about for yourself. Then stop following it. Just don't make a mistake and break the wrong standard.'

Of course, this placed him in a very awkward and uncomfortable position. Our standard operating procedures were actually very good. He had no idea which one was causing all the problems. Over the next few weeks and months, he found himself challenging the wisdom of almost every rule. He broke or changed several and found the results were better than if he had followed the book blindly.

I had achieved the results I wanted. He suffered for a while but I think it paid off for him. The last I heard, he was a senior VP in a very well-respected company. I have repeated this exercise several times since then with the same type of people. It doesn't always work, but the results are often worth the effort.

The opposite of too many rigidly followed rules is just as bad. Having no rules and just doing whatever you want merely leads to anarchy. The same is true when you have a maverick who never follows any rules, but breaks them all out of pure devilment. Such people not only create a great deal of disruption, but can put your entire organisation at risk.

Over the years, I have only had dealings with that type of individual once. I tried a similar ploy with him and explained that there was one rule he absolutely had to follow or he would be dismissed. It worked to a degree, but I must admit that he remained more trouble than he was worth. Perhaps, with more practice, I will learn how to handle his type as well.

You and your organisation need rules and need to follow them, if not blindly, then at least wisely. Otherwise, you will never improve because there are no benchmarks to show where improvements are possible. Your actions will be too random without some guidelines. Consistency and dependability are impossible. Chaos reigns and catastrophe follows.

The balance between having rules but breaking them when needed and accepting the associated risks when you do so, seems to work as a valid compromise. It also improves the rules. You achieve a condition called 'controlled chaos' which, I believe, every organisation should strive for. You have to be structured enough to keep on top of things but flexible enough to allow creativity to thrive. The financial benefits are impressive, the skills the staff build up are more so and, just as important, it's fun.

Do I follow the rules? You bet I do! Except sometimes.

Have you ever noticed that the spectacularly successful are just like the rest of us, only different? Have you ever wondered why some people with genius IQs drive taxi-cabs while some fairly average intellects become heads of large organisations? What makes them different from you and me? Maybe the following will provide a small clue.

Rule of business life no. 74

Some rules are made to be ignored

He had done it to me again! My face burning with the scarlet red of embarrassment, I walked into my office swearing at myself. I couldn't believe it had happened. That was the third time!

Our offices were located in a typical, multi-storey building as anonymous as all the rest in town. The toilets were located on the landings between each floor, with male and female facilities on alternate landings. I was on the first floor and the CEO on the fifth. Although we had elevators, I mostly used the stairs when I went to his office. It was good exercise – and it gave me time to prepare.

I was returning from a meeting with him and, candidly, my mind was numb. I just couldn't cope with the scope of his vision when the ideas emerged that fast. He was ignoring every rule of business I had ever been taught. It was absolutely brilliant!

So I walked straight into the women's toilet on my way down the stairs.

As I said, this wasn't the first time, either. He just kept producing these wonderful ideas. I don't think the women were too impressed with that as an excuse, however. It had to stop. His ability to surprise me had to be curtailed. I needed to determine how to do this before I gained a totally undeserved reputation.

A few months later, we were drinking coffee in an airport lounge. We were discussing things casually when I asked him why he was able to break so many rules without getting burned. He described an event early in his career which gave me an insight into the way his mind worked.

'It happened way back when I was still young and quite naïve,' he said. 'I had just started a job as a marketing manager with a new firm and had finished my first advertising layout. I sent it to all the people who needed to approve it and was very eager to see what they thought. Then I got a call from my boss, the VP of Advertising.

'He told me I had it all wrong – it was a total disaster. According to him, I had no idea at all what the company was about and I must never have met a customer in my life. He wanted me to start the whole exercise again. This time, I was to follow the rules.

'Five minutes later, I got another telephone call. This one was from his boss, an executive VP of Marketing. He thought my layout was wonderful. To listen to him, you'd have thought I had worked for the company for the last twenty years. He told me I really understood the rules of the game.

'That was when I decided,' he concluded, 'to ignore both of them. Basically, that's what I do. I ignore other people's rules. I try to form my

217

best judgement first, without prejudice. Then, and only then, do I see what others think. If I feel I'm still right, then I go ahead.'

That was it. He just assumed that the rules did not apply to him. He didn't necessarily break them. Neither did he follow them. He simply ignored them.

This gave him the option of thinking matters through to their natural conclusions. It allowed him the freedom to be creative. It was an attitude that helped turn him into a superstar.

There's a big difference between rules and laws. You must obey the law. To do otherwise is unacceptable. Not only will breaking laws be extremely prejudicial to your career; you could end up in jail.

Rules, however, are a different matter. They don't always apply to the circumstances you may have to handle. Breaking a rule means that you have determined that it is of no value, not just now but in any circumstances. Breaking all the rules means you are merely a maverick and not someone to be taken seriously.

But ignoring a rule falls into a separate category. All it indicates is that, in your judgement, this rule doesn't apply this time. There are many rules we ignore for the very good reason that they don't mean anything today. For example, I read somewhere, and although it may not be true it is still a useful example, that taxis in London are supposed to carry a spare bale of hay for their horses. It's a rule that once made sense but is now meaningless.

Businesses have multiple versions of this bale-of-hay condition. We have forms that some old, outdated procedure says must be filled in, but who does so? With new business systems in place, some rules are no longer needed but they haven't been updated. Most of the time, it's easier simply to ignore these rules than try to eliminate them.

There are no guarantees in life. If you ignore rules, you may or may not succeed. There is a risk if you attempt it. Ignoring rules can be equivalent to breaking them. It's fine when you're right, but deadly when you're not. Regardless, it's always worth checking to see if the rule you're supposed to follow is merely disguising a bale of hay.

There seems to be some glamour or panache associated with rule-breakers, as long as they get away with it and no one is hurt. Can you ever make progress without endangering yourself and others around you? Are there rules that should be broken? Maybe there are, if you keep your eyes and mind open to the possibilities around you.

Rule of business life no. 73

And some rules are made to be broken

They certainly are strange people. Some of those in Personnel, I mean. I suppose I'll never completely understand most of them. They try so hard but they just can't seem to relate to line managers. Still, their intentions are good and, like most business people, I try to accommodate their weird little concepts. It's not just an attempt to humour them, honest. Well, maybe it is.

This policy of appeasement once paid unexpected dividends. I took my entire management team on a three-day team-building exercise organised by Personnel. We did all the things one learns to expect. We took the personality profile tests – and cheated to confuse the amateur psychologists in Personnel. We went through the workshops – and never let them know we had seen it all before. There was nothing to be gained by disappointing them, after all. We even let them sit in on our drinking sessions in the evenings – and deliberately gave them some choice material to scribble down as they tried surreptitiously to take notes. I must admit, I enjoyed myself immensely.

On the last day, the personnel folk decided we should play a game to teach us how to practise better teamwork. We were divided into two groups competing against each other. Each team was given an egg, two balloons, some tape, some string and a small towel. The goal was to drop the egg about thirty feet from an upper-floor window without letting it break. The team who could get their unbroken egg down fastest would be the winner.

It must be a cultural phenomenon. Only the British could develop something as cock-eyed as that. I was certainly out of my depth. Luckily, one of the people on my team was a sly old dog who knew what to do.

'Listen,' he explained, 'It's simple, at least in theory. You're supposed to blow up both balloons, put the egg in the middle and tape the balloons together. The rest of the stuff they gave out is just junk to confuse us. The only problem is that it won't work. The window is too high and the damned egg will break no matter what we do. Now, I'm sure at least one of the guys on the other team knows how to do this, so we have to work out a better way.'

The contest was held and it began exactly as predicted. Each team sent a member to the top floor while the rest of us waited on the patio below. The other team dropped their egg, firmly taped between the two balloons, but to no avail. The balloons broke and so did their egg.

Then our guy calmly walked down the stairs, our egg cradled gently in his hands. He took his time, stopping at each landing to take a bow. He was an expert in deliberately rubbing salt into the eggs – er, wounds of the other team.

The people from Personnel were furious. We were cheating, they claimed. Maybe, but we brought the egg down without breaking it. We broke the rules, they went on. Perhaps, but what we did wasn't specifically prohibited. We were not practising teamwork, they cried in fury. Wrong. We had used everyone on the team. Finally, the truth came out. We were supposed to fail so that they could show us how to cope with failure. Bull. Show me someone who knows how to lose and I'll show you a loser.

Calling something a 'risky business' is a redundant expression. All business activity is risky at some time or other. Even when you attempt to minimise or eliminate risks, you are merely changing their nature. Accept this as a fact, then add one more truth to the equation. If you take risks, then, sooner or later, you will lose. Expecting anything else is not just being foolish; it's downright stupid.

An old saying claims it's better to be a hammer than a nail, but we don't always have a choice. Most of us are either not good enough or not lucky enough to be a hammer. Even those who may feel they are hammers will be viewed as nails by those bigger or more powerful. Now you have an unpleasant choice to make. You can bury yourself or stick out. You may be hammered if you do the latter, but at least you get noticed.

But don't be silly about it. There's nothing to be gained if you just stand there, wave your hands and tell others to hammer you. It will happen often enough without your begging for it. Always look for options. Don't follow other people's rules unless they actually help you. Find new ways to accomplish your purpose without taking unnecessary risks. And, if you absolutely have to take a risk, do it in a way that no one expects. Even if you lose once in a while, the attempt will at least make it a little more enjoyable.

There are exceptions to every rule. You, I am sure, have already spotted some of the ones inherent in the rules I have created. That's to be expected. It was never my intention that you should agree with me. I just want you to think about some issues that may have escaped your attention.

Please feel free to tell me about the rules you really dislike. After all, the best way to learn more is to listen to the arguments of those who disagree. I would also be interested in your favourite rules. I can be contacted through my Internet E-Mail address: socks4hippos@compuserve.com.

Quick review – a summary of the rules

Part I   Rules about work

1.   Don't put socks on the hippopotamus
Avoid doing any work that does not need to be done. We are all too busy to take on useless activities. Challenge the need to act before doing so.

2.   Don't kill frogs
Adding small elements of incremental work to already existing tasks can upset the balance. Check that the added work is really valuable and necessary. If it is, try to eliminate other activities so your staff don't become too stretched.

3.   Activity ain't productivity
It is better to leave people idle for short periods than to make up artificial work to keep them busy. This 'make-work' can become a habit which is difficult to break. Then, when you need their efforts for essential tasks, they are tied up in these useless activities and are not available.

4.   You can't dig a well from the bottom
It is necessary to attend to all the boring details to accomplish a task successfully. Just knowing the end goal is not enough. You must do what is necessary to achieve it.

5.   Don't make soup in a basket
You have to ensure the entire organisation is able to do the job. This means you cannot concentrate on one area exclusively while allowing another to suffer. Don't give all your energy to one area only to have the entire company fail because of negligence in other parts.

6. Pick the low-lying fruit first
When faced with too much to do, eliminate all the non-essential jobs. When too much still remains, do the easiest work first. That improves morale and frees up even more time for the hard tasks.

7. Don't let the best be the enemy of good
Everything has to fit together. It is always acceptable to do (or buy or hire) something good that integrates easily with everything else. Trying to achieve the best, when the cost means it doesn't work except in isolation, usually results in general failure.

8. If it ain't broke, you haven't tried hard enough
Everything wears out over time, but that doesn't mean you will always view it as broken. Sometimes, when something has been acceptable for too long, it merely means you're not seeing the problems. Ask why things work, not just if they are broken.

Part II   Rules about advancement and promotion

9. Never ignore what you don't understand
When confronted by something you don't understand, remember that ignorance is an unforgivable sin in business. Instinct is not adequate. Take the time and exert the patience needed to reach a true understanding.

10. Preparation is half the battle
It is always better to be fully prepared. When that's not possible, at least have an opinion about what can be done. Then keep your opinion to yourself while you continue making better preparations.

11. Trying is nice – succeeding is better
Hard work is not enough. Nor is talent. Excuses are useless. You must deliver results if you want to be successful. Nothing else matters in the end.

12.   It's hard to stand up and look around when there's a sword hanging over your head
Don't allow yourself to be placed in a position where you cannot succeed. When someone tries to force you into that type of situation, get out.

13.   If you don't want to dance, don't come to the party
Success brings certain obligations with it. You have to fulfil them or you will not be allowed to continue. You must accept the accountabilities of your position or you will fail to keep it.

14.   If you don't make dust, you'll eat dust
You have to take some chances if you want to succeed. Success will not happen if you only seek security. Playing safe means standing still.

15.   A closed mouth gathers no feet
When you don't know something, don't try to pretend you do. One of the worst things you can do is bluff. When you have nothing meaningful to say, keep quiet. Even when you can say something, make sure it's something that needs to be said. Keeping the mouth shut has seldom hurt a career.

16.   Squeaky wheels get replaced, not lubricated
Whining and complaining gets you nowhere in business. Don't call attention to yourself unless you have something relevant to add to the activities going on.

Part III   Rules about management

17.   Steering is not the same as rowing
There is power in the creative element of work. But it is unwise to mix the power of the 'idea' with the power of command. You end up making decisions about your own ideas and that disenfranchises others in the company.

18.   Be scared ...
Fear is not an altogether bad thing in business. It keeps people on their

toes and interested in what is going on around them. Too much fear, though, is bad and must be avoided.

19.   ... But don't let your hands shake
We all feel fear from time to time, but you must keep it under control. It will be disastrous if those who work for you sense your fear.

20.   The more *you* do, the less gets done
Delegation is necessary, not just something to be desired. When you try to achieve too much by yourself, too little gets done.

21.   If you're right too often, you're wrong
There's a great temptation to prove how good you are, but you should avoid doing it. Usually, you have to prove someone else is wrong in order to show that you are right. This leads to morale and motivation problems.

22.   Some spotted leopards are just big pussy-cats
People can change if you give them a chance. Never write people off as losers because of hearsay. Give most people an opportunity to correct their failings and they'll at least try hard to do so.

23.   Rubber bands snap
There are many ways to exert pressure and cause behaviour changes. The financial incentive works well but can backfire. Be careful not to encourage greed to creep into the organisation. It can be destructive.

24.   No situation is so bad that a manager can't make it worse
Many managers make the mistake of trying to manage too much. They would be better off if they did less and allowed their people to work with greater independence.

Part IV   Rules about leadership

25.   Sweep the stairs from the top down
When things go wrong, the leaders must accept accountability. When they go very wrong, the leaders must be the first to go.

26. Even blind squirrels find some nuts
Arrogance based on success is barely acceptable. When the success comes from one lucky break, it is intolerable. A little humility is never out of place.

27. If all you can hear is yesterday's praise, you've gone deaf
Leaders must encourage those who are willing to disagree. They cannot afford to become deaf to their critics.

28. You can fool some of the people some of the time – but you can fool yourself all the time
You must not believe your own press releases. Your company only wrote them to display strengths and hide weaknesses. If you pay too much attention to them, you run the risk of forgetting where improvements are needed.

29. Dreams are for bedrooms, not boardrooms
Daydreaming is acceptable in children, not in members of corporate boardrooms. When you want to achieve something, go ahead and do it. Don't just dream about it.

30. If you're wreckless today, you'll be reckless tomorrow
Too much success can breed arrogance. Guard against it. Remember, success can be a lousy teacher.

31. Over-simplification is the practice of the lazy
Too many leaders over-simplify and then make the excuse that they are trying to keep things clear. This creates far more problems than it solves. The real cause is laziness, not a desire for simplicity.

32. There's no limit to how softly a large hammer can hit
Being a leader brings with it a great deal of power. That doesn't mean you should use it. The best leaders seldom resort to using power in order to ensure tasks are accomplished.

Part V   Rules about change

33.   If you want to be tied to the past, marry a museum curator
Just because something was true years ago doesn't mean it's true now. Looking to the past for lessons may be acceptable but you should not spend too much time on it. The real action is in the future.

34.   Sacred cows are full of it
All companies have traditions. Some are good and some are not. You must learn to separate them and purge yourself of the bad ones, regardless of the amount of resistance.

35.   Innovation requires no know
If you believe you know all there is to know, you stop asking questions. If you want to create an innovative environment, you must assume you know nothing. That attitude allows you to learn more.

36.   The pace of change always exceeds the pace of understanding
Changes are taking place rapidly. It will be impossible to keep up with all of them. You need good staff and you need to trust them.

37.   Take care of the baby
Quality is a worthwhile issue and should never be overlooked. However, you can take anything too far, including concern about quality. Sometimes, you can do more harm than good.

38.   Rowing the boat will cause it to rock
You can't make progress without hurting someone. Don't be surprised when you hear complaints – and don't let it stop you.

39.   There's a difference between conducting a test and being a guinea pig
Change may be needed but that doesn't mean you are not responsible for those affected by it. Management has a requirement to be compassionate as well as analytical. If you are cold and unfeeling towards those who work for you, your bosses will assume its acceptable to feel the same way towards you.

40. The first step in training mules is to gain their attention

People are stubborn. You sometimes have to shock them to gain their attention. After that, progress will be easier.

41. Hype springs eternal

Be careful before embarking on a new change programme. Not all of them are good and even fewer are good for your particular company. Support the programme after analysis, not after hearing the latest hype.

Part VI   Rules about risks

42. If you never make a mistake, you'll never make anything

If you take enough risks, sooner or later you will fail. However, you must take some risks to accomplish anything meaningful. You just have to accept this and try to keep the amount of loss under control.

43. Listen for the dog that doesn't bark

Sometimes, it is the absence of information that gives us the greatest clue that something is wrong. Keep this in mind when analysing data before taking a risk. Look for what is hidden.

44. Time spent on reconnaissance is never wasted

Find out as much as possible before committing yourself and your company to a risky venture. Be careful, though. There is a temptation to take data gathering too far. Avoid illegal and unethical acts.

45. Play it by ear and lose your head

Don't take risks based merely on instinct. Analyse everything carefully before deciding. Your instincts are important but you should not depend on them exclusively.

46. Money talks – don't let yours say goodbye

There are times when companies, especially big ones, forget how important money is. Treat every penny as your own and you'll make fewer mistakes.

47. If you stand in the middle of the road, you can be hit from both directions

You have to choose sides in the game of business. If you try to keep everyone happy, you'll be the first to lose.

48. Never fight a foreign war when your own soil is not secure

Don't push an expansion programme beyond the company's ability to support it. Make sure your business infrastructure is sound and check the capabilities of your local competitors before committing to an aggressive expansion.

49. Don't freeze in the headlights

When you see things start to go wrong, react immediately. Don't wait until you have solid proof. That may be too late.

Part VII   Rules about organisations

50. Size doesn't matter – it's how you use it that counts

Large organisations do not have to be awkward and inefficient. They can operate with the same speed and flexibility as smaller ones. You just have to make sure you empower people in the right way.

51. If you're putting two bulls together, build a bigger pen

Two or more dominant people can coexist in the same team and at the same level but they must be allowed the freedom to expand their area of control to accommodate themselves. If done right, this can be a very powerful technique to spark dramatic growth.

52. Duelling speakers ruin the music

Matrix management rarely works, but it can if a little common sense is used. Remember, the line boss closest to the people being managed in a matrix structure is the real boss. Any other is just an influence manager.

53. It's hard to go exploring when you're defending the castle

Department managers can spend too much time defending themselves and their people. Everyone would be better off if they interacted more with the rest of the company and spent less time being defensive.

54. Accountants should be on tap – not on top
When you are promoted, you must take up your new position, not hold on to your old one. If you don't let go, it will be impossible for you to represent your new position.

55. Teamwork: an illusion searching for a delusion
For the most part, true teamwork does not exist. It's merely an illusion in the mind of the boss. However, teamwork is possible although not in the sense that most business people try to represent it.

56. There's no such thing as friendly fire
Internal fighting hurts the company more than any competitor ever will. You must avoid it at all costs.

Part VIII   Rules about communications

57. Lapses in language lead to lamentable lies
English is a slippery language and we can create confusion rather than clarity if we do not use it carefully. But it's the lies we tell ourselves that hurt us most.

58. Don't distort, just report
Many issues in business are boring. There is a temptation to add some excitement by exaggerating. This can be dangerous, not just exciting.

59. You can't see through a blizzard of paper
We generate far too much paperwork in business. This sometimes makes us wish we could eliminate all the paper, but that would be foolish. Some paperwork is as necessary as other paperwork is wasteful. The trick is to determine which is which.

60. Listen with your eyes
Language is not the only way we communicate. Body language and general conduct are also good indicators that we must pay attention to.

61. Milk in the cow never turns sour
Some information is meant to be confidential, so be very careful. There's more than one way information is divulged.

62. A rattled sabre makes noise – a drawn one doesn't
Be subtle in your communications. People who bluster loudly often miss key elements of what is being said. And they always miss what hasn't been said but is nevertheless implied.

63. There's always some kid with a crayon
Every work needs review and editing. If called on to do it, however, don't carry it to extremes. The original intent can too easily be lost.

64. The best excuses are silent
Never make excuses. Even the best 'reason' can and will be seen by someone as an excuse.

Part IX   Rules about people and relationships

65. Say what you'll do – do what you say
Credibility is one of the most important assets we have in business. It can easily be lost if there is a discrepancy between your words and your actions.

66. A sword in the hand doesn't allow for handshakes
Aggression has its place in business relationships, especially when negotiating for your firm. However, it can be taken too far and can cause a great deal of damage. You should save it for the last resort.

67. If you're doing all the talking, no one is doing the thinking
We all love the sound of our own voices. The danger of talking too much is that others will think that you have all the answers. That may cause them to stop thinking for themselves.

68. If they snooze, you lose
Business can be boring, but you can't let people become bored. It's necessary to 'entertain' them to keep their interest.

69. Doing nothing is often the best thing to do

Doing nothing because you don't know what to do or because you run out of time is inexcusable. However, it is perfectly acceptable to do nothing when this is a conscious decision. Sometimes it is the only good decision.

70. Don't throw rocks when you need hand grenades

In the age of downsizing and flat organisation structures, businesses can sometimes cut too much. When you dismiss staff, you may be losing the ammunition and skills you'll need tomorrow. Think all the issues through carefully before acting.

71. Every contact may be your last chance

Customer relations should never be forgotten. In this age of consumerism and intolerance of business arrogance, you may only get one chance, so treat your customers with the greatest respect.

72. Make your boss a partner

Anything is possible if your boss is a partner. This means you must share both successes and failures. It also means you never deliver surprises, pleasant or otherwise.

Part X   Rules about rules

73. Some rules are made to be followed

Almost all rules make sense to some extent, and following them provides a certain degree of safety. While you shouldn't be too rigid in your compliance, you should think about each rule carefully and understand its benefits.

74. Some rules are made to be ignored

Some rules can be safely ignored, at least by some people at certain times. Ignoring rules simply means that you follow your own. But you must be consistent when you use this strategy.

233

75.   And some rules are made to be broken

Some rules are foolish and you should never pay attention to them. Breaking certain rules gives you a tremendous amount of power and flexibility. Just be sure that you have thought everything through first.

A Systematic Approach to

Getting Results

Surya Lovejoy

Every manager has to produce results. But almost nobody is trained
in the business of doing so. This book is a practical handbook for
making things happen. And whether the thing in question is a
conference, an office relocation or a sales target, the principles are the
same: you need a systematic approach for working out:

- exactly what has to happen
- when everything has to happen
- how you will ensure that it happens
- what could go wrong
- what will happen when something does go wrong
- how you will remain sane during the process.

This book won't turn you into an expert on critical path analysis or
prepare you for the job of running the World Bank. What it will do is
to give you the tools you need to produce results smoothly, effectively,
reliably and without losing your mind on the way.

Gower

Gower Handbook of Management Skills

Third Edition

Edited by Dorothy M Stewart

'This is the book I wish I'd had in my desk drawer when I was first a manager. When you need the information, you'll find a chapter to help; no fancy models or useless theories. This is a practical book for real managers, aimed at helping you manage more effectively in the real world of business today. You'll find enough background information, but no overwhelming detail. This is material you can trust. It is tried and tested.'

So writes Dorothy Stewart, describing in the Preface the unifying theme behind the Third Edition of this bestselling Handbook. This puts at your disposal the expertise of 25 specialists, each a recognized authority in their particular field. Together, this adds up to an impressive 'one stop library' for the manager determined to make a mark.

Chapters are organized within three parts: Managing Yourself, Managing Other People, and Managing the Business. Part I deals with personal skills and includes chapters on self-development and information technology. Part II covers people skills such as listening, influencing and communication. Part III looks at finance, project management, decision-making, negotiating and creativity. A total of 12 chapters are completely new, and the rest have been rigorously updated to fully reflect the rapidly changing world in which we work.

Each chapter focuses on detailed practical guidance, and ends with a checklist of key points and suggestions for further reading.

Gower

It's Not Luck

Eliyahu M Goldratt

A Gower Novel

Alex Rogo has had a great year, he was promoted to executive vice-president of UniCo with the responsibility for three recently acquired companies. His team of former and new associates is in place and the future looks secure and exciting. But then there is a shift of policy at the board level. Cash is needed and Alex's companies are to be put on the block. Alex faces a cruel dilemma. If he successfully completes the turnaround of his companies, they can be sold for the maximum return, but if he fails, the companies will be closed down. Either way, Alex and his team will be out of a job. It looks like a lose-lose situation. And as if he doesn't have enough to deal with, his two children have become teenagers!

As Alex grapples with problems at work and at home, we begin to understand the full scope of Eli Goldratt's powerful techniques, first presented in *The Goal*, the million copy best-seller that has already transformed management thinking throughout the Western world. *It's Not Luck* reveals more of the Thinking Processes, and moves beyond *The Goal* by showing how to apply them on a comprehensive scale.

This book will challenge you to change the way you think and prove to you that it's not luck that makes startling improvements achievable in your life.

Gower

The Management Skills Book

Conor Hannaway and Gabriel Hunt

From managing employee performance to chairing meetings, and from interviewing staff to making retirement presentations, the list of skills demanded of today's manager seems endless. How can you be effective in all these areas?

If you are a practising manager, this book is for you. It is designed to answer your need for support in your day-to-day work.

Over 100 brief guides cover essential management skills. Each guide gives you all you need to know without cumbersome technical details. Look up the subject you need, and apply the ideas immediately.

The Management Skills Book was written with today's busy managers in mind. It is an ideal introduction for new managers, and a great reminder of the essentials for the more experienced.

Gower

Mind Skills for Managers

Samuel A Malone

How good are you at managing multiple tasks? What about problem solving and creativity? How quickly do you pick up new ideas and new skills?

Managers in the '90s are measured against some tough criteria. You may feel that you're already doing everything that you can, and you're still being asked for more. But in one area you've got over 90% of unused capacity ... your brain.

Mind Skills for Managers will help you to harness your mind's unused capacity to:

- develop your ability to learn
- generate creative ideas
- handle information more effectively
- and tackle many of the key skills of management in new and imaginative ways.

Sam Malone mixes down-to-earth ideas with techniques such as Mind Maps, checklists, step-by-step rules, acronyms and mnemonics to provide an entertaining, easy-to-use guide to improving your management techniques by unleashing the full power of your mind.

The skills in this book need to be practised. The best approach is to take one idea at a time and apply it. By following the book you will learn a whole range of 'mind skills' and be rewarded by measurable improvements in your performance.

Use and implement the ideas and you will think better, think faster and work smarter.

Gower

Monkey Business

Why the Way You Manage is a Million Years Out of Date

Gary Johnson

We accept evolution as historical fact. In today's sophisticated business environment our ape-like ancestors have been left far behind us. Or have they?

Far from it, says Gary Johnson. Primeval instincts are still driving many of our business decisions, without us being aware of it, and sometimes with disastrous consequences. Understanding this helps us to recognize 'irrational' behaviour in ourselves and our colleagues, and gives us the opportunity to over-ride what our instincts are telling us.

Johnson uses hundreds of persuasive and entertaining examples from scientific research and from business, providing fresh answers to questions such as:

Why does stress hamper creativity? Answer: Because stress for our ancestors was an immediate physical threat, prompting the 'fight or flight' response, a rush of adrenalin, and a shutting down of creative thought until the danger has passed. Great for dealing with sabre-toothed tigers, but not for making that crucial business decision.

Monkey Business is about fundamental truths, not about the latest management theories. Reading it is guaranteed to make you see yourself, your colleagues, and the way you work in a new light.

Gower

The New Unblocked Manager

A Practical Guide to Self-Development

Dave Francis and Mike Woodcock

This is unashamedly a self-help book, written for managers and supervisors who wish to improve their effectiveness. In the course of their work with thousands of managers over a long period the authors have discovered twelve potential 'blockages' that stand in the way of managerial competence. They include, for example, negative personal values, low creativity and unclear goals.

By means of a self-evaluation exercise, the reader first identifies the blockages most significant to them. There follows a detailed explanation of each blockage and ideas and materials for tackling the problem.

This is a heavily revised edition of a book that, under its original title, *The Unblocked Manager,* was used by many thousands of managers around the world and appeared in ten languages. The new edition reflects the changed world of management and owes much to the feedback supplied by practising managers. In its enhanced form the book will continue to provide a comprehensive framework for self-directed development.

Gower

Proven Management Models

Sue Harding and Trevor Long

This unique volume brings together, in a standardized format, 45 models for management diagnosis and problem-solving: all chosen for their proven value to senior management and MBA tutors alike. They cover strategy, organization, human resources and marketing, and range from well-known techniques such as Breakeven Analysis and Situational Leadership to less familiar approaches like Five Forces and the Geobusiness Model.

Each entry contains:

- a diagrammatic representation of the model
- the principle on which the model is based
- the underlying assumptions
- the issues involved
- guidance on using the model
- related models
- further reading.

The models are indexed by subject and there is also a matrix showing how they are related to each other.

The result is a reference guide that will be invaluable to practising managers, consultants and management students alike.

Gower

Superboss 2

David Freemantle

You too can be a SUPERBOSS!

David Freemantle will persuade you that every manager can take action today to become a SUPERBOSS. In this entertaining book, a revised and updated version of a worldwide bestseller, he describes more than 130 effective ways of managing people.

Amusing, stimulating and often provocative, *Superboss 2* is a treasure trove of practical advice for anyone aspiring to managerial excellence.

Gower

Using Management Games

Second Edition

Chris Elgood

The benefits of using management training games are clear: they allow theory to be put into practice in a risk free environment, and encourage teamworking and decision-making. But as their popularity has rightly increased over the last few years, the range of games available has become bewildering. How do they differ from one another? How do they compare with other ways of learning? How do you identify the most appropriate games for your training objectives?

Chris Elgood provides a welcome guide to different types of game, from those designed to increase group effectiveness, such as icebreakers, puzzles and communication games, to others for developing organizational awareness or interpersonal skills, such as simulations or role-plays. For each, he explains the methods by which they promote learning and the situations for which they are best suited.

The popularity of management games has increased so rapidly that this new edition has been completely rewritten. The growth of computer-controlled games is reflected, as is the importance of games in developing teamwork, and the significance of debriefing.

Gower

The "How To" Guide for Managers

John Payne and Shirley Payne

• Encourage your team to suggest their own objectives
• Prevent fires rather than fight them
• Decide! You'll never have all the information you would like

These, and another 107 'ideas', form the basis of John and Shirley Payne's entertaining book. Whether you're newly promoted or an old hand at managing, it will help you to improve your performance and avoid some of the pitfalls you may not even have been aware of.

Written in a practical, no-nonsense style, the Guide focuses in turn on the eleven key skills of management, including setting objectives, decision making, time management, communication, motivating, delegating and running effective meetings. A questionnaire at the beginning enables you to identify those chapters that will give you the maximum benefit. Or read through the whole book - as the authors say, using their ideas can't guarantee success, but it will increase your chances.

Gower